Plight and Fate of Children
During and Following
GENOCIDE

Plight and Fate of Children

During and Following

GENOCIDE

GENOCIDE:
A CRITICAL BIBLIOGRAPHIC REVIEW
VOLUME 10

Samuel Totten, editor

Transaction Publishers
New Brunswick (U.S.A.) and London (U.K.)

Library of Congress Catalog Number: 2013032563
ISBN: 978-1-4128-5355-2
Printed in the United States of America

Library of Congress Cataloging-in-Publication Data

Plight and fate of children during and following genocide / Samuel Totten, editor.
  pages cm. — (Genocide: a critical bibliographic review ; volume 10)
  Includes bibliographical references and index.
  ISBN 978-1-4128-5355-2
1. Genocide. 2. Children—Crimes against. 3. Crimes against humanity—History—20th century. 4. Crimes against humanity—History—21st century. I. Totten, Samuel.
  HV6322.7.P59 2014
  362.88083—dc23

                                                    2013032563

Dedication

To Patrick Murinzi Minega and all other
children victimized by genocide, war, and violence.

Contents

Introduction

Samuel Totten

Generally, when I make my way through museums dealing with genocide I find myself feeling sad and angry but I forge on and make my way through the exhibits. This, I have done, time and again, beginning back in 1978 when I first visited Yad Vashem, the Holocaust Martyrs' and Heroes' Remembrance Authority in Jerusalem, the US Holocaust Memorial Museum in 1993, and the tiny museum on the Armenian genocide located in the basement of a church in Deir et Zor (Syria) in 2005. But then, in 2006, as I made my way through the museum at the Kigali Genocide Memorial Centre in Rwanda, I entered the "Children's Wing," and within ten minutes my heart was shattered. I had only managed to view a tenth of the photographs and accompanying information in the room, but I simply could not go on. I literally wanted to scream and flay away at a world that would allow such horrific injustice and atrocities to be perpetrated.

I shall never forget the last photo and captions that ripped my heart apart. It was the sweetest picture of a young man, Patrick, seven years of age, I've ever seen. His smile and bright sparkling eyes exuded joy. Then, I read the captions:

Name: Patrick Murinzi Minega
Favorite Sport: Swimming
Favorite Sweets: Chocolate
Favorite Person: His Mum
Personality: Gregarious
Cause of Death: Bludgeoned with Club

Over the years (during which I served as a Fulbright Scholar at the Centre for Conflict Management at the National University of Rwanda, and on subsequent research trips when Rafiki Ubaldo, a survivor of the 1994 genocide, and I conducted interviews for our book, *We Cannot*

1

Forget: Interviews with Survivors of the 1994 Genocide in Rwanda), I returned to the Kigali Genocide Memorial Centre several times in order to try to view all of the photographs and captions in the "Children's Wing." Each and every time I'd only get so far before I was overwhelmed with sorrow, and, yet again, would depart without having viewed the entire exhibit. To this day I've not viewed the entire exhibit.

The killing of infants, preschoolers, school-age children, and preadolescents should be beyond the pale. Unfortunately, and sadly, it is not—at least not for those who are apt to committing crimes against humanity and genocide. And it's not just killing that the latter engage in, but also the torture and butchery of babies and young children.

When perpetrators kill infants and children there is often a sadistic tone and tenor to their actions. They seem to enjoy exhibiting their perverted power over the victim population. They seem to enjoy crushing the spirits of those parents and siblings who are forced to watch their children and babies and young brothers and sisters, respectively, be brutalized in the most horrific ways possible. They seem to enjoy instilling terror into the victim population by ripping apart, crushing the skulls of, slicing the heads off of, and stabbing and shooting helpless and totally innocent members of the victim population.

Not even fetuses are safe from the ravages perpetrated by genocidaries. In just about every genocide one reads about, some perpetrators have ripped open the wombs of pregnant mothers, pulled out the fetuses, and destroyed them in front of the mother's eyes. It makes for ghastly reading; but that, obviously, is nothing next to what the horrified mother and her loved ones live through. In most instances, the mother, who is carved up as if she were some inanimate piece of meat, ends up dead.

There are, of course, numerous reasons why children are targeted during periods of genocide. Children are brutalized and killed by perpetrators in order to terrorize targeted groups and force them to flee from those areas coveted by the perpetrators or by those perpetrators who wish to "cleanse" an area of those "others." By attacking the victim group's children, perpetrators believe that the targeted group is more likely to flee for safety and thus abandon their homes, villages, and/or farms.

Children are also targeted by genocidaires in order to cut off the "lifeblood" of the targeted group. Time and again during genocide, male infants and young boys have been targeted due to the perpetrators' perception of them as potential foes and thus a security threat. This was certainly the case during the 1994 Rwandan genocide: "The targeting of Tutsi children along with adults carried the idea of 'self-defense' to its logically absurd and genocidal end. To encourage assailants to kill children, some instigators stated that even the youngest could pose a threat; they often reminded others that Paul Kagame or Fred Rwigema, RPF commanders who led the guerilla force, had once been babies too" (Human Rights Watch 2003, n.p.).

Female infants and young girls are targeted because they constitute the future bearers of children of the targeted group. In various societies (such as in Darfur, where Muslims perceive those girls and women who had been raped as "damaged" and not worthy of remaining with their families and fellow villagers), perpetrators targeted women knowing full well that, in many, if not most, cases, the babies conceived of the rapes would be considered "Arab" or "Janjaweed babies," and thus ostracized by their own family members and fellow villagers, and, in the end, would not grow up to produce more foes of the perpetrators.

In those cases where children have been forced to fight alongside military, militia or rebel troops, they are perceived as "fair game," since they pose a danger to the opposition. This is just one more reason as to why children should never be recruited to serve with any group of combatants.

This volume, the last I shall be editing for the *Genocide: A Bibliographical Series* (more on that below), is comprised of the following chapters by the following authors: (1) Australia's Aboriginal Children: Stolen or Saved? by Colin Tatz; (2) Hell Is for Children: The Impact of Genocide on Young Armenians and the Consequences for the Target Group as a Whole by Henry C. Theriault; (3) Children: The Most Vulnerable Victims of the Armenian Genocide by Asya Darbinyan and Rubina Peroomian; (4) Children and the Holocaust by Jeffrey Blutinger; (5) The Fate of Mentally and Physically Disabled Children in Nazi Germany by Jeffrey Blutinger; (6) The Plight and Fate of Children vis-à-vis the Guatemalan Genocide by Samuel Totten; (7) The Plight of Children during and following the 1994 Rwandan Genocide by Amanda Grzyb; (8) The Darfur Genocide: The Plight and Fate of the Black African Children by Samuel Totten; (9) Sexual and Gender-Based Violence against Children during Genocide by Elisa von Joeden-Forgey; and (10) Child Soldiers: Children's Rights in the Time of War and Genocide by Hannibal Travis and Sara Demir.

I wish to sincerely thank each author for his/her contribution on this most disturbing of issues. The significance of the volume hardly needs explanation or justification.

As mentioned above, I have decided to conclude my editorship of this series with this volume. It has been an honor to serve as its editor. In doing so, I have had the pleasure of working with dozens of scholars of genocide studies as we collaborated to produce six volumes, including this one, in the series: Volume 5: *Genocide at the Millennium* (2005); Volume 6: *The Prevention and Intervention of Genocide* (2007); Volume 7: *The Plight and Fate of Women during and following Genocide* (2009); Volume 8: *Genocide of Indigenous Peoples* (2010); Volume 9: *Impediments to the Prevention and Intervention of Genocide* (2013); and Volume 10: *The Plight and Fate of Children during and following Genocide*.

Genocide: A Critical Bibliographic Series was created and inaugurated by Dr. Israel W. Charny in 1988. After editing the series for fifteen years (1988–2003), he turned the series over to me. I've edited the series for the past ten years (2003–2013). I am now pleased to turn the series over to two new editors: Dr. Elisa von Joeden-Forgey and Dr. Henry Theriault. Both are well-known and respected scholars of genocide studies. Both have also contributed to the genocide bibliographical series. I am confident that they will bring a fresh perspective to the series and produce highly informative and thought-provoking volumes in the years ahead.

I wish to thank Transaction Publishers for its dedication to publishing the series, and in particular I wish to think Dr. Irving Louis Horowitz, the founder of Transaction Publishers and Ms. Mary Curtis, President of Transaction Publishers, for their unwavering support of the series. I also wish to thank all of the scholars over the years who contributed to the series while I was an editor. Without them, there would be no series to speak of. Last but certainly not least, I wish to sincerely thank Dr. Israel W. Charny for providing me with the opportunity to edit the series over the past decade and for allowing me to, as it were, carry his baby into the future. Had it not been for his innovative efforts, the series would not exist.

Reference

Human Rights Watch. 2003. "Lasting Wounds: Consequences of Genocide and War for Rwanda's Children." New York: Author. http://www.unhcr.org/refworld/docid/3f4f595a12.html (accessed at August 20, 2013).

1

Australia's Aboriginal Children: Stolen or Saved?

Colin Tatz

Introduction

Why are Aboriginal children included in this volume? They weren't murdered systematically as 1.2 million Jewish children were during the Holocaust. They were not institutionalized in euthanasia centers, deliberately emaciated, and then "put down" by lethal injection. They were not rounded up and killed by the Nazis as the Romani children were. They were not killed as Tutsi children were by extremist Hutu during the 1994 Rwandan genocide. Nor were they "spared"—as Armenian, Assyrian, and Pontian Greek children were—when parents were coerced into their "Turkification" by adoption, forced marriages, or sexual chatteldom.

Aboriginal children are included herein because they were forcibly removed from their parents, from the early 1800s to the late 1980s, to fulfill a religious as well as an eugenicist fantasy, that their placement in a variety of "assimilation homes" would end their Aboriginality by moving them into the white, Christian, and "civilized" mainstream. Other alleged (and contradictory) motives were concerns about child abandonment or neglect by their parents, and hence their need of protection; fear by some well-wishers that white or "mixed-blood" contact would hasten the demise of "full-blood" Aborigines; and fear (by many) that a "hybrid colored population of very low order" threatened the prevailing civilization. Churchmen, police, government officials, and even private citizens were the instruments of forcible removal. Despite claims about "the best interests of the child" and "loving protection," removals were not voluntary, consensual, or because of "reckless and depraved indifference"—what American law defines as wanton,

5

morally deficient behavior, lacking regard for human life, and hence criminally blameworthy.

Another question that needs to be addressed is this: Why is the forcible transfer of children of one group to another group considered as criminally heinous as the deliberate ending of procreative, "feeble-minded," or biological life? First, the 1946–1948 Genocide Convention's (the UN Convention on the Prevention and Punishment of the Crime of Genocide; hereafter, UNCG) drafting committees were heavily influenced by the horrific racial policies and practices of that decade. Some UN delegates may have remembered the fate of Armenian children. None, though, would have known about the Australian Aboriginal experience, deliberately hidden from public view for so long. Second, the first draft of the UNCG defined three categories of genocide: biological, physical, and cultural. The drafters excluded cultural genocide, but later, by the smallest of margins, agreed to an exception by way of Article II(e), "forcible transfer of children." Thus, child transfer came to be equated as an act of genocide with biological and physical killing, causing serious bodily and mental harm, inflicting conditions of life calculated to destroy a group, and sterilization. Whether we agree with such synonymy of unequal behaviors (and outcomes) is irrelevant. Forcible transfer of children has been a genocidal and criminal act since January 1951 when the UNCG went into force, and is likely to be so for the next fifty years in the catalog of crimes scheduled by the (2002) statute of the International Criminal Court.

Child Removal—With Intent

Are the "Stolen Generations"—the term current since the 1980s—an ethical or conceptual category, a collective which "simply" suffered one or another form of mistreatment, relocation, dislocation, or separation? Or were they individuals removed by duress and force to special institutions to be divested of their Aboriginality?

Notions of assimilation, including "retention" and separation of children, usually of mixed descent, began as early as 1814. New South Wales Governor Lachlan Macquarie created a "Native Institution" at Parramatta to "civilize" children for at least ten to twelve years, preparing boys for agricultural work and girls for domestic service, with no parental visits and no holidays-at-home time. All the children absconded and the institution closed in 1820. "Retentions" were prevalent at Yarra Government Mission (1837–1839), Buntingdale Mission (1838–1848), and Merri Creek Baptist School (1845–1851)—all of which were institutions in that part of New South Wales that was to become the separate colony of Victoria in 1851. Employers across the spreading frontiers also "retained" children, often for "work" purposes. After the *Victorian Aborigines' Protection Act of 1869*, statutes in Australian colonial/state jurisdictions allowed governmental guardianship of all Aboriginal children, with power to remove children of mixed descent in order to absorb them either culturally or physically into the general population (Tatz 2011a, 96–97).

Child removal gained momentum after federation in 1901 and lasted another three or four generations. For well over a century, across the continent, between 20,000 and 35,000 children, possibly 50,000—often the progeny of Aboriginal women and white cattle ranch workers, crop growers, miners, and adventurers—were taken away to dormitories, reformatories, hostels, mission properties, and especial "assimilation homes." The assimilation homes that were run by govenremnt staff and by church agencies flourished. Several were in urban domains, some in settled rural areas, but most were in remote Australia. Over time, Western Australia had no less than eighty-four such state-run institutions, another fifty-nine were run by various church denominations, and seven were nondenominational homes (for all children). Most had a longish life. New South Wales closed Kinchela Boys' Home (established 1924) in 1970; Colebrook Children's Home in South Australia (1927) terminated in 1972; the Retta Dixon Home in Darwin (1946) ceased in 1980; Western Australia closed one of its major institutions, Sister Kate's Orphanage (1933), in 1987; and the last such mission institution in Bomaderry (NSW) (1908) shut down in 1988.

In northern Australia, "yellafellas," the common derogatory term used for "half-castes," were embarrassments to a society desperate to maintain its whiteness and were quickly taken to institutions to extinguish their Aboriginality (Choo 2001, 143–51). Private shame led to removals becoming a cornerstone of action by state and federal administrators. Australians always assumed that their culture and color genes were the stronger. Dr. Cecil Cook, Chief Protector of Aborigines in the Northern Territory, had no doubt about it: "Generally by the fifth and invariably by the sixth generation, all native characteristics of the Australian Aborigines are eradicated. The problem with our half-castes will quickly be eliminated by the complete disappearance of the black race, and the swift submergence of their progeny in the white" (Gray 2011, 61).

Australian eugenics was not simply an ad hoc policy of "misguided child welfare," which has been the inevitable theme and counterclaim by denialists of removal with intent.

The "Science" of Removal

In Western Australia, harsh views about aboriginals were a regular occurrence. In 1904, Father Nicholas Emo told the Royal Commission on the Condition of the Natives that "the children ought to be sent to the mission schools (where there are Sisters or Matrons), while the half-castes should be sent to reformatories" (Choo 2001, 144). In his opinion, "the half-caste girls are in general of a very vicious temperament" (Choo 2001, 144). In 1909, the Chief Protector in Western Australia, Charles Gale (1909), quoted one of his traveling protectors, James Isdell: "The half-caste is intellectually above the aborigine, and it is the duty of the State that they be given a chance to lead a better and purer life than their mothers. I would not hesitate for one moment to separate any half-caste from its Aboriginal mother, no matter how frantic her momentary grief might be at the time. They soon forget their offspring" (7).

It was but a "maudlin sentiment" to leave children with their Aboriginal mothers, Isdell added: "They forget their children in twenty-four hours and as a rule [were] glad to be rid of them" (Haebich 2000, 233).

In 1911, the State Children's Council in South Australia was the major body concerned with the welfare (and removal) of children. Cameron Raynes (2009, 2–13) and Anna Haebich (2000, 199) cite an "unequivocal statement" of the intent to "put an end to Aboriginality" or at least significant manifestations of it—such as the kinship relationships, communality and reciprocity systems, birth, circumcision and mourning rituals, earlier than "normal" sexual development, and color (if possible). The Council wrote on the proposal to remove "half-caste, quadroon and octoroon" Aboriginal children, paying "special attention" to the girls: "The Council is fully persuaded of the importance of prompt action in order to prevent the growth of a race that would rapidly increase in numbers, attain a maturity without education or religion, and become a menace to the morals and health of the community. The Council . . . feels that no consideration . . . should be permitted to block the way of the protection and elevation of these unfortunate children" (Raynes 2009, 13).

Several of the key state bureaucrats—Charles Gale and Dr. Walter Roth early in the century, and later, Auber Octavius Neville in Western Australia, John William Bleakley in Queensland, Dr. Cecil Cook in the Northern Territory, and a few years later, William Penhall in South Australia—were educated men and were doubtless aware of the eugenicist principles prevalent in Europe and the United States. Ultimately, their ideas were consummated at a national summit of ministers and their officials in Canberra in 1937: "The destiny of the natives of Aboriginal origin, but not of full blood, lies in their ultimate absorption by the people of the Commonwealth and it is therefore recommended that all efforts shall be directed to this end" (quoted in Tatz 2003, 88–94). These men never defined absorption, but the kernel of their ideas was physical distance from tribal kin and, ideally, disappearance of color and ethnicity. These bureaucrats were part of a Western tradition which has long contended that some lives are more valuable, more worthy, than others. They were hardly the pioneers of what came to be called "racial hygiene" in the early twentieth century, but their ideas go to the heart of genocidal thought and action, that is, resorting to biological solutions to social (and racial) problems (Aly, Chroust, and Pross 1994, 1).

Neville presented a three-point biological plan. First, keep "full-bloods" in inviolable reserves where they are destined to die out. Second, take all "half-castes" away from their mothers. Third, control marriages so that "pleasant, placid, complacent, strikingly attractive, auburn-haired, and rosy-freckled" quarter- and half-blood Aboriginal maidens marry into the white community. In doing so, it would be possible to "eventually forget that there were ever any Aborigines in Australia" (quoted in Beresford and Omaji 1998, 48).

Neville also asserted that: "The native must be helped in spite of himself! . . . Even if a measure of discipline is necessary it must be applied, but it can be applied in such a way as to appear to be gentle persuasion . . . the end in view will justify the means employed" (quoted in Haebich 2000, 259). Here, indeed, is the quintessence of Australian genocidal intent—the erasure of the Aboriginal presence, one way or another. Dr. Cecil Bryan recommended the following to the 1934 Moseley Royal Commission regarding the treatment of Western Australian Aborigines: "I am come to the Commission to ask that steps be taken to breed out the half-caste, not in a moment, but in a few generations, and not by force but by science. I mean the application of the principle of the Mendelian law" (quoted in Haebich 1988, 320).

Some of these notions became official practices. The "full-blood" people in isolated reserves didn't die out, an abiding and enduring premise of both those who had a care and concern for Aborigines and those who despised or attacked them. After 1937, some reserves were phased out but dozens of new ones were established and older ones reinforced by tougher regulations. Coaxed (or even coerced) Christian marriages, as proposed by A. O. Neville, were never going to succeed but child removal by policemen and other officials became the order of the day.

Public Awareness

Whatever explanations and rationalizations were offered before 1949, there can be no justification of forcible child removal after Australia ratified the UNCG in June 1949. And yet, it persisted.

In the late 1970s, the Aboriginal Child Care Agency in Victoria and in South Australia agitated against child removal and in 1980, a New South Wales Link-Up movement began to fight removals and retrieve children. Ultimately, the long-suppressed saga of child removal started to come into some public discussion several years after Peter Read's 1981 pioneering monograph helped bring the phrase "Stolen Generations" into Australia's political vocabulary. That "dissociating the children from [native] camp life must eventually solve the Aboriginal problem" was official New South Wales practice. To leave them where they were, "in comparative idleness in the midst of more or less vicious surroundings," the government claimed, would be "an injustice to the children themselves, and a positive menace to the State" (Read 1981, 7). Read found 5,625 removals in that jurisdiction between 1883 and 1969. In the documentary records, there was space allocated for a column headed "Reasons for [Aborigines Welfare Board] Taking Control of the Child." The great majority of entries carried the handwritten entry, "For Being Aboriginal" (Read 1981, 6). After 1939, removals in that state required a hearing before a magistrate.

Read stated on the ABC television's *7.30 Report* (April 3, 2000) that 50,000 was the likely number of removed children across the country. Several denialists claim that "only" 10 percent of children were forcibly removed. Arithmetic doesn't alter the precepts of the UNCG, and here the word "only" is both mischievous and obfuscatory. The matter of intent to destroy in "whole or in part" is certainly not specific in the

UNCG: we know intuitively what "whole" is, but the term "in part" is both unclear and unresolvable.

By 1980, when the Link-Up movement began in New South Wales and spread to other states, the finding and reuniting with removed family members had become the single-most important issue in Aboriginal life (Bradfield 1997, 13–22). Strident Aboriginal voices persuaded the federal Labor government to initiate an inquiry into "the separation by compulsion" of Aboriginal children from their families. The word "separation" in the formal terms of reference seemed to infer that some reuniting was once envisaged. That was never the intention: children were to be separated forever from their Aboriginality.

The inquiry report, *Bringing Them Home* (HREOC 1997), headed by Sir Ronald Wilson, a former High Court Justice, was something of a bestseller: "A finding of genocide was presented: the essence of the crime was acting with the intention of destroying the group, not the extent to which that intention was achieved" (HREOC 1997, 272). The removals were intended to "absorb," "merge," and "assimilate" the children "so that Aborigines as a distinct group would disappear" (HREOC 1997, 270–75). The inquiry researchers and writers understood the UNCG and its flaws and complexities, and they did take the trouble to consult on the question of genocide and its meanings. Much of the hostility to the findings has come from people who insist that genocide was, and can only be, the footage we see of Bergen-Belsen bulldozers, dismembered bodies in Rwandan streets, and serried skulls in the Tuol Sleng Genocide Museum in Cambodia.

"In Their Best Interests"

Several former officials have admitted that while the practices were based on the notion of the rescuability of "half-caste" children, the removals were "for their own good" and not done heartlessly. For example, Colin Macleod (1997), a former Northern Territory public servant in the late 1950s, insists that removals were necessary because children, especially girls, were in danger of being sexually misused as "part-time concubines," their offspring rejected, neglected, or injured by their clans or relatives (174–75). Boys, he claims, were at the "crossroads," caught between Aboriginal community restrictions (which he called "incumbent problems") and being "raised as Europeans with all the benefits that entailed (voting, drinking, better education, and jobs)" (Macleod 1997, 174–75). He posits stark choices and asserts that "rescue" was the essence of the removals which he saw or was involved in: "Many of the children taken away were being given a chance to live and not die, to have a life beyond childhood without being permanently maimed" (Macleod 1997, 176).

Leslie Marchant (2003), a former Western Australian bureaucrat, insists that public servants didn't steal children but "protected them and their families, as we were charged to do by law, as the records show" (32–34). William Rubinstein (2009), a history professor in Australia and in Wales and author of *Genocide: A History*, offers a quite remarkable "revelation" in his aptly entitled *Quadrant* article, "The Biases of Genocide Studies" (56–58). The families of those removed "could be described as classically dysfunctional and in a state of familial social collapse: probably illiterate, unemployable mothers who in some cases engaged in prostitution" (Rubinstein 2009, 57). The crux, he explains, is that there was "almost always an absent father or multiple absent fathers" (Rubinstein 2009, 57). Had they been "full-blood" children and removed *en masse* as part of "a deliberate centrally-directed intentional policy," *that* could have been genocide (Rubinstein 2009, 58). But they were "half-European," "by-products" of casual or paid sex and, most significantly, *without fathers* (or *multiple fathers*) and hence were removed "to improve their life's chances"—and that can't be genocide (Rubinstein 2009, 57).

The *Bringing Them Home* report discussed this issue and concluded that "mixed motives," such as the benefits argued by men like Macleod, "are no excuse" for the forcible removal of children (HREOC 1997, 273–74). Or, as the moral philosopher Raimond Gaita (1997) contends, "the concept of good intention cannot be relativized indefinitely to an agent's perception of it as good" (21). If we could, he writes, then we would have to say that Nazi murderers had good, but radically benighted intentions, because most of them believed they had a sacred duty to the world to rid the world of the "race" that polluted it.

Margaret Jacobs (2009), who has published an important account of settler colonialism, "maternalism," and child removal in the American West and in Australia, concludes that "[child removal] reformers . . . sought to undermine the intimate bonds between indigenous children and their families and to replace them with a new loyalty and affiliation to institutional authorities" (31). Defenders of such practices ignore these bonds; they insist that the offset is that "good" has come out of these practices, and that many removed children have made outstanding contributions to society as activists, professionals, writers, artists, dancers, and sportspeople. Such positive outcomes, however, are not an issue in the context of genocide. These hindsight speculations are, in reality, no more than rationalizing pleas about needing to understand the times, the places, and the deeds; they are but appeals for mitigation, about leavening the negatives with positives, and they are used, often shamelessly, as an evasion or alleviation of both responsibility and accountability.

The Current State of Affairs

Denialism

Denialism rests quintessentially on assertion and contention rather than on research or any effort to demonstrate or affirm viewpoints. The contrast between two Western Australians could not be clearer. Thus, historian and anthropologist Anna Haebich published two books on the fragmentation of families and removal of children (Haebich 1988, 2000), and in a total of 1,138 pages, she attributed her interviews, research sources, and archival documents. Here, indeed, is evidence, not assertion. In contrast, Leslie Marchant penned three unsourced pages in *Quadrant* magazine to claim that he, personally, protected three (unnamed) children from neglect and danger, so he asserted that there was no child removal whatsoever in the West (Marchant 2003).

The *Bringing Them Home* report, and the general public dismay that ensued, led to the birth of a small but voluble denialist *industry*, mainly from a clique of right-wing journalists, a handful of retired public servants, a similar number of politicians, and a quintet of academics. First came the federal government bureaucrats who denigrated the whole Stolen Generations issue. Then, the Minister for Aboriginal Affairs defended their view, contending that since an *entire generation* was not removed but perhaps "only" one in ten children, one could not use the phrase "Stolen Generation(s)" (Herron 2000, in Senate Legal and Constitutional References Committee, Executive Summary, 2).

Bizarre moral equations and wild assertions abound. Suggestions about theft of children against parents' wishes are, some argue, inherently "absurd" (McGuinness 1999, 2), a "deliberate falsification of our history" (McGuinness 2001, 2–4) and "a calumny against the nation" (Brunton 1998, 24). Some also argue: even though the whole story is "a silly fairy tale," removal of children was good for them; Aboriginal pluses in history outweigh the minuses and so we can delete the minuses; the "stolen generation myth is both racist and genocidal and is killing Aboriginal children right now" (Bolt, *Herald Sun*, 2011); and,

13

at most, Australian racism is no more than "a sentiment rather than a belief, involving rejection of, or contempt for, or simply unease in the presence of, people recognized as different" (Minogue 1998, 15). The postulates of the denialists are stark and disturbed: it didn't happen; it couldn't have happened; it happened too long ago to prove; it was a hoax, a monument to false memory syndrome; the facts are open to different interpretations; what happened was not genocide; it wasn't theft of children but their rescue and protection; the earlier silence of academics makes the whole "story" suspicious now; there are no moral issues involved, only the "mistaken" and "fabricated" facts; reports of genocide are nothing but "sensation-mongering" and "unsupported hyperbole"; and the *Bringing Them Home* document revealed just how "well and truly the quality media has been taken for a ride" (McGuinness 2001, 2; see also Brunton 1998; McGuinness 1999, 2001; and Windschuttle 2000, 2002).

The late Padraic McGuinness was editor of *Quadrant* magazine from 1997 to 2007. The repository of almost all of this denialism, its articles are presented as opinion pieces, with nary a documented interview, a single source or reference. McGuinness styled himself and his colleagues as "Witnesses for the Defense," never explaining what it was they were defending. Keith Windschuttle is now the editor of *Quadrant* magazine, a man whose self-professed role is that of "Historian as Prophet and Redeemer" (Windschuttle 2002, 9–18). Singularly lacking any academic, field, or practical credentials in Aboriginal affairs, these "Witnesses" postulate, *inter alia*, that the charge of genocide is either an absurdity, pedantry, or mischief; an invention of white academics, some of whom, like historian Henry Reynolds, are arrogant and facetious, or like historian Ann Curthoys, are "red diaper babies" (Windschuttle 2006, 19), or like the author (Tatz), exhibit a "disagreeable self-hatred of [his] Jewish identity" (Brunton 2000, 41). Anthropologist Ron Brunton (2000) attacked the National Inquiry, concerned at the "role of suggestion in creating false memories of events that never really happened" (41–42). He castigated the failure to distinguish "truly voluntary" and "coerced" removals. He asserted that Tatz' "silence" over the years made it look suspicious that this "doyen of genocide studies" "suddenly" used the word genocide. Had Tatz and others spoken out earlier, Brunton (1998) argued, "this certainly would have brought a very rapid end to the supposed genocidal process (23). The late anthropologist Kenneth Maddock pointed to the "significant silence" of anthropologists who never mentioned genocide and talked of the "absurdity" of imputing evil to the Aboriginal authorities in Darwin. Besides which, his three academic acquaintances who worked with these very authorities—Colin Tatz, "the outspoken political scientist," the prehistorian Carmel White, and the anthropologist John Bern—"were of Jewish background and interested in Israel." Even they, with Zionistically attuned antennae, "caught not a whiff of genocide" (Maddock 1998, 2000).

Windschuttle, a former lecturer in social policy and media studies, is in a special class as a denialist. Singularly, he has contrived, by massive and indefatigable industriousness, to build a case that 20,000 Aborigines killed and some 35,000 children removed is all a fabrication by men and women operating under an "academic mask of respectability" (Windschuttle 2000, 2010). He never suggests why or how these otherwise reputable men and women, praised nationally and internationally for their meticulous research, have somehow collaborated and conspired in such blatant and deliberate falsification, or worse, concoction. Nor does he explain why so many removed Aborigines who had lost family, together with a major social movement like Link-Up, began such a concerted search for missing parents and siblings. Nor does Windschuttle explain how and why all states and most police forces have apologized for what they did and how Tasmania and Western Australia have been "conned" into a minor form of reparations for these actions.

Explaining Denialism

Why the denials? Some of them are racial animus, pure and simple. A senior public servant turned politician, John Stone, declared that all this was but the "misplaced remorse" of Australians and the "well-groomed pseudo Aborigines ... whose sole personal achievement has been to climb aboard the lushly-funded gravy train while holding out their hands for even more gravy," now part of the political culture (cited in *Australian Financial Review* 1995, n.p.). In April 2011, Melbourne journalist Andrew Bolt penned almost identical views on "white-skinned" Aborigines posing as "real" Aborigines for financial gain—only this time there were major repercussions when, in September 2011, a superior court found him guilty of breaching the federal *Racial Discrimination Act*, a judgment that led the conservative federal opposition to state that when in office it will abolish the prohibition of racial vilification because it "inhibits free speech" (*The Age* 2011; Tatz 2011b, 49–50).

15

Political scientist Robert Manne (2001) is less concerned with their denialists' motives than with what he calls the heart of the campaign, namely, "the meaning of Aboriginal dispossession" (102–4). There is, he argues, "a right-wing and populist resistance to discussions of historical injustice and the Aborigines" (Manne 2001, 102). Separation of mother and child "deeply captured the national imagination" (Manne 2001, 104). That "story had the power to change forever the way they saw their country's history"—hence the imperative to destroy that story (Manne 2001, 104).

I share Mannes's point but contend that denialism is centrally about the place of morality in Australian politics. It is either a promotion of an especial Australian moral gene, in which there is, by definition, no place for genocidal thoughts or actions, or it is an attempt to excise morality from political considerations—to create an amoral, economically centered body politic. I'm not quite sure which it is, and it may turn out to be both.

Australians are insecure about who and what we are, and where we are—a small number of predominantly white, Christian people surrounded by hundreds of millions of non-Christian Asians. The assimilationist tradition is powerful: we need to feel and to be seen as one, and in such oneness there isn't room for counter cultures, let alone for divergent views of our history. We don't see ourselves as "having a history" in any pejorative sense. Aboriginal nationalism, with its insistence on a preceding and parallel past and an unequal present, is disturbing, even distressing, a threat to a nation worried about fracturing, about cracks appearing in the temple of homogeneity. The nineteenth-century belief that Aborigines were dying out, or would die out, is an enduring one (McGregor 1997). Many would prefer that it endure forever. We need to be seen as "genuinely benevolent." We want noble origins to feel that we are in a "good" country, one dedicated to both the belief and the practice of egalitarianism as decent colonists and decent democrats.

Critical Challenges

Admissions of Culpability

The prevailing tenor in the 1990s and early 2000s was that the present generation cannot be held guilty, or responsible, for the misdeeds of our forebearers. The first public admission by a senior government figure was made in 1992. Prime Minister Paul Keating's speech in the Sydney suburb of Redfern admitted the taking of traditional Aboriginal lands, the murders, dispossessions, the alcohol, diseases, the taking of children from their mothers, the smashing of traditional life, and their exclusion from society and its benefits (Moores 1995, 377–82). (Historically, Redfern in inner Sydney became the locale of the largest concentrated Aboriginal population in New South Wales. The area known as "The Block" has been an overcrowded site of clashes with police, demolition of slums, refurbishment, and is now accepted as a permanent place of Aboriginal living and cultural activity.) What shocked the nation was the admission rather than the contents. Between 1997 and 2001, state and territory governments, most police departments, churches, mission societies, city and shire councils proclaimed both sorrow and apology for the general treatment of Aborigines and specifically for the forcible removal of children.

Bringing Them Home was published in April 1997. Between May 1997 and October 2001, apologies poured forth (a list of which was issued by the Australian Human Rights Commission: http://www. humanrights.gov.au/sites/default/files/content/pdf/social_justice/ bringing_them_home_report.pdf.) In May, South Australia apologized for "the mistakes of the past" ("including any relevant actions of South Australia Police"), regretting "the forced separation of some Aboriginal children." In June, New South Wales (NSW) apologized unreservedly "for the systematic separation of generations of Aboriginal children from their parents, families and communities" regretting parliament's passing laws and endorsing policies which produced such grief. In May 1998, the NSW Police Commissioner offered an apology on behalf of his service. In June 1997, the Australian Capital Territory (ACT) Legislative Assembly apologized for the hurt and distress for something that was "abhorrent"—"the past policies of forced separation."

In August 1997, Tasmania's parliament regretted the "removed children"; in September that year, Victoria State apologized for children "removed from their families" and expressed "deep regret at the hurt and distress" caused. The police indicated that enforcing policies "that now are acknowledged as racist" is a "significant cause of distrust of police." In May 1999, the Queensland government apologized for the "Indigenous children [who] were forcibly separated," but the police service did not. Western Australia apologized for the removal of children, an act that "encompasses acknowledgment by the Western Australian Police Service of its historical involvement in past policies and practices of forcible removal."

In November 2000, the Senate Legal and Constitutional References Committee produced its report (Senate Legal and Constitutional References 2000) on the federal government's implementation of the recommendations made in the *Bringing Them Home* report. It recommended a "Motion of National Apology and Reconciliation," a "gesture of good faith" by the Northern Territory parliament (which came about in October 2001), and the establishment of a "Reparations Tribunal." This committee produced compelling evidence as to why the conservative federal government should do what it had steadfastly refused to do.

That coalition, in office from 1996 to 2007, was adamant that were the nation to offer an apology it would open the way for costly compensation claims. Nor, said Prime Minister John Howard, could he apologize on behalf of migrant groups who had nothing to do with these events. He told talkback radio that he wanted Australians to "feel relaxed and comfortable about their past," he didn't wish to wake up each day to hear that Australia has had "a racist, bigoted past," and, accordingly, he would attempt a national school history program that accentuated "positive achievements" (Radio 2UE, October 24, 1996; *Sydney Morning Herald*, October 25–26, 1996). Despite his offer of a personal apology, his government was adamant in its refusal to issue any official acknowledgment of these events (Tatz 2003, 164–70).

The Australian Labor Party won the November 2007 election and Prime Minister Kevin Rudd set about a national apology. On February 13, 2008, the nation came close to a standstill as the national apology was televised from federal Parliament for several hours. Some of the wording is general but there are specific references to the children:

- We apologise for the laws and policies of successive Parliaments and governments that have inflicted profound grief, suffering and loss on these, our fellow, Australians.
- We apologise especially for the removal of Aboriginal and Torres Strait Islander children from their families, their communities and their country.
- For the pain, suffering and hurt of these Stolen Generations, their descendants and for their families left behind, we say sorry.
- To the mothers and the fathers, the brothers and the sisters, for the breaking up of families and communities, we say sorry.
- And for the indignity and degradation thus inflicted on a proud people and a proud culture, we say sorry (Hansard 2008, 167–73).

This was grand theater, made much more so by the intransigence of the former government. When state and local governments apologized years earlier, the press notices were there, recognized but somewhat muted. The delayed and therefore much-awaited national apology was climactic and, in a real sense, a *tremendum* in the national psyche.

Reparations and Law Suits

A dramatic day—but everyone (other than the victim population) was happy enough that the rider to the apology was that there would be no reparations. That kind of money, said the government, could be better spent elsewhere. Human rights lawyer Andrea Durbach (2008) has well described the saga of reparations in the widest sense as "splintered efforts" to remedy gross human violations—"sporadic, piecemeal and devoid of any national conviction" (1).

Here we have people now acknowledged as victims but who are not considered "appropriate" recipients of any restitution. Given that Tasmania is generally regarded as the area where the greatest genocidal actions occurred, it is perhaps ironic that this state is Australia's only domain that has initiated financial reparation. In November 2006, the Tasmanian Parliament passed the *Stolen Generations of Aboriginal Children Act*. In January 2008, Premier Paul Lennon declared that while "cash is a mere gesture," the lives of 106 claimants had been "deeply affected by this flawed policy of separation" (*The Australian*, January 29, 2008, n.p.). Of the 106, 84 were paid approximately $A55,000 each and each family of deceased claimants received approximately $A4,700. Western Australia established *Redress WA* in 2008 to acknowledge and apologize to adults who as children were abused and/or neglected while they were in state care. Written applications were sought for *ex-gratia* payments, adjudicated by a panel on a scale of severity of the abuse. No specific sums were indicated but an idea can be gained by the figures of $A5,000 to $A10,000 in the event of death before the adjudication. The Redress program was available for a very short term and lapsed in September 2011.

The Australian public was more generous in spirit. Many more people accepted the *Bringing Them Home* findings than rejected them (HREOC 1999, 27–47). Hundreds of thousands were prompted to sign "sorry books" located in public places; thousands stood in lines to listen to removed children telling their stories; many more thousands planted small wooden hands on lawns and beaches signifying hands held up in an admittance of guilt or sorrow; and even more thousands marched in solidarity across major city bridges. The first National Sorry Day was held in 1998 (and thereafter commemorated every May 26). From inception, the National Sorry Day Committee has worked assiduously to have the *Bringing Them Home* recommendations implemented and for Stolen Generations history to be incorporated into all school syllabuses.

Several Stolen Generation groups have resorted to civil law in search of recognition of their experience and compensation for their usually troubled lives. Two dozen cases have been heard in various jurisdictions. Most have focused on sexual assaults while incarcerated, or on breaches of fiduciary care, arguing that state or territory administrations had, by removing them, not cared for them appropriately. Most have lost on technicalities and several have spent enormous sums on legal fees and extensive trips to Darwin (Cunneen and Grix 2004; Buti 2008). But it is important to note that not one case has sought to establish *directly* that Australia bound itself to the Genocide Convention in 1949 and that forcible child transfer is the essence of the Genocide Convention Article II(e). The Howard federal government spent between $A15 and $A20 million defending one case alone (brought by Lorna Cubillo and Peter Gunner, both removed at age eight) in the Northern Territory (Rush 2008, 30). Even though the plaintiffs lost the case on a technicality, *Quadrant* writers openly celebrated the result as victory for those who had always said Australia was "not guilty" (Bennett 2000; Meagher 2000). A short-lived "victory" because the benchmark has now been set by South Australia's Supreme Court. On August 1, 2007, it awarded Bruce Trevorrow $A525,000 (and a further $A250,000 in interest) for being treated unlawfully and for being falsely imprisoned when he was removed from his mother and handed to a white family when he was only thirteen months old (Buti 2008). Following his decease in 2008, the South Australian government appealed the verdict, claiming it didn't want the money back, but only wanted "clarity" on points of law. In March 2010, the full court rejected that appeal.

Tellingly, Howard's refusal to apologize lest it open such legal doors was always in vain. There has been no shortage of complainants and the significant Trevorrow case has perhaps opened more legal avenues of restitution than can be accommodated by a limited and (doubtless tokenistic) reparations program.

Conclusion

Elazar Barkan (2000) has dealt eloquently with *The Guilt of Nations*, the matter of restitution and the negotiating of historical injustices. Australia has now moved, as have other western states, to a willingness to acknowledge the past, even the recent past, but it has yet to arrive at the logical consequence of that position—that the victims deserve consideration. Roy Brooks, an esteemed American law professor and author of numerous books on atonement and forgiveness, has edited a pertinently titled book, *When Sorry Isn't Enough* (1999). He doesn't address the Australian case in a separate chapter, but he may well have one in his next edition. Most removed children I know have moved beyond their original goals: to find family and to have the authorities acknowledge that something happened to them. As they find out more about the injustices, and as their frustration increases at our poor record of negotiating them, so also action will increase for exemplary and penalty damages.

References

Aly, Götz, Peter Chroust, and Christian Pross. 1994. *Cleansing the Fatherland: Nazi Medicine and Racial Hygiene*. Baltimore, MD: The Johns Hopkins University Press.

Barkan, Elazar. 2000. *The Guilt of Nations: Restitution and Negotiating Historical Injustices*. New York: WW Norton & Company.

Bennett, David. 2000. "The *Cubillo* and *Gunner* Cases." *Quadrant* 44, no. 11: 35–43.

Beresford, Quentin, and Paul Omaji. 1998. *Our State of Mind: Racial Planning and the Stolen Generations*. Fremantle, WA: Fremantle Arts Centre Press.

Bolt, Andrew. 2011. "It's Hip to be Black." *Herald-Sun*. April 15. n.p.

Bolt, Andrew. n.d. "Statement by Shandow Attorney General George Brandis." *The Age*. September 30, 2011.

Bradfield, Stuart. 1997. "With the Best of Intentions: The Removal of Aboriginal Children and the Question of Genocide." BA Honours thesis, Politics Department, Macquarie University, Sydney (available online).

Brooks, Roy, ed. 1999. *When Sorry Isn't Enough: The Controversy Over Apologies and Reparations for Human Injustice*. New York: New York University Press.

Brunton, Ronald. 2000. "Betraying the Victims: The 'Stolen Generations' Report." Available at: www.gwb.com.au/2000/pc/stolen1.html (accessed April 4, 2000).

Brunton, Ronald. 1998. "Genocide, the 'Stolen Generations' and the 'Unconceived Generations.'" *Quadrant* May, 42, no. 5: 19–24.

Buti, Antonio. 2008. "The Stolen Generations and Litigation Revisited." *Melbourne University Law Review* 32, no. 2: 383–419.

Choo, Christine. 2001. *Mission Girls: Aboriginal Women on Catholic Missions in the Kimberley, Western Australia, 1900–1950.* Perth, WA: University of Western Australia Press.

Durbach, Andrea. 2008. "'The Cost of a Wounded Society': Reparations and the Illusion of Reconciliation." *NSW Law Research Series 4.* www.austill.edu.au/journal/UNSWLRS/2008/4.

Gaita, Raimond. 1997. "Genocide, the Holocaust and the Aborigines." *Quadrant* 41, no. 7–8: 17–22.

Gale, C. F. 1909. *Report of the Chief Protector.* Perth, WA: Parliament, Votes and Proceedings, vol. 2, West Australian State Archives (653/213/1909).

Gray, Stephen. 2011. *Brass Discs, Dog Tags and Finger Scanners: The Apology and Aboriginal Protection in the Northern Territory, 1863–1972.* Darwin, NT: Charles Darwin University Press.

Haebich, Anna. 1988. *For Their Own Good: Aborigines and Government in the South West of Western Australia.* Perth, WA: University of Western Australia Press.

———. 2000. *Broken Circles: Fragmenting Indigenous Families 1800–2000.* Fremantle, WA: Fremantle Arts Centre Press.

Hansard (House of Representatives debates). 2008. "Apology to Australia's Indigenous People." 13 February, 167–73.

Herron, Senator John. 2000, "Minister for Aboriginal and Torres Strait Islander Affairs, Federal Government Submission to Senate Legal and Constitutional References Committee, Inquiry into the Stolen Generation [*Healing*]," March. Canberra, ACT: Commonwealth of Australia.

HREOC [The Human Rights and Equal Opportunity Commission]. 1997. *Bringing Them Home: Report of the National Inquiry into the Separation of Aboriginal and Torres Strait Islander Children from their Families.* Sydney, New South Wales: Human Rights and Equal Opportunity Commission.

———. 1999. *Social Justice Report 1998.* Sydney: Human Rights and Equal Opportunity Commission.

Jacobs, Margaret. 2009. *White Mother to a Dark Race: Settler Colonialism, Maternalism and the Removal of Indigenous Children in the American West and Australia, 1880–1940.* Lincoln: University of Nebraska Press.

Macleod, Colin. 1997. *Patrol in the Dreamtime.* Sydney: Random House.

Maddock, Kenneth. 1998. "The 'Stolen Generations': A Report from Experience." *Agenda* 5, no. 3: 347–53.

———. 2000. "Genocide and the Silence of the Anthropologists." *Quadrant* 44, no. 11: 11–16.

Manne, Robert. 2001. *Quarterly Essay: In Denial—the Stolen Generations and the Right.* Melbourne: Morry Schwartz, Black Inc.

Marchant, Leslie. 2003. "From the Diary of a Protector of Aborigines." *Quadrant* 47, no. 4: 32–34.

McGregor, Russell. 1997. *Imagined Destinies: Aborigines and the Doomed Race Theory, 1880–1939.* Melbourne: Melbourne University Press.

McGuinness, P. P. 1999. "Poor Fella My 'Stolen Generation.'" *Quadrant* 43, no. 11: 2–4.

———. 2001. "The Erosion of the 'Stolen Generations' Slogan." *Quadrant* 45, no. 4: 2–4.

Meagher, Douglas. 2000. "Not Guilty." *Quadrant* 44, no. 11: 26–34.

Minogue, Kenneth. 1998. "Aborigines and Australian Apologetics." *Quadrant* 42, no. 9: 11–20.

Moores, Irene. 1995. *Voices of Aboriginal Australia: Past, Present, Future.* Springwood, NSW: Butterfly Books.

Raynes, Cameron. 2009. *The Last Protector: The Illegal Removal of Aboriginal Children from Their Parents in South Australia.* Kent Town, SA: Wakefield Press.

Read, Peter. 1981. *The Stolen Generations: The Removal of Aboriginal Children in New South Wales 1883 to 1969.* Sydney: NSW Ministry of Aboriginal Affairs.

Rubinstein, William. 2009. "The Biases of Genocide Studies." *Quadrant* 53, no. 5: 56–59.

Rush, John. 2008. "*Cubillo and Gunner* revisited: a question of national character." *Australian Indigenous Law Review* 12: 25–31.

Senate Legal and Constitutional References Committee. 2000. *Healing: A Legacy of Generations: The Report of the Inquiry into the Federal Government's Implementation of the Recommendations Made by the Human Rights and Equal Opportunity Commission in Bringing Them Home,* Commonwealth of Australia, November. Sydney, NSW: Government of Australia.

Tatz, Colin. 2003. *With Intent to Destroy: Reflecting on Genocide.* London: Verso.

———. 2011a. "The Destruction of Aboriginal Society in Australia" In *Genocide of Indigenous Peoples: Genocide—A Critical Bibliographic Review,* ed. Samuel Totten, and Robert K. Hitchcock, Vol. 8, 87–116. New Brunswick, NJ: Transaction Publishers.

———. 2011b. *Genocide in Australia: By Accident or Design?* Melbourne: Monash Indigenous Centre and Castan Centre for Human Rights Law. http://www.law.monash.edu.au/castancentre/projects/tatz-essay.pdf

Windschuttle, Keith. 2000. "The Myths of Frontier Massacres: (Part III) Massacre Stories and the Policy of Separation." *Quadrant* 44, no. 12: 6–20.

———. 2002. "The Historian as Prophet and Redeemer." *Quadrant* 46, no. 12: 9–18.

———. 2006. "The Return of Postmodernism in Aboriginal History." *Quadrant* 50, no. 4: 9–23.

———. 2010. *The Fabrication of Aboriginal History: The Stolen Generations.* Sydney: Macleay Press.

Annotated Bibliography

Uncovering the Stolen Generations

Chisholm, Richard. *Black Children: White Welfare? Aboriginal Child Welfare Law and Policy in New South Wales.* SWRC Reports and Proceedings, 52. Kensington, NSW: Social Welfare Research Centre, University Welfare New South Wales, 1985, 144 pp.

In tandem with Peter Read's 1981 work, Richard Chisholm was one of the first scholars to raise the issues of Aboriginal child welfare and placements in New South Wales.

MacDonald, Roweena. *Between Two Worlds: The Commonwealth Government and the Removal of Aboriginal Children of Part Descent in the Northern Territory.* Alice Springs: IAD Press, 1995, 78 pp.

A significant collection of official documents and correspondence that provides incontrovertible evidence of governmental policy and practice of child removal. This invaluable book is based on several public exhibitions by National Archives Australia.

Read, Peter. *The Stolen Generations: The Removal of Aboriginal Children in New South Wales 1883 to 1969.* Sydney: NSW Ministry of Aboriginal Affairs, 1983, 20 pp.

This short account introduced the public to the concept and the reality of forcibly removed children, the stolen rather than the separated children. Peter Read uses the word genocide to describe child removal.

Official Inquiries

Bleakley, J. W. *The Aboriginals and Half-Castes of Central and North Australia.* Melbourne: Government Printer, 1929, 65 pp.

The Director of Aboriginal Affairs in Queensland was invited to provide the federal government with a report on the Northern Territory. The eugenicist ideas of the time come though clearly.

Human Rights and Equal Opportunity Commission. *Bringing Them Home: Report of the National Inquiry into the Separation of Aboriginal and Torres Strait Islander Children from Their Families.* Sydney: Human Rights and Equal Opportunity Commission, 1997, 689 pp.

This significant report traces the history of laws, policies, and practices in each state and territory which led to the removal of children; describes the consequences of removal on children, families, and communities, including intergenerational effects; recommends reparation and compensation principles as well as professional support services needed by those affected by removal. The report justifies its use of the term genocide. It details lists of all Aboriginal and child welfare statutes.

Senate Legal and Constitutional References. *Healing: A Legacy of Generations: The Report of the Inquiry into the Federal Government's Implementation of the Recommendations Made by the Human Rights and Equal Opportunity Commission in Bringing Them Home.* Sydney, New South Wales: Commonwealth of Australia, 2000, 416 pp.

An important sequel to the *Bringing Them Home Report.* The authors examine the responses by governments to the fifty-four recommendations made by the National Inquiry, finding that many of the key changes, some two hundred, had been ignored. Most remain unaddressed at this time (2013).

Western Australian Government. *Report of the Royal Commission Appointed to Investigate, Report and Advise Upon Matters Relating to the Condition and Treatment of Aborigines.* [H. D. Moseley]. Western Australia, Votes and Proceedings, 2. Perth: Government Printer, 1935, 24 pp.

The Moseley Royal Commission examined proposals to extend the powers of A. O. Neville, the Chief Protector of Aborigines, and the social policy of removal of children from their parents. Submissions detailed accusations of child slavery, abuse, and mistreatment and the evidence given by mothers of the removed children. While concluding there were "problems" with the policy, Moseley recommended continuation of Neville's regime. Anna Haebich (1988, 2000) addresses fully the evidence of mothers and other witnesses.

Meston, Archibald. *Report on the Aboriginals of North Queensland, (Under Instructions from the Queensland Government)*. Brisbane, Queensland Parliament Votes and Proceedings, 4 (85). Brisbane, Queensland: Government Printer, 1896, 18 pp.

Archibald Meston, appointed by colony Queensland to investigate what was, in effect, genocide, was one of the first to report that "boys and girls were frequently taken from their parents . . . with no chance of their returning."

Scholarly Treatments

Beresford, Quentin, and Omaji, Paul. *Our State of Mind: Racial Planning and the Stolen Generations*. Fremantle, WA: Fremantle Arts Centre Press, 1998, 295 pp.

Examines (a) why governments introduced the child removal and assimilation policies, (b) what was decided at the 1937 conference of state and Commonwealth officials on Aboriginal affairs policy, and (c) the influence of the eugenicist and assimilationist, A. O. Neville.

Choo, Christine. *Mission Girls: Aboriginal Women on Catholic Missions in the Kimberley, Western Australia, 1900–1950*. Perth, WA: University of Western Australia Press, 2001, 350 pp.

A detailed analysis of attempts by Catholic missionaries, men and women, to control the lives, identities, bodies, values, marriage, and sexual behavior of Aboriginal girls from the age of seven upward.

Gray, Stephen. *Brass Discs, Dog Tags and Finger Scanners: The Apology and Aboriginal Protection in the Northern Territory 1863–1972*. Darwin, NT: Charles Darwin University Press, 2011, 229 pp.

An overview of racial policies and practices by the federal and territory governments. It includes a chapter on the eugenicist views of the Chief Protector of Aborigines, Dr. Cecil Cook.

Haebich, Anna. *For Their Own Good: Aborigines and Government in the South West of Western Australia, 1900 to 1940*. Perth, WA: University of Western Australia Press, 1988, 413 pp.

A detailed account of the *Aborigines Act* 1905, the impoverishment of Aboriginal communities, child removal, and institutionalization, A. O. Neville's regime, the struggle for identities, and the Moseley Royal Commission of 1835.

Haebich, Anna. *Broken Circles: Fragmenting Indigenous Families 1800–2000*. Fremantle, WA: Fremantle Arts Centre Press, 2000, 726 pp.

The most comprehensive and seminal account of forcible child transfer in the various states and territories of Australia: official policies and practices, the Aboriginal reaction to these interventions, and the resultant fragmentation of Aboriginal families. The author documents political campaigns by Aborigines from the 1970s to the 1990s to regain control of their children.

Jacobs, Margaret. *White Mother to a Dark Race: Settler Colonialism, Maternalism and the Removal of Indigenous Children in the American West and Australia, 1880–1940*. Lincoln, NE: University of Nebraska Press, 2009, 557 pp.

A significant comparison of colonial practices of child removal in the western United States and Australia. The author diagnoses the "misdiagnosis" of the problem: insatiable demand for land, together with homogenization as white

Christians were the problem, not the native peoples. Even the "maternalists" misconceived the issues.

McGlade, Hannah. *Our Greatest Challenge: Aboriginal Children and Human Rights*. Canberra, ACT: Aboriginal Studies Press, 2012, 284 pp.

The significance of this work is in the detailed treatment of sexual abuse of stolen children and the treble trauma of loss of family, loss of human dignity and the introduction of sexual violence in Aboriginal communities.

Moses, A. Dirk, ed. *Genocide and Settler Society: Frontier Violence and Stolen Indigenous Children in Australian History*. New York: Berghahn Books, 2005, 325 pp.

This edited collection includes three chapters on the Aboriginal Stolen Generations. Anna Haebich's compelling essay deals with the concept of "erasing the Indigenous presence" in the southwest of western Australia.

Raynes, Cameron. *The Last Protector: The Illegal Removal of Aboriginal Children from their Parents in South Australia*. Kent Town, SA: Wakefield Press, 2009, 102 pp.

This short work uncovers remarkable archival material showing the way in which William Penhall and his department removed Aboriginal children contrary to child protection laws in force in South Australia in the mid-twentieth century.

Tatz, Colin. *Genocide in Australia: By Accident or Design?* Melbourne: Monash Indigenous Centre and Castan Centre for Human Rights (online and hard copy editions), 2011, 100 pp. http://www.law.monash.edu.au/castancentre/projects/tatz-essay.pdf

This monograph is an expansion and elaboration of earlier essays by Colin Tatz that analyze the intent, motives, methods, manner, and outcomes of Australia's genocidal history, including the physical killing phases through to child removal practices.

Van Krieken, Robert. "Rethinking Cultural Genocide: Aboriginal Child Removal and Settler–Colonial State Formation." *Oceania* 75, no. 2 (2004): 125–51.

Discusses genocide and the removal of Aboriginal children, the legislative and administrative bases as well as welfare and genocide involved in Australian child removal.

Denialism

Manne, Robert. *Quarterly Essay: In Denial—the Stolen Generations and the Right*. Melbourne: Morry Schwartz, Black Inc., 2001, 113 pp.

A critical account of the right-wing campaign against the *Bringing Them Home* report. Robert Manne analyzes the nature and motives of those who deny the historical mistreatment of the Australian Aborigines, particularly the conservative newspaper columnists and the *Quadrant* editor, the late P. P. (Paddy) McGuinness.

Windschuttle, Keith. *The Fabrication of Aboriginal History: The Stolen Generations*, 1881–2008. Sydney: Macleay Press, 2010, 656 pp.

This is a sequel to Keith Windschuttle's first volume which disputed genocidal massacres. In this volume he concludes that "almost all" removals of Aboriginal children were conducted "on the same child welfare policies that applied to white children," and were "neither racist nor genocidal." There are, he argues, "no 'Stolen Generations.'" This long work is the culmination of

Windschuttle's numerous articles in *Quadrant* magazine on how scholars—
"under the mask of respectability"—have, he alleges, fabricated and concocted
a shameful history of which Australia is not guilty.

Law Suits, Reparations, Public Responses

Buti, Antonio. "The Stolen Generations and Litigation Revisited." *Melbourne University Law Review* 32, no. 2 (2008): 383–419.

This legal analysis consolidates what has been written to date on legal cases brought by removed Aboriginal children. While the focus is on the Bruce Trevorrow case (*Trevorrow v. South Australia* [No. 5] (2007) 98 SASR 136), there are important references to earlier trials which were unsuccessful.

Cunneen, Chris, and Julia Grix. *The Limitations of Litigation in Stolen Generations Cases*. Research Discussion Paper No.15. Canberra: Aboriginal Studies Press, 2004, 48 pp.

The pursuit of court action by Joy Williams, Alex Kruger, George Bray, Lorna Cubillo, Peter Gunner, Valerie Linow, and Christopher Johnson. The limitations of the legal system are carefully analyzed. The authors argue for a reparations-style tribunal in place of existing legal processes.

Durbach, Andrea. "'The Cost of a Wounded Society': Reparations and the Illusion of Reconciliation." *NSW Law Research Series 4*, 2008. www.austill.edu.au/journals/UNSWLRS/2008/4.

An important dissection of Australia's poor record in negotiating historical injustices and responding to requests or demands for apology, compensation, and restitution.

Kruger, Alec, and Gerard Waterford. *Alone on the Soaks: The Life and Times of Alec Kruger*. Alice Springs, NT: IAD Press, 2007, 342 pp.

Alec Kruger was one of the first of the Aboriginal Stolen Generation to seek redress in the courts. His case failed on a number of technical rather than substantive grounds. He describes his "stolen" experience and his court travails (see *Kruger v.The Commonwealth; Bray v. The Commonwealth* (1997) 190 CLR 1).

Aboriginal Viewpoints

Bird, Carmel, ed. *The Stolen Children: Their Stories: Including Extracts from the Report of the National Inquiry into the Separation of Aboriginal and Torres Strait Islander Children from their Families*. Sydney: Random House Australia, 1998, 194 pp.

Some five hundred removed children gave evidence to the National Inquiry. Most were given in confidence, their names withheld. This collection constitutes compelling testimony of, and the impact on, each removed child.

Cummings, Barbara. *Take This Child . . . From Kahlin Compound to the Retta Dixon Children's Home*. Canberra: Aboriginal Studies Press, 1990, 139 pp.

An Aboriginal view of the impact of institutionalization on part-Aboriginal people in the Northern Territory. The author grew up under the "dormitory system," which began with the Kahlin Compound, and was later transferred to Bagot Reserve and the Retta Dixon Home which was administered by the Aborigines Inland Mission.

Kennedy, Roseanne. "Stolen Generation Testimony: Trauma, Historiography and the Question of 'Truth.'" *Aboriginal History* 25 (2001): 116–31.

A vital discussion of the attempts to both validate and negate the value of oral testimony given by Aboriginal children removed from their families. The author castigates the search for "clinical" testimony devoid of emotion or what has been labeled "collective hysteria."

Mellor, Doreen, and Anna Haebich, eds. *Many Voices: Reflections on Experiences of Indigenous Child Separation.* Canberra, ACT: National Library of Australia, 2002, 324 pp.

Possibly the best collection of comments, quotations, and documents relating to governmental policies, institutions, memoirs, testimonies, and biographies of removed children.

Read, Peter. *A Rape of the Soul So Profound: The Return of the Stolen Generations.* Sydney: Allen & Unwin, 1999, 215 pp.

Nearly twenty years after his initial monograph on the Stolen Generations, historian Peter Read examines the impact of removals on a number of victims. Many remain forever broken, while others have overcome their often inhumane experiences.

Simon, Bill, Des Montgomerie, and Jo Tuscano. *Back on the Block: Bill Simon's Story.* Canberra, Aboriginal Studies Press, 2009, 170 pp.

Simon is a church pastor living in Sydney's famous "Block" in the inner Sydney suburb of Redfern. Removed to Kinchela Boys' Home, he found his mother when in his thirties. "I had turned into someone that not many mothers would have wanted for a son."

Tatz, Colin. "Genocide in Australia." In *Centuries of Genocide: Eyewitness Accounts and Critical Views*, ed. Samuel Totten and William S. Parsons, 4th ed., 55–87. New York: Routledge, 2012.

An overview of Australia's eras of physical killing of Aborigines on the frontiers and the systematic removal of Aboriginal children across the continent. It includes poignant extracts from Aboriginal eyewitness accounts of their removal and incarceration.

2

Hell Is for Children: The Impact of Genocide on Young Armenians and the Consequences for the Target Group as a Whole

Henry C. Theriault

Any discussion of genocide against Armenians during World War I and after must begin with the caveat that it was part of an overarching genocidal process targeting Greeks, Assyrians, and Armenians. Due to geographical, political, ideological, and practical variations, the treatment of the different groups was not identical; but, be that as it may, there are sufficient parallels to justify some generalizations in terms of the impacts on victims. For instance, while their uses and contexts differed, one can draw a parallel between the effects of the Greek labor battalions and the reduction of Armenian soldiers to slave-like labor and conditions, as well as forced labor on the Baghdad Railroad. That said, regarding the fate of children, the main distinction now is that the fate of Armenian children has become the topic of focused academic analysis and documentary filmmaking, while the treatment of the other groups' children largely remains integrated in the broader literature as it is in the primary sources. Even this, though, is beginning to change, especially with Australian scholar Panayiotis Diamadis's (2012) new article on "Children and Genocide," which includes an extended section on "The Hellenic, Armenian and Assyrian Genocide." While most of the scholarship discussed in this chapter focuses on Armenians, much of what is developed can be applied to Greeks and Assyrians without significant qualification. What is more, the author expects that in coming years a more integrated approach to these three victim groups will become the norm and that comparative work on the fate of children will be part of this trend.

While there is one classic treatment of children in the *Survivors: An Oral History of the Armenian Genocide* (Miller and Miller 1993), there still has not been sustained attention on the issue, as denial, historiography, geopolitics, and long-term resolution/justice remain dominant in the discourse. However, even in Turkey, there are signs that this situation is changing.

Developing a Framework of Analysis

There are two interrelated ways to understand the impact of the Armenian genocide on children. The first and most obvious way is to look at how genocide affected children specifically. Material considerations are one axis of analysis: Were children targeted along with adults? Under what conditions and how were children killed—direct killing versus disease, starvation, thirst, etc.? Were children forcibly transferred from the victim group? And so on. The other axis is psychological considerations: What did children who later died as well as those who survived witness, and how did it affect them? What happened to the ethnic and religious identity of children who suffered genocide, especially those forcibly or voluntarily removed from families? What kind of resilience or resistance did children demonstrate? And so on. Long-term effects must be differentiated from short-term effects. For instance, what were the effects of childhood malnutrition on growth and adult health?

The second way to understand the impacts of genocide on children is through their implications for the group. Similar to the first way, material and socioconceptual axes refine the issue. On the one hand, to what extent was the prevention of children being conceived and born practiced, which, in turn, could constitute a means of destroying the target group? To what extent were children transferred from the victim to the perpetrator group? And so on. On the other hand, what were the effects of the traumas sustained by children on the future development of their group? Did the trauma experienced and the destruction of their childhood (itself in a sense a target of genocide) negatively (or positively) affect their own parenting practices and thus the social dynamics of their group? And so on.

While for a variety of oft-rehearsed reasons, the United Nations' definition of genocide in the UN Convention on the Prevention and the Punishment of the Crime of Genocide (UNCG) is contested, to the credit of its developers, it is quite a useful framework for considering the impact of genocide on children and the consequences of that impact on the target group. Two of the five listed methods of carrying out genocide focus on children: the prevention of live births in the group and the forcible transfer of children from one group to another. The impact of genocide on children and its consequences for the group are thus explicit in the UN definition.

The other three methods—direct killing, creation of conditions that result in death, and infliction of bodily or mental harm—also readily apply to children and suggest possible distinctions from adults, for instance in the kinds of mental harm inflicted or the susceptibility of children to difficult physical conditions such as food or water deprivation. But, despite these differences, in actual cases of genocide these three methods are routinely applied to victim subsets that include children. Thus, children suffer these harms alongside or parallel to[1] adults from their group. In the Armenian case, for instance, Talat Pasha gave an explicit order to subject children to the same destruction as adults (Charny 1999).

This suggests a complicating factor. Children, particularly adolescents, are often treated by perpetrators as adult members of the target group. For instance, twelve-year-old boys might be killed as potential soldiers, while twelve-year-old girls might be raped "as women" or forced into sexual slavery or prostitution.[2] Thus, we might examine the impact of this treatment as harms to children understood against an objective category of "child," but we might also look at it relative to the perpetrators' self-understanding of their actions toward those who are objectively children. Did perpetrators view themselves as harming children? Given younger ages of marriage and a shorter overall life expectancy in the Ottoman Empire than that of most contemporary scholars of genocide, a possible difference must be recognized in the present analysis.

The Fate of Children

This section sketches out the various ways in which the 1915–1923 Armenian Genocide affected children, culled from accounts detailed in the Annotated Bibliography (which is included at the end of this narrative). First, of course, children were targeted along with others in the general population of Armenians remaining after Armenian men were killed and Armenian men in the military had either been enslaved or killed. Children, especially younger children, were susceptible to hunger, disease, and exposure, as well as less able to keep up with deportation caravans and thus often left behind to die. Conditions of starvation and thirst made it more difficult, if not impossible, for nursing mothers to produce milk. Babies were targeted for death along with others, but there are accounts of particularly cruel killings of babies by, for instance, soldiers throwing them in the air and catching them on bayonets (Housepian 1999, 63). Fetuses were also targeted, for instance, when pregnant women's abdomens were slashed and fetuses ripped out.

There was also rampant sexual abuse of girls, including a chilling account in Donald Miller and Lorna Touryan Miller's (1993) *Survivors: An Oral History of the Armenian Genocide*:

> References to sexual abuse abound in our interviews, but one of the most graphic accounts was of a young girl who was raped by one of the Turkish leaders of a town through which their caravan passed. Gendarmes went through the caravan and found an especially pretty twelve-year-old girl. They dragged her away from her mother, telling the weeping woman that they would return her. And, in fact, the child was returned, but she had been terribly abused and died. (102–3)

Girls were also forced into sexual slavery or "marriage," while accounts abound of girls and boys also being forced into domestic slavery. In his description of the horrific destruction of Armenians from Erzerum, Hilmar Kaiser (2002) provides many details about the rape, kidnapping, enslavement, and starvation of children. This includes the sale of children and women who had "entered Muslim households" in the hope of being saved from the genocide: "The prices of an Armenian child's life was low. Sometimes it cost 2 Medjidie, sometimes 8 piastres, or just a handful of flour" (Kaiser 2002, 167).

There also many cases in which Armenian children were taken into Turkish homes in order to be assimilated into Turkish families, culture, and society. In effect, the effort was made to make them into "Turks." The isolation and vulnerability of such children presumably assisted the forced assimilation process, though there is a good deal of survivor testimony about children who later ran away and reclaimed their Armenian identity. Some children were also rescued by the League of Nations' Commission of Inquiry for the Protection of Women and Children in the Near East and other initiatives. It is difficult to know what percentage remained, however, because the history of such children has largely been lost, with the exception of some memoirs about those who remained in their new situations. The growing awareness in Turkey of those who remained with their Turkish families has raised complex identity issues for them and their progeny.

An area of growing interest is the fate of those orphaned in the Armenian genocide, whether they were rescued by compassionate Muslims, escaped from captivity, or simply survived death marches that claimed the lives of adult family members. Tens of thousands ended up in orphanages, and many of them eventually made their way to places such as Canada and the United States. Bared Maronian's film, *Orphans of Genocide* (Maronian 2013), includes a segment on a Turkish-government-run orphanage intended to Turkify Armenian orphan victims of the genocide. This formal institutionalization of Turkification actually fits the UN definition discussed above—it was the intentional transfer of children from one group to another.

The long-term psychological effects of childhood victimization in the genocide are evident in many survivor testimonies made by elderly survivors. Some appear to remember what happened to them vividly, even in old age, and react emotionally to it, for instance, by breaking down in tears during the process of remembering (Jones 1992). Miller and Miller (1993) address, in depth, the different forms of long-term psychological damage to the children, and this phenomenon is confirmed by numerous other scholars (Boyajian and Grigorian 1986; Kalayjian et al. 1996; Kalayjian and Shahinian 1998). Lost childhood is a broader phenomenon and suggests developmental challenges, as does the general context of being more or less targeted for genocide.

Later Generations

While not strictly speaking part of the specific topic of this bibliographic review, it is worth mentioning that in recent years the issue of the intergenerational transfer of trauma as well as the various material, social, cultural, political, and other impacts of genocide on later generations have emerged as important areas of discussion. For the purposes of this treatment of the impact of the Armenian genocide on children, the issue is the effect of the genocide on the childhoods of later generations. Levon Boyajian and Haigaz Grigorian (1986) identify a number of effects on the development of the children and grandchildren of survivors. One very disturbing finding is that children of survivors "grew up in many instances with a sense that life was a serious business; that because of [the Armenian genocide] and the sufferings of their parents, they were required to be serious and, in some sense, almost sad; that they did not have the right to be happy and cheerful" (Boyajian and Grigorian 1986, 181).

Works by grandchildren of survivors, such as Arlene Voski Avakian's *Lion Woman's Legacy: An Armenian-American Memoir* (Avakian 1992), Peter Balakian's *Black Dog of Fate: An American Son Uncovers His Armenian Past* (Balakian 1997), and Markar Melkonian's *My Brother's Road: An American's Fateful Journey to Armenia* (Melkonian 2005), have added to the understanding of the long-term impact on the personal, social, ethical, and political development of later generations of Armenians. Avakian's complex feminist engagement with her Armenian identity through her relationship with her grandmother's genocide narrative, Balakian's scholarly and artistic development, and Monte Melkonian's path from "all American kid" to radical political activist and military leader also highlight the agency of later generations of Armenians in responding to and reconstructing Armenian identity. Similarly, Fethiye Çetin's *My Grandmother: An Armenian-Turkish Memoir* (Çetin 2012) offers insight into the effects of having as a grandmother a Turkified child survivor of the Armenian genocide and the process she followed to learn about her grandmother.

The Primacy of the Text

The range of types of text relevant to Armenian children in the genocide begins with works that detail or discuss broader elements of the genocide that include victimization of children. For instance, eyewitness reports by US consular officials and others include many details of the treatment of specific groups of Armenian victims in particular places at particular times. These include accounts of children being killed along with adults; children being abandoned, kidnapped, or given or sold to Turks or others; sexual violence against children, primarily girls; children's bodies visible among the killed; and so forth. Survivor narratives not only include such details, but also often include more personalized accounts that focus in on particular children and individual stories. Scholarly analyses similarly refer to children as part of the overall victim group, but generally in an abstract way and without separating them out: as part of the "women, children, and elderly" Armenians who remained in the villages and towns in eastern Asia Minor after the Armenian men in the military had been killed and remaining local Armenian men had been removed for deportation, slave labor, or massacre. Because especially recent scholarship on the Armenian genocide tends to present the geopolitical and internal political dynamics, histories, and tensions that led to genocide, or the overall process of genocide as a means of confirming the facts against denial, children tend not to be separated out for analysis.

One ground-breaking exception to this is Donald Miller and Lorna Touryan Miller's *Survivors: An Oral History of the Armenian Genocide* (Miller and Miller 1993), which features a chapter specifically on "The Experiences of Women and Children," with subsections devoted to children. Miller and Miller's innovation is not merely to describe the treatment of children (and women) specifically, but to discuss and analyze the distinct elements of that treatment and its effects on victims *as children* (*and women*). For instance, based on survivor narratives, Miller and Miller (1993) detail the psychological impact of the children's separation from parents and families, and their social development in a context of isolation and the desperate struggle to survive. Not only is the separation from an adult on whom one is dependent a unique experience in the victim group (adults certainly experience intense psychological harm from separation—especially separation from children, but the separation itself is of a different nature) and so objectively distinct from the experiences of other victims, but it also has impacts on the child developmentally and materially that are different from effects on adults.

This suggests an important aspect of the fate of children in the Armenian genocide and explains why survivor narratives and other material provide fertile ground for further research on this topic. As with Miller and Miller but also with most if not all documentaries, such as the BBC's *Hidden Holocaust* and Araz Artinian's *Twenty Voices: The Last Testimonies of the 1915 Armenian Genocide Survivors*, much of the academic and documentary research on the genocide was begun only in the 1970s, 1980s, or 1990s with those remaining survivors who had been young or adolescent children at the time of the genocide.[3] Thus, contemporary testimony and research—and thus virtually all films, videos, etc.—on the experiences of Armenians are actually skewed toward children's experiences.

Miller and Miller's (1993) *Survivors* also offers another interesting and rare element. One of the survivor accounts presented by Miller and Miller includes a case in which Turkish boys killed an Armenian baby by holding it by its legs, swinging it, and smashing its head repeatedly on a stone wall. While the bulk of perpetrator appears to have been by adult males, this incident suggests that sometimes

35

children participated as well. Eyewitness and survivor accounts of the genocide—Grigoris Balakian's Balakian's memoirs *Armenian Golgotha* is a good example (Balakian 2009)—includes not infrequent descriptions of the participation of Turkish and other women in the genocidal process, whether inflicting violence, looting, or taking Armenian children.

In addition to eyewitness accounts, survivor testimony taken by others, survivor narratives composed by the survivor himself or herself, and scholarship and documentary films offering analyses of these primary sources are also important to discuss. The photographs of genocide are of great significance, especially Armin T. Wegner's well-known contributions, which document the extermination of Armenians. The various available photographs, taken as representative of the deportations and other genocidal processes to which Armenians were subjected, feature again and again the corpses of children (often starved), children on deportation marches, and children suffering as they try to gain admission to or live in orphanages and refugee camps (Hofmann and Koutcharian 1992).

Two other categories of texts should be mentioned. First, there have long been strains of Armenian and of external literature on the Armenian genocide, most famously Franz Werfel's *The Forty Days of Musa Dagh*, first published in German in 1933 and later published in 1934 in English(Werfel 2012). Initially dominated by poetry, in recent decades many Armenian-authored novels—in Armenian as well as other languages (including English)—have been published, sometimes to great acclaim. Similarly, fictional films by Armenians as well as others have been produced, including the celebrated *Ararat* by Atom Egoyan in 2002. These literary and cinematic works have tended to follow the broader pattern of eyewitness and survivor narratives in containing a good deal on the treatment of children but integrated into an overarching story focused on the genocide and its aftermath. For instance, *Ararat* engages in a fictionalized way the struggle of artist Arshile Gorky to deal with the trauma of his childhood experience of the genocide, including the death of his mother. While literary or filmic fiction should never be conflated with historical accounts of the genocide nor with scholarly analyses of the genocide, fiction does offer another approach to the issue and allows exploration of the impact of the genocide in more speculative but important ways as well as helping those inside and outside the victim community to "image" the genocide in a way that goes beyond statistics or flat histories.

The very feature of literary and cinematic presentations of horrific mass violence that makes them potentially unreliable sources of historical knowledge—that the writers, directors, actors, etc., control the narratives and thus, in a sense, manipulate the audience—is what can bring out particular features of the effects on children in ways that go far beyond a detached analytical rendering of them and can present the kinds of internal and social struggles that are very hard to document through historical records and yet which are central to the experience of genocide.

Sophisticated new work vis-à-vis literary, cinematic, and artistic response to the Armenian genocide has emerged in recent years, some that provides unique insights into the experiences of children in the Armenian genocide. These include Rubina Peroomian's *And Those Who Continued Living in Turkey after 1915* (Peroomian 2008) and Kim Theriault's *Rethinking Arshile Gorky* (Theriault 2009). Peroomian brings attention to bear on the new literature in Turkey focused on "hidden" Armenians; that is, Armenians who as young women or children were forced or otherwise ended up in Turkish homes and who were to varying degrees Turkified—including women who later escaped but left behind children they were forced to bear typically as one of multiple wives. This is important not only in highlighting the fate of direct child victims, but also in bringing into view indirect child victims who were denied their partial Armenian heritage and deprived of their Armenian mothers when they escaped bondage. Theriault (2009) offers a novel analysis of the impact of the Armenian genocide on Gorky, going beyond the discussion of the effects of the trauma on his later life, to trace out the ways in which the childhood trauma of genocide influenced and drove his globally celebrated artistic innovations, especially the development of Abstract Expressionism.

This literary and artistic focus suggests the second additional type of text. Though they have been (in the author's view, wrongly) routinely dismissed as sources of historical documentation, histories based on direct survivor experiences passed down in families and communities provide an interesting alternative epistemology for engaging the Armenian genocide.[4] Because public discussion of the genocide was long limited due to the lack of public awareness and the relentless denial campaign that has been mounted by successive Turkish governments, for many decades, the communication of experiences of the genocide in Armenian families and communities, particularly to later generations and non-Armenians who were friends with Armenians

37

appears to have been, next to religious commemoration, the main form of exposure of both Armenians and non-Armenians in their orbits (Robert Dole being a good example) to the details of the genocide. While typically presenting a partial and constrained perspective, it is precisely the personalization of these accounts that has given them so much meaning for the progeny of survivors. That many developed as intentionally non-public internal texts whose audiences were primarily of single families has allowed Armenians a private space of remembrance—and even grieving—that is protected from denial, geopolitics, and the like. These accounts of the genocide have also helped to explain to post-survivor generations why they live, sometimes as outsiders, far from the traditional Armenian homeland and how they came to have the complicated Diasporan or mixed identities they have. While some accounts have become oral histories in the technical sense of being recorded and even made their way into other kinds of texts, such as published books and documentary films, they seem to have a heavier impact on fiction writing and poetry. What is more, the privacy of internal accounts, especially as they intertwine across families from the same area in the Ottoman Empire, provides a foundation for intimate and trusting connection and community building among Armenians. These internal histories, focused on children or otherwise, have not become a major area of study, perhaps because of their important private functions within Armenian communities and families as well as the fact that there are powerful political, academic, and literary/artistic voices that are able to present the genocide internally and externally. The need to proclaim the injustice done to Armenians and bear witness to it might be balanced by the need for a space in which the genocide can be engaged in a non-public manner.

Critical Challenges Facing the Field

Five primary challenges exist. First, because the Armenian genocide occurred close to a century ago, almost no survivors are alive today and of those who are alive, few were old enough during the genocide to, later, be able to offer new testimony in response to questions specifically focused on the fate of children in the genocide. While much can be culled from existing records, these are limited by the interests of the eyewitnesses, interviewers, or even survivors who created them. For instance, given relatively recent advances in trauma psychology, researchers would ask different questions from contemporaneous interviewers, who did not have such a frame of reference. Present researchers are restricted to indirect or fortuitous elements in the available eyewitness accounts and survivor testimonies, which increases the speculativeness of analysis while limiting the amount of available relevant data. It should be noted that the situation is no different for diplomatic or other governmental sources, which are limited by political frameworks, status of the writer, and so on.

Second, there is no central repository for or searchable electronic database of audio or video testimonies by survivors and eyewitnesses of the Armenian genocide. Collections are scattered in various locations (including Los Angeles, California; Watertown, Massachusetts; New York City; and Toronto, Ontario, Canada) and access is limited by geography and funding, as well as varying proprietary issues. Digitization of the many thousands of recorded testimonies should be a priority and funds should be raised for it. What is more, some kind of general researcher protocol should be developed to store copies of available accounts and testimonies in a central repository and to allow access to any legitimate researcher after those initially collecting or otherwise controlling the testimonies and accounts have had a reasonable period of time (perhaps ten years) to research and publish on them.

Third, perpetrators' treatment of children, especially adolescent girls, as if they were adults for purposes of forced marriage or sexual slavery and rape, seems to affect how this subgroup of children is approached in the literature. It is a welcome change that after decades of relative silence about the sexual abuse and enslavement of women in the Armenian genocide, the issue is now researched and discussed relatively frequently. That said, much of the attention on the gender of the victims has tended to obscure the fact that much of the violence against women was violence against those who were not adults. This is not to suggest that women suffered any less than girls, but that the age of victims must be taken into account in analyzing what was done, why perpetrators did it, and how it affected victims. Research should take account of both gender and age. Along with this tendency not to distinguish girls from women (see Miller and Miller 1993) when discussing sexual violence, there is no sustained attention to sexual abuse of boys. Because the topic was presumably even more avoided than sexual violence against women and girls, there is virtually nothing in the sources of which the author is aware, thus constituting a research gap on this issue.

Fourth, the continuing aggressive and robust denial campaign by the Turkish government and its supporters and the focus on recognition and justice issues in the Armenian community mean that scholarship and public attention on the Armenian genocide privileges (1) evidentiary material and (2) historical, political, philosophical, and even sociological and psychological research focused on justice issues such as reparations and Armenian-Turkish relations as matters of politics and society. Attacks by deniers on the reliability of privately as well as publically disseminated survivor testimony of the Armenian genocide, such as Norman Itzkowitz's mocking of the narrative of an Armenian "grandmother" as unreliable and unworthy of scholarly attention (H. Theriault 2001), reinforces the sense that "soft" sources on the Armenian genocide that are not useful in political activism or legal action are of less importance generally as regards the genocide. This is not to suggest that a focus on legal and political questions is not appropriate or important, but that the cost of this—partially imposed by deniers—is an unnecessary downplaying of other legitimate approaches to understanding the Armenian genocide—and especially the experiences of children.

Finally, discussion of the fate of Armenian children to the extent that it has occurred has taken place in isolation from discussions of the fate of Assyrian and Greek children. A more comprehensive approach is necessary because to some extent the genocidal processes were intertwined or unified, but also because both similarities and differences in the experiences of children in each group are important for understanding the genocidal process at work. For instance, were Greek children forcibly Turkified at the same rate as Armenian children? Were there orphanage opportunities for Assyrian children at the same level as for Armenian children? And so on.

The Probability of Progress

Little can be done at this point about the first challenge, that of the fact that it is no longer possible to gather direct survivor and eyewitness testimony and that the record of the Armenian genocide is thus fixed. But each of the other challenges can be addressed.

Developing the kind of protocols and central repository for survivor and eyewitness accounts will require significant funding as well as agreements among institutions and individuals in control of sets of accounts. The first important steps are already being taken, beginning with the 2010 agreement between the Shoah Foundation and the Armenian Film Foundation (AFF) for the Shoah Visual History Archive to host the AFF's approximately 400 video testimonies by Armenian genocide survivors, with the goal of becoming a repository for other sets of video testimonies as well ("Garabedian to Speak," 2012). While in the short term, and especially with the hundredth anniversary of the beginning of the Armenian genocide coming in less than three years, the focus is likely to remain on political history and justice issues. Such initiatives are likely to have support in the coming years. For example, a major reparations proposal (McCalpin et al. 2012) calls for funding for education and scholarship on the Armenian genocide. If the Armenian genocide issue is addressed through recognition and reparation, then reserving and supporting access to survivor and eyewitness accounts could become a focus in the post-reparations period and could be supported by compensation funds.

Increased attention to sexual violence against girls as children, in addition to as women, is a matter of shifting analytical frameworks and simply requires an interest in making the shift. Pointing the issue out in the present chapter and in other venues could help to create that interest.

The impact of deniers on "soft" accounts of the Armenian genocide is likely to continue until progress toward a just resolution of the issue is made. If and when denial loses its prominence or effectiveness, it is likely that research on the Armenian genocide will broaden and increase in areas that are not focused on historical proof and justice.

Finally, Diamadis's article on Greek, Assyrian, and Armenian children is blazing a trail toward a new integrative analysis on children and other issues. This reflects a broader shift toward recognition of an Ottoman genocidal process against Christian minorities that appears to have taken hold.

Notes

1. Separation of subcategories of a victim group is not uncommon.
2. This phenomenon has long been epidemic around the world outside of the context of genocide (see below).
3. The reasons for this are multiple, but the main reasons are: (1) after the Armenian genocide, the Armenian community was left largely to itself to try to recover from material deprivation, social fragmentation, and psychological traumatization, and reaching a point of relative stability at which public discussion of the genocide was materially and psychologically possible took about half a century; (2) Armenians learned from US civil rights and other liberation or protest movements around the world how to advocate for recognition of their history; (3) interest in genocide, generally, and in the Armenian genocide, in particular, by scholars and the

public emerged and grew only in this period; and (4) the independence of Armenia brought back into the forefront of regional politics the presence of Armenians and their relationship to Turkey.

4. These privately disseminated accounts of the genocide should not be conflated with survivor testimonies or narratives that are presented or summarized in books and films. Private histories internal to families and communities are precisely what survivor testimony or narrative is when it is not recorded in writing or electronically, or otherwise publically available or disseminated. Because of the nature of these internal, private histories of the Armenian genocide, the author relies on his own extensive personal experience with the internal, private histories of his family and friends.

References

Artinian, Araz (Wr. and Dir.). 2004. *Twenty Voices: The Last Testimonies of the 1915 Armenian Genocide Survivors* (Long Version). DVD. 84 minutes. Color. Information Films, Inc., and Araz Artinian Productions (Prods.). Available at: http://www.youtube.com/watch?v=Dm-DXeKoaOQ.

Avakian, Arlene Voski. 1992. *Lion Woman's Legacy: An Armenian-American Memoir*. New York: The Feminist Press.

Balakian, Grigoris. 2009. *Armenian Golgotha: A Memoir of the Armenian Genocide, 1915–1918*. Trans. Peter Balakian, and Aris Sevag. New York: Alfred A. Knopf.

Balakian, Peter. 1997. *Black Dog of Fate: An American Son Uncovers His Armenian Past*. New York: Broadway Books.

Boyajian, Levon, and Haigaz Grigorian. 1986. "Psychosocial Sequelae of the Armenian Genocide." In *The Armenian Genocide in Perspective*, ed. Richard G. Hovannisian, 177–85. New Brunswick, NJ: Transaction.

Çetin, Fethiye. 2012/2008. *My Grandmother: An Armenian-Turkish Memoir*. New York: Verso.

Charny, Israel W., ed. 1999. "Source Document: Telegrams by Turkish Leaders Ordering the Armenian Genocide." In *The Encyclopedia of Genocide*, ed. Israel W. Charny, 96. Santa Barbara, CA: ABC-CLIO.

Diamadis, Panayiotis. 2012. "Children and Genocide." In *Genocide Perspectives IV: Essays on Holocaust and Genocide*, ed. Colin Tatz, 312–52. Sydney, New South Wales: The Australian Institute for Holocaust & Genocide Studies/ UTSePress.

Egoyan, Atom (Wr. and Dir.). 2002. "Ararat." DVD. 115 minutes. Color. Robert Lantos and Atom Egoyan (Prods.).

"The Hidden Holocaust." (Produced in 1992 by Channel 4 BBC Television in the UK, 60 Minutes, Color).

Hofmann, Tessa, and Gerayer Koutcharian. 1992. "'Images that Horrify and Indict': Pictorial Documents on the Persecution and Extermination of the Armenians from 1877 to 1922." *Armenian Review* 45, no. 1–2: 53–184.

Housepian, Marjorie. 1999. "The Unremembered Genocide." In *The Encyclopedia of Genocide*, ed. Israel W. Charny, 64–64. Santa Barbara, CA: ABC-CLIO.

Jones, Michael (Director). Victor Price (Writer). (1992). "The Hidden Holocaust." Secret History. Channel 4 (UK). Television. 50 Minutes. Color. 27 July. Michael Jones. Available at: http://www.youtube.com/watch?v=jwfy9uItdMg

Kaiser, Hilmar. 2002. "'A Scene from the Inferno': The Armenians of Erzerum and the Genocide, 1915–1916." In *Der Völkermord an den Armeniern und die Shoah (The Armenian Genocide and the Shoah)*, eds. Hans-Lukas Kieser, and Dominik J. Schaller, 129–86. Zurich: Chronos.

Kalayjian, Anie, and Siroon P. Shahinian. 1998. "Recollections of Aged Armenian Survivors of the Ottoman Turkish Genocide: Resilience through Endurance, Coping, and Life Accomplishments." *Psychoanalytic Review* 85, no. 4: 489–504.

Kalayjian, Anie, Siroon P. Shahinian, E. L. Gergerian, and L. Saraydarian. 1996. "Coping with Ottoman Turkish Genocide: An Exploration of the Experience of Armenian Survivors." *Journal of Traumatic Stress* 9, no. 1: 87–97.

Maronian, Bared (Writer and Director). 2013. "Orphans of the Genocide." KPTV 18 (USA). Television. 110 minutes. Color. April 18. Armenoid Productions, Inc. (Producer). Purchase from Armenoid Productions, 1913 NW 49th Avenue, Coconut Creek, FL 33063; 954-646-0944. More information available at: http://www.armenoidteam.com/.

McCalpin, Jermaine O., Ara Papian, Alfred de Zayas, and Henry C. Theriault. 2012. *Resolution with Justice: Reparations for the Armenian Genocide—The Report of the Armenian Genocide Reparations Study Group*. Unpublished Draft. September.

Melkonian, Markar. 2005. *My Brother's Road: An American's Fateful Journey to Armenia*. New York: I.B. Taurus.

Miller, Donald E., and Linda Touryan Miller. 1993. *Survivors: An Oral History of the Armenian Genocide*. Berkeley and Los Angeles: University of California Press.

"Orphans of the Genocide." (Produced in 2012, 105 minutes, Color, DVD. Distributed by Armenoid Productions, Inc., Coconut Creek, Florida).

Peroomian, Rubina. 2008. *And Those Who Continued Living in Turkey after 1915: The Metamorphosis of the Post-Genocide Armenian Identity as Reflected in Artistic Literature*. Yerevan: Armenian Genocide Museum-Institute.

Theriault, Hank (sic). 2001. "Universal Social Theory and the Denial of Genocide: Norman Itzkowitz Revisited." *Journal of Genocide Research* 3, no. 2: 241–56.

Theriault, Kim S. 2009. *Rethinking Arshile Gorky*. University Park, PA: Pennsylvania State University Press.

Werfel, Franz. 1934/2012. *The Forty Days of Musa Dagh*. Boston, MA: David R. Godine.

Annotated Bibliography

Publications

Anush, Armen. *Passage Through Hell: A Memoir*. Translated by Ishkhan Jinbashian. Studio City, CA: H. and K. Manjikian, 2005, 123 pp.

> Told from the perspective of a boy age nine at the beginning of the Armenian genocide, this memoir describes the destruction of Armenians on a death march to Der-Zor in intimate and detailed terms. Through its author's own reactions and his account of those around him, it presents a complex account of the evolving psychological impact of the genocide on individuals as well as the overall group of victims.

43

Anush was a writer and there is a literary quality to his narrative. While this could suggest that the reported emotional responses were based on his reflections later, and even if this is true, the work offers important insights not just into what happened on the death marches and around Der-Zor, but its long-term psychological effects on survivors, particularly those who experienced the genocide as children. Yet, the memoir was written (in Armenian) in 1955 and pushes matters in the opposite direction, as this was before there was widespread public attention on genocide in general and before Armenians recovered sufficiently to begin public education efforts about the genocide (which was post-1965). This makes it unlikely that Anush's recollections are mediated through a genocide studies or Armenian genocide history framework. The emotional reactions are different from, for instance, Grigoris Balakian's (see *Armenian Golgotha: A Memoir of the Armenian Genocide, 1915–1918*, trans. Peter Balakian with Aris Sevag. New York: Alfred A. Knopf, 2009) analytical approach to his experiences in the genocide, which attempt to theorize the genocide and report on its general features through analysis of his own experiences: Anush explains the individual psychological reactions he had to his experiences in a very direct and personal way, but which nevertheless provides important insights on the general genocidal process and impact.

Sexual violence is also part of the narrative:

> What had transpired during that awful night? Only years later did I learn the facts. Guided with lanterns, the soldiers had meandered among the deportees, picked six girls, and dragged them to their tent. But the girls had refused to do the soldiers' bidding. In fact, they fought for their honor and their lives. Just then two Armenian women had entered the tent, grabbed a couple of rifles, and killed two of the soldiers. The other soldiers had attacked the women and killed them. They had also murdered all the women gathered around the tent and cut all six girls to pieces. (23)

Though not theorized, this also shows the agency of Armenians, including children, an important corrective to the general impression of passive victims.

The memoir also details the preying on the deportation caravan of various people, including "boat captains, merchants and robbers" (30) and "strangers" who "attacked our caravan and robbed us blind, taking everything we had: blankets, knapsacks, clothes, and shoes" (33).

One unfortunate incident in the first few days of the deportation involved Assyrian women attempting to profit from helping the victims. One promised to

> get us out of there thanks to her friendship with the police chief. All she needed was to find out where we had hidden our treasure and to be handed 30 gold coins as payment for the chief, so that our business could be taken care of swiftly.
>
> Mother told her we had no treasure but immediately gave her the 30 gold pieces.
>
> Once paid, the Assyrian woman was never seen again. (8–9)

While likely not widespread, this highlights the complex position of victim group members relative to one another.

Finally, this memoir includes mention of the fact that generally boys over twelve years old, but some as young as ten years old, were killed along with adult Armenian males. While the perpetrators might have considered them potential military threats, it is crucial to remember that these were often elementary- or middle-school-aged children, even by the standards of the day.

Bjørnlund, Matthias. "'A Fate Worse Than Dying': Sexual Violence During the Armenian Genocide." In *Brutality and Desire: War and Sexuality in Europe's Twentieth Century*, edited by Dagmar Herzog, 16–58. New York: Palgrave Macmillan, 2009.

This is a nuanced and incisive description and analysis of sexual violence against women and girls in the Armenian genocide. While it covers some previously trod ground, it also includes important new applications of the growing literature on mass rape beyond the Armenian case and presents new understandings of the role of sexual violence and, to a lesser extent, forced assimilation in the Armenian genocide.

It is not a fault of the author that the article does not separate out the treatment of girls, as the chapter's focus is gender violence. Its analysis of gender violence during the course of the Armenian genocide is so useful that, for those focusing in on the sexual violence against girls, it is an invaluable background resource.

Boyajian, Levon, and Haigaz Grigorian. "Psychosocial Sequelae of the Armenian Genocide." In *The Armenian Genocide in Perspective*, edited by Richard Hovannisian, 177–85. New Brunswick, NJ: Transaction, 1986.

Even though published a quarter century ago, this article is noteworthy for the nuanced and sophisticated theoretical apparatus it applies to the survivors of the Armenian genocide, many of whom were children during the genocide. The authors discuss various psychological and social impacts of the Armenian genocide on survivors as well as on later generations. In regard to the latter issue it was cutting edge and was one of the first, if not the first, works on the Armenian genocide to draw attention to the issue of the intergenerational transfer of trauma. Drawing on early psychological work on the *Holocaust*, the authors approach the psychological effects on Armenian genocide on survivors, opening up a new line of inquiry that has proven fruitful.

Çetin, Fethiye. *My Grandmother: An Armenian-Turkish Memoir*. Translated by Maureen Freely. New York: Verso, 2008/2012, 114 pp.

This is the memoir of a Turkish woman who discovers that her grandmother was in fact a survivor of the Armenian genocide who was kidnapped and forced into servitude in a Turkish home. Not only was she forced to work as servant girl but she was also forced to convert to Islam and assimilate to Turkish identity. As such, the memoir provides an elucidating look into the world of those Armenian boys, girls, and women who were taken or given to Turks (to save their lives), forced to work and reside in Muslim homes, and were neither rescued nor managed to escape to freedom in the aftermath of the genocide.

Though Çetin does not avoid the harsh reality of the genocidal process, including using the phrase "agonizing death march" to characterize what

Armenian women and children in her grandmother's area went through after the men had their throats cut and were thrown into the river (54), in contrast to the brutal conditions reported by many others who escaped or were rescued from Turkification, her grandmother's life was not unpleasant. Even if she was reminded of her "servant girl" status in the Turkish household in which she was raised, she was treated well, and even indulgently, by its patriarch. What is more, her marriage and family life seemed positive and loving, and she was respected in her town and assertive and confident in her interactions with others. Even so, two things come through clearly in Çetin's complex narrative: first, her grandmother experienced deep sorrow regarding her childhood, and second, she struggled to retain her identity, along with other converted Armenian genocide survivors.

Çetin also engages the issue of the intergenerational effects of the Armenian genocide, both the trauma and the ways in which the genocide created complex, unsettled identities for later generations. In describing her grandmother's story, she describes her own grappling with her newly discovered family history of suffering and her newly fragmented identity. The work, as a result, is sophisticated yet genuine.

Dadrian, Vahakn N. "Children as Victims of Genocide: The Armenian Case." *Journal of Genocide Research* 5, no. 3 (2003): 421–37.

This important article offers a comprehensive account of how children were killed in the Armenian genocide. While Vahakn Dadrian does note the taking of Armenian girls into domestic or other types of slavery, his focus is on killing methods. Dadrian explicitly goes beyond the treatment of deportees en masse, that is, the general tendency in the literature to treat women, the elderly, and children of different ages as if subject to uniform treatment. He uses a wealth of primary documentation to focus in on the specific treatment of children.

There are three killing methods he highlights: mass drowning (especially of infants), mass burning of live children, and sexual violence that ended in killing either immediately or after a period of captivity. He also mentions mass poisoning of Armenian infants by Ali Saib, Director of Public Health in Trabzon.

Dadrian also discusses the important topic of Turkish male perpetrators raping Armenian boys. While rape of women and girls is euphemistically but frequently mentioned in primary eyewitness accounts and survivor narratives, sexual violence against Armenian boys is not. Dadrian's article thus adds an important dimension to our understanding of the fate of children and the Armenian genocide more generally.

The specific eyewitness and survivor testimonies Dadrian references are uniformly chilling, to say the least.

Diamadis, Panayiotis. "Children and Genocide." In *Genocide Perspectives IV: Essays on Holocaust and Genocide*, edited by Colin Tatz, 312–52. Sydney, New South Wales: The Australian Institute for Holocaust & Genocide Studies/UTSePress, 2012.

This insightful, well-conceived, and fresh look at the issue of children as victims of genocide in the Ottoman Empire does three very important things. The first is that it expands the discussion beyond Armenians to include Ottoman Assyrians and Ottoman Greeks, both of whom suffered genocide in the 1914–1923 period. While Assyrians were a smaller group concentrated in only some of the areas where Armenians were located, their treatment was quite similar to Armenians, adjusted geographically, and the effects arguably more devastating, as the global Assyrian community continues to struggle, through today, to support its identity and garner public awareness of the genocidal violence against it. There are more differences between the Greek and Armenian experiences, due to many obvious factors, not the least of which was the existence of an independent Greece outside the Ottoman Empire and the fact that mass violence against the Greeks began in 1914 rather than 1915 and continued in new forms into the 1920s, for instance, through the genocidal Greek labor battalions (see Speros Vryonis, Jr., "Greek Labor Battalions Asia Minor." In *The Armenian Genocide: Cultural and Ethical Legacies*, edited by Richard Hovannisian, 275–90. New Brunswick, NJ: Transaction, 2007).

Second, Diamadis's article provides an account of the evolution of the forcible transfer of children from subordinate to dominant groups (a method of genocide) from antiquity to the middle of the twentieth century. The author provides substantive discussions of cases representative of key historical eras that line up well with the kinds of typologies developed by Frank Chalk and Kurt Jonassohn, Roger Smith, Helen Fein, and others in past decades (ancient genocides after military victory, colonial genocides, etc.). The evolutionary sequence he sketches is convincing and valuable, and to the present author's knowledge nothing like this has been developed on this topic before. Situating the Ottoman Turkish case within this multimillennia history brings both consistencies and differences into relief. Bringing the Ottoman Turkish case into proximity to the Australian and North American indigenous cases provides the foundation for important future research.

Third, Diamadis manages to integrate graphic and precise primary accounts of the treatment of children with insightful theoretical and comparative points. In this way, he productively avoids the "data dumping" tendency of some historical works on genocide and related issues.

As a forty-page article is limited by its nature and thus an author cannot be criticized for not being more comprehensive, a book-length expansion of this paper by its author would constitute an even more important contribution to the field of genocide studies and beyond.

Facing History, and Ourselves National Foundation, Inc. *Crimes Against Humanity and Civilization: The Genocide of the Armenians Resource Book.* Brookline, MA: Author, 2004, 198 pp.

This is a comprehensive and accessible introduction to the Armenian genocide, and one that is appropriate for use with high school students. It covers a whole range of issues, from Armenian life before the genocide to the challenges facing bystanders. Among other strengths, it includes insightful study questions at the end of each section, and questions that can stimulate student reflection and discussion. It interweaves primary sources, including photos, narrative and descriptive passages, and summaries of relevant scholarship. The selected primary sources feature references to children as victims of death marches, girls as victims of sexual violence, and the Turkification of Armenian children.

Hofmann, Tessa, and Gerayer Koutcharian. "'Images that Horrify and Indict': Pictorial Documents on the Persecution and Extermination of the Armenians from 1877 to 1922." *Armenian Review* 45, no. 1 (1992): 53–184.

This article features seventy-three authenticated photographs of the Armenian genocide (87–126) and its immediate aftermath of refugee suffering (127–59), with contextualizing captions and commentaries as well as an accompanying article discussing methodological, among other issues, regarding the photographs as documentation of the genocide. The collection of images is an extremely important contribution to documentation and understanding of the Armenian genocide. In the photographs, the suffering of children on death marches and in encampments is apparent again and again. There are also pictures of children as refugees or orphans in the aftermath of the genocide.

As an interesting aside, the authors discuss the complicated position of Armin T. Wegner, who photographed deportation marches and other aspects of the genocide at great risk to himself, advocated for Armenians after World War I, and was jailed and tortured for opposition to the Nazis. During World War I, however, even as he showed some of his photographs at a presentation on January 26, 1918, he "expounded the official Turkish version" of what was happening to Armenians (57). The authors attribute this to "the German military censorship that had blocked the truth in Germany about the Armenian Genocide during the World War" (57–58).

Kloian, Richard D. *The Armenian Genocide: News Accounts From the American Press (1915–1922)*. 3rd ed. Berkeley, CA: Anto Publishing, 1985/1988, 388 pp.

Many of the articles contained in this unique collection of US news articles mention or discuss the treatment of children. While there is no framework of analysis specifically geared toward children, the descriptions in many of the articles offer valuable details of the plight of children on the deportation marches and elsewhere.

Mazian, Florence. "The Patriarchal Armenian Family System: 1914." *Armenian Review* 36, no. 4 (1983): 14–26.

This very interesting and unique article provides a comprehensive description of typical Armenian family patterns prior to the Armenian genocide. It especially focuses on gender hierarchy within the family. The ultimate conclusion is that Armenian families were typically male dominated, which is more characteristic of authoritarian political contexts, but that there were more egalitarian trends in the years prior to the genocide. Both points suggest perhaps that dependence on men in the context of genocide created a crisis or breakdown when the men were removed or otherwise not able to protect their families, but women did have the beginnings of the tools to assume a leadership role for the benefit of their children. At the very least, the article provides a glimpse into the family lives of children immediately prior to the genocide.

Miller, Donald E., and Linda Touryan Miller. *Survivors: An Oral History of the Armenian Genocide*. Berkeley and Los Angeles: University of California Press, 1993, 242 pp.

Simply put, this is *the* essential work on the issue of children in the Armenian genocide. Even two decades after its publication, the theoretical framework used by the authors for their interviews and analysis of the results as well as their sensitivity to a full range of issues—from remembrance of life before the deportations to the various emotional and ethical responses survivors developed in later life—provide a comprehensive model for research and reflection. This work advanced understanding of the impact of the Armenian genocide on children more than any other. Presenting the genocidal process in general but then adding sections treating the experiences of children as children is tremendously valuable. Readers begin to understand what the survivors experienced, what they thought about it at the time, how they made sense of it in later life, and, to an extent, how it has affected their lives.

An important element theorized by Miller and Miller is the agency of Armenians, including children. Not only do the authors highlight the resilience and resourcefulness of even young children in surviving and maintaining the identity and family relations, but they also document women, and especially adolescent girls, committing suicide in order to avoid rape by the perpetrators or death on the terms of the perpetrators.

The book is based on interviews of one hundred survivors of the Armenian genocide gathered in the late 1970s and 1980s, when survivors were typically seventy years of age or older. Most of the survivors interviewed had been children during the genocide and, though Miller and Miller recognize the possible impact of public discourse on the genocide in the intervening years, provide consistent and impressively accurate answers to the structured set of questions that they were asked. One of the strengths of the presentation of the narratives of the survivors is the way in which Miller and Miller juxtapose multiple survivor testimonies presenting related facts and reflections such that each at once reinforces the main point being made and at the same time adds something new to the reader's understanding. What is more, analytical points are integrated into the sections featuring narratives, such that evidence and inference are linked closely and clearly: the book is frequently at the same moment emotionally wrenching and crisply analytical. The work is as much a guide on how to do oral history research as it is an exemplar of the form.

Given the prominence this book has attained, as well as its uniqueness in the literature, a new and expanded edition that included appendices of extended edited transcriptions of direct survivor recordings would be welcome most welcome.

Peroomian, Rubina. *And Those Who Continued Living in Turkey after 1915: The Metamorphosis of the Post-Genocide Armenian Identity as Reflected in Artistic Literature*. Yerevan: Armenian Genocide Museum-Institute, 2008, 277 pp.

This work analyzes fiction and memoirs produced in Turkey by individuals who publicly identify as Armenians, as well as individuals who do not. The author discusses the ways in which Armenians and other authors of later generations have engaged the Armenian genocide itself and/or contemporary struggles over identity in the post-Armenian genocide world. While Peroomian's concerns are broader than the plight and fate of children during and after a period of genocide, there are interesting elements relevant to the impact of the Armenian genocide on direct child victims as well as the intergenerational transfer or effects of trauma.

Literary studies of fiction and memoir that take the Armenian genocide as a topic add value to fiction and memoir. While on their own, fictional works and memoirs have had important impacts on discourse about and appreciation of the impact of the Armenian genocide, critical scholarly analyses not only present interpretations based on critical techniques that can increase readers' appreciation of such works but also are able to separate reliable memoir and fictional accounts of the Armenian genocide from those that are not. In this way, Peroomian's study extends the impact of the works in question while also authenticating them as legitimate relative the wealth of factual data available on the Armenian genocide. The insights gained through authors' reflections can thus be seen to be anchored in reliably represented direct experience of, or accurate knowledge about, the genocide and thus as offering legitimate insights into the genocide, if of a different kind from historical sources, political analyses, and so on.

Sarafian, Ara (Comp.). *United States Official Records on the Armenian Genocide 1915–1917*. Princeton, NJ: Gomidas, 2004, 704 pp.

An invaluable collection of primary eyewitness accounts of particular events of the Armenian genocide, many of which served as the basis of the elements of the Bryce/Toynbee report (James Bryce and Arnold Toynbee. *The Treatment of Armenians in the Ottoman Empire, 1915–1916: Documents Presented to Viscount Grey of Falloden by Viscount Bryce*, ed. Ara Sarafian. Reading, England: Taderon, 2000). Many of the documents contained in the *United States Official Records on the Armenian Genocide* include descriptions of the deportation, killing, selling, kidnapping, etc., of Armenian children.

Shemmassian, Vahram L. "The League of Nations and the Reclamation of Armenian Genocide Survivor." In *Looking Backward, Moving Forward: Confronting the Armenian Genocide*, edited by Richard G. Hovannisian, 81–112. New Brunswick, NJ: Transaction Publishers, 2003.

This is another one of the many excellent historical pieces on little-discussed aspects of the Armenian genocide published in collections edited by Richard Hovannisian, which add essential specificity and detail to knowledge and understanding of the Armenian genocide and its impact. Vahram Shemmassian details the issues engaged by and activities of the League of Nations' Commission of Inquiry for the Protection of Women and Children in the Near East, which was constituted in response to the Romanian representative's highlighting of "Eastern slave markets, where women and children were sold, which we know were flowishing [*sic*] in Armenia and Asia Minor. . . . Now with the return of Peace and relaxation of passport formalities it is to be feared that the traffic will take a new lease of life." (82)

Among many, three important aspects of the article are especially noteworthy. First, Shemmassian provides a wealth of useful, contextualized statistics on how many children had been transferred to Turkish, as well as other, groups, which are broken down in places by age, gender, and type of captivity. He also provides information about the children's eventual fate. The scale of the problem was staggering: a 1921 Commission estimate indicated that after about 90,000 "Armenian orphans" had already been rescued, "[s]till, 73,350 Armenian orphans were believed to remain in Turkish institutions and homes" (88)—thousands of whom would be rescued through the work of the Commission. Second, within the framework of his knowledge of the genocide and assimilation methods and making use of the research and insights of the Commission members themselves, Shemmassian presents a nuanced analysis of the process of assimilation that varied by the characteristics of children (age, gender, and so on), region, type of group forcing assimilation, etc. For instance, a report from one Commission member "dwelled primarily on the Turkish methods of brainwashing Armenian children" (87), while in other cases, different methods were used, including brutality, threats, and the offering of trinkets as gifts. The article conveys well the vulnerability of children in a genocidal context. He points out the practical and psychological obstacles to reclamation, including on the one hand that "Muslim nomadic society . . . was reluctant to give up its coveted wartime spoil unless forced to do so" (94), which the League of Nations was not prepared to do, and, on the other hand, the facts that some who had been girls during the genocide had later been "sold in marriage" (104) and that many captives had given birth to the children of the captors.

The work of the Commission centered on just two areas, Constantinople and Aleppo, so many of the captive Armenians had no chance for rescue. What is more, there was an interesting split between Commission activities in the two locations. The League of Nations took great pains not to assign any responsibility for the existence of the orphans or their need for rescue, attributing them instead to the general wartime conditions. This meant that Turkish orphans were treated the same as Armenian and other Christian orphans, so the mechanisms of coercion and force were not, at least explicitly, part of the analysis applied to the situation. The League and its Commission's operation in Constantinople were committedly neutralist and officially aimed at "'reconstruction' of families torn apart" by generic war and "'reconciliation' among peoples" (85–86), a problem that Armenians would of course face regarding denial and other issues as the legacy of the genocide extended further in time. In the Aleppo area, however, Shemmassian reports a clearer understanding that what the Commission was facing was the effect of a mass extermination and assimilation campaign and an exclusive focus on the victims of that process (see 94).

Stone, Frank A. "Young People Caught Up in a Catastrophe: Survivors of the Armenian Genocide of 1915." *Genocide & Human Rights*. Special issue of *Journal of Armenian Studies* 4, no. 1–2 (1992): 137–63.

This is a very interesting application of the methodology of "literary sociology" (which is clearly explained in the article) to six published memoirs by survivors focused on their experiences of genocide. Five of the six survivors were children at the time of the genocide. The article offers useful accounts of key experiences of the memoir authors and their community more broadly during the Armenian genocide, as well as a comparative analysis revealing typical types of experiences and reactions to them (though the author stresses the individual, personal nature of each experience). Patterns emerge that help to organize our understanding of the genocide and its particular effect on children:

> The accounts that we have examined make it clear that the victims of a genocide experience many forms of violence. They are subject to verbal abuse and accusations. The security of their goods and property is removed and they are quickly impoverished. They encounter religious bigotry and prejudice. Their personal relationships are destroyed as grandparents, parents, siblings, relatives, and neighbors lose their lives. They have a well-founded, constant fear of physical abuse, molestation, and rape. Infectious diseases are rampant. Starvation becomes

> commonplace. There is a lack of sanitation and means of maintaining personal hygiene. In the end, some of the victims must seek shelter from the violence all around them by becoming attached to the households of their enemies. (161)

The last point is crucial to understanding the experience of children in the Armenian genocide. Though adults suffered similar fates, they could be expected to have more developed coping mechanisms. Children went through these horrors during the time that their personalities and individual identities were being formed, and thus these experiences shaped them in a foundational way. At the same time, children developed active survival strategies, a point developed at length and deeply by Miller and Miller (1993).

Tachjian, Vahé. "Gender, Nationalism, Exclusion: The Reintegration Process of Female Survivors of the Armenian Genocide." *Nations and Nationalism* 15, no. 1 (2009): 60–80.

This article looks at the attempts to reintegrate the tens of thousands of Armenian women and girls who had been taken, or, by circumstances, forced or coerced, into Turkish, Kurdish, or other homes; into prostitution; or other related situations. While focused on Armenian women and not specifically Armenian girls or children, frequent examples of adolescent or mid-teen Armenian girls forced into domestic and/or sexual slavery at those ages or younger emphasize that the term "Armenian woman" in this case applies to girls as well. Vahé Tachjian offers a complex and balanced account of the contending attitudes among Armenian leaders about whom to reintegrate and how. The account includes a treatment of the ideological foundations of some of the views. He is at once sensitive to the facts (1) that all discourse and decisions regarding this population of victims occurred in a post-geno-cide context and so reactions in the victim group must be judged relative to the experience of genocide and continuing oppression and (2) that this discourse and decision making could have coercive and exclusionary effects on women and girls. Tachjian details the specific circumstances of different women and girls to explain the difficulties of their situations and own decision making.

One point that should be mentioned, though, is the presence of a slight inaccuracy. Tachjian (2009) states that:

> the nationalist ideology of the "Committee for Union and Progress" [CUP] had not exhibited the same ferocity and extremis in the case of young Armenian girls, women, and children as it had in that of Armenian males of all ages. CUP ideology tolerated the integration of women into Muslim society, provided, of course, that these individuals no longer lived in a group, but were isolated in their new Muslim environment and certain to lose their national identity. These women and children were often regarded as spoils of war, slaves, or even objects of sexual slavery. In essence, the tactic deployed by the CUP was to prevent the perpetuation of the national identity of this component of Armenian society. Thus, rather than being physically destroyed, women and chil-dren were transferred from one group to another, always with the *idée fixe* of changing their national identity. (65)

The attitude of the CUP described here shows that the CUP's ideology was just as negative regarding women and children as it was regarding men. While the author probably has in mind the possibility allowed women and children to convert to Islam, this choice was typically forced or coerced and could subject the genocide victim to hellish torture and degradation lasting months, years, or the rest of her/his life.

Theriault, Kim S. *Rethinking Arshile Gorky*. University Park: Pennsylvania State University Press, 2009, 243 pp.

Arguably the most sophisticated scholarly analysis of Gorky's work, this monograph argues persuasively for the bold claim that the development of Gorky's trail-blazing Abstract Expressionism has its roots in his childhood experience of the Armenian genocide, coupled with his post-genocide dislocation to the United States as a displaced refugee who attempted to fit into his new societal context while grappling with the consequent trauma of the genocide and still retaining (and asserting) elements of his Armenian identity. The author expands this relationship between art and life to exposure to Armenian art and architecture in Gorky's childhood:

> ... Gorky used the transient flesh of landscape in his paintings as inspiration, but Gorky also combined this with memory. Just as Gorky had found in Modernism spatial complexities that reminded him of Armenian art, he found that the American landscape reminded him of homeland and facilitated the memory of impressions that he superimposed in his paintings. The transience of memories filtered through years of exile and childhood recollections combined with the observed American landscape into a mutation of the familiar ... Gorky's idea of universality was something he pursued from the beginning of his career, and it was embodied through the incorporation of Gorky's own personal story into the work ... (150)

The author's deep relating of Gorky's life and art provides a useful excess beyond the theory, using his biography and art as a means of understanding the trauma of genocide in various dimensions, from the loss of Gorky's mother to the struggle against the forces taking his identity away from him:

> A number of his friends have commented that Gorky would often turn his jacket inside out, making it look like a peasant outfit, and dance Armenian dances that he remembered from his boyhood ... Handkerchief dancing was not something that people did at New York parties in the 1930s. Stuart Davis [another top artist] told Gorky once, 'We don't do that here' ... indicating that Gorky's self-expression and ethnic identification were unacceptable in such circumstances. (170–71)

Films

"Grandma's Tattoos." (Written and directed by Suzanne Khardalian. 58 minutes, Color and B/W, DVD. Produced by PeA Holmquist in 2011. Available from The Cinema Guild, 115 W. 30th Street, Suite 800, New York, NY 10001, www. cinemaguild.com).

This film presents the journey of discovery made by the filmmaker as she attempts to understand the tattoos her grandmother had on her face. Suzanne Khardalian uncovers the tortured past of her grandmother, raped by a Turkish man at age ten and kidnapped and forced into sexual/domestic slavery, at which time she was tattooed. The strength of the film is the analysis of the grandmother's caustic and somewhat antisocial personality as the result of the trauma she suffered as a child in the genocide. At the same time, the film overall is rather amateurish and fails to draw on the ever increasing and rich scholarship on the victimization of Armenian women and girls or the vast amount of material on the long-term psychological effects of childhood sexual victimization. As a result, the film presents as mysterious and unknowable the general facts and depth of the grandmother's horrific experiences, rather than using the extensive scholarly resources to make reasonable inferences based on what was known of the grandmother's early and later life. In this way, the film misses the opportunity to provide viewers, via a gripping survivor, with unique and powerful insights into (plus a substantial analysis of) the execution of the Armenian genocide and its long-term impact—issues that most are unlikely to be exposed to in other ways.

"The Hidden Holocaust." (Produced in 1992 by Channel 4 BBC Television in the UK, 60 Minutes, Color/Black and White).

A version of this film was shown in the United States on A&E network's *Time Machine*. While the historical framework developed in the film is somewhat dated and in some ways simplistic—for instance, in how it treats the religious differences between Armenians and Turks—the film offers a great deal through its inclusion of survivor interviews and a segment featuring renowned journalist Robert Fisk and others uncovering the skeletal remains of genocide victims in Der-Zor. The survivor narratives are chilling, including a woman relating attempts to bury a child victim of the Armenian genocide only to have him dug up by dogs and a man telling of how as a child he was one of about fifteen survivors out of thousands forced into a cave, soaked in kerosene, and immolated. The persistence of the emotional pain at losses of mothers and other family members conveys the deep long-term effects of the genocide.

Maronian, Bared (Writer and director). "Orphans of the Genocide." (Written and directed by Bared Maronian. 60 minutes, Color and B/W. DVD. Not yet available for purchase), 2013.

This cutting-edge documentary expands previous discussions of orphans of the Armenian genocide in two notable ways. First, it offers an in-depth treatment of the "Georgetown Boys" (and girls), 109 Armenian orphan boys and 29 orphan girls raised at the Georgetown Armenian Boys Farmhouse starting in 1923. The film engages a range of issues, including the long-term impact of the Armenian genocide but also the benefits of resettlement in Canada and being raised at the farmhouse. Besides including an account of internationally known scholars Drs. George and Lorne Shirinian's father and mother, who were both orphans raised in the Farmhouse, the film offers important insights into the complex process of immigration with contending forces toward identity preservation and assimilation. At one point, the boys were given Anglo names in place of their Armenian names, to support their assimilation into Canadian society. The boys resisted this attempt to obscure and push abandonment of their Armenian heritage and eventually kept their Armenian names and identities.

Second, it looks at much more cynical attempts at altering the identity of Armenian orphans via a segment focused on an orphanage in Antoura, Lebanon. This Ottoman government-run institution was devoted to the intensive genocidal Turkification of Armenian children. The extent of the mistreatment there has been confirmed by the recent discovery of the skeletal remains of hundreds of Armenian children interred in the building that housed the orphanage.

"Twenty Voices: The Last Testimonies of the 1915 Armenian Genocide Survivors" (Written and directed by Araz Artinian Produced in 2004, 84 minutes, Color and Black and White. DVD. Araz Artinian Production, 20 Voices Museum Project, P.O. 26007, C.P. Normandie, Montréal, Quebec, H3M, 3E8, Canada).

Distributed on a limited screening basis, this film is an arrangement of video interviews of twenty elderly survivors about their experiences in the Armenian genocide. The audio of some portions of the interviews, along with biographies and photographs of each of the survivors, are available on the "20 voices" website at http://www.twentyvoices.com.

The interviewees were children at the time of the Armenian genocide. In the interviews, they describe their direct experiences and reactions to what they experienced as children, though often with adult reflection on the impact of the trauma they suffered. There are a number of noteworthy aspects of the film and interactive website, which include the drawing of survivor testimony from all areas of the Ottoman Empire in which the Armenian genocide was perpetrated and the range of experiences of the survivors, from being orphaned to be taken into a household to be Turkified and later getting away or being rescued. Araz Artinian's filming method is also to be commended: she conducted interviews in a physically minimalist form, with a simple background, which highlights the interviewees' words and faces in a unique manner.

It is also worth noting that the "Twenty Voices" interviews are featured in another documentary by Artinian, "The Genocide in Me" (2005, DVD, 53 minutes, color), which explores the complex impact of the genocide on Artinian's life. It is important to recognize that it was as children that later generations of Armenians have typically been impacted by the Armenian genocide, even if developed knowledge of it has only come later for many of them.

3

Children: The Most Vulnerable Victims of the Armenian Genocide

Asya Darbinyan and Rubina Peroomian

[A]ttempts have been made to discern certain features or patterns that stand out with respect to the genocidal treatment of children. This attempt provides a perspective through which children are viewed as a distinct sub-category within the overall victim population—Vahakn Dadrian in "Children as Victims of Genocide."

Introduction

As a result of the systematic destruction of Armenian life in the Ottoman Empire during the period between 1894 and the establishment of the Republic of Turkey in 1923, an estimated 1.5 million people lost their lives and some 500,000 fled the country. The 3,000-year presence of Armenians in their homeland was reduced to a mere 50,000, residing as a more or less accepted minority in Istanbul, with thousands of forcibly or voluntarily Islamized Armenians living discreetly and anonymously throughout Turkey. In this darkest quarter century in the history of the Armenian people, children suffered not only as members of the targeted population but also in their unique predicament of vulnerability and helplessness. It is difficult to place an exact number of how many children lost their lives and/or were abducted and taken into Muslim households or Turkish orphanages never to be found. This number is certainly in the hundreds of thousands, possibly as high as three quarter of a million. By the destruction of the children of the Armenian population, the Young Turks obliterated the natural growth of the nation for many years to come.

In May 1915, Great Britain, France, and Russia issued a joint declaration in which the treatment of Armenians in the Ottoman Empire was defined as "new crimes of Turkey against humanity and civilization" (The Armenian Review 1984, 65). The events of 1915, however, were just the culmination of the genocidal acts against Armenians. What are often overlooked are the pre-1915 massacres: the Hamidian massacres of 1894–1896 and the Cilician massacres of 1909. The survivors of the latter continued living in their ravaged homes and ransacked towns and villages, and rebirth was possible despite continuing discrimination and persecution. The Armenian Church and the Armenian cultural, political, and benevolent associations took charge of rebuilding the nation. Armenian as well as foreign organizations established orphanages to house the orphan leftovers of the massacres. Children grew up in a familiar environment and entered society relatively well-equipped with the necessary survival tools. Hovhannes Mugrditchian (1996) remembers one such orphanage in the Monastery of Sis, established in 1898, and Reverent Yeznik Der-Sarkissian, the superintendent, who treated the orphans like the true father they had lost (10). In his memoir, Mugrditchian (1996) wrote: "The superintendent of the orphanage, a wonderful man . . . looked after us like an ideal father, and I always remembered him with great affection" (p.10).

Eventually, between 1915 and 1923, a more total destruction occurred in calculated phases. First, Armenian men were conscripted into the Ottoman army and liquidated. Then Armenian community leaders and intellectuals were arrested and killed. Finally, women, children, and the elderly were deported to the Syrian Desert.

The Pre-1915 Massacres

"Fifty thousand orphans made so by the Turkish massacres of Armenians is the official estimate received at the State Department from US Consul Berghotz, at Erzeroum," reported the New York Times on December 18, 1896. According to this report, provisional relief was provided and orphanages were being set up in Urfa, Caesarea, and elsewhere.

The reports of representatives of different countries about the massacres of Armenian people in 1894–1896 raised a wave of Armenian relief efforts across the globe, which resulted in various organizations and committees rushing relief workers and aid to the Armenians.

For example, Clara Barton, the head and founder of the American Red Cross, was permitted to enter the Ottoman Empire in 1896. Barton remained there for more than five months coordinating the relief work in different provinces of the empire.

Five expeditions of the American Red Cross were also sent to the desolated interior, two of which were headed by physicians. Their objective was to distribute food, medicine, and tools to begin the massive reconstruction of the devastated towns and villages (Barton 1898, 316–17). John D. Rockefeller gave the first of hundreds of thousands of dollars that he and his family contributed to Armenian relief.

Both Germany (Lepsius 1897, 276; Ehmann 1921, 2 and 9) and various Scandinavian countries also responded to the massacres. Danish and Swedish members of "Women Missionary Workers" (KMA) assisted German orphanages in Kharberd (Harput), Marash, Van, and Mush (Azadian 1995, 179–84, 191, and 201). In 1903, the KMA founded "Emmaus," the first Danish orphanage in Mezre. Karen Jeppe and Maria Jacobsen, two Danish missionaries who were later referred to as "Danish mothers of Armenian orphans," arrived in Turkey in 1903 and 1907, respectively, and remained with Armenian refugees and orphans throughout World War I as well.

Swiss missionaries opened a number of orphanages for Armenian orphans in Sivas, Bursa, Pardizak, and other cities in Turkey, and assistance was also provided by "Friends of Armenia" from Great Britain (Azadian 1995, 179–84, 191, and 201).

To some extent, the relief work by foreign missionaries and Armenian organizations satisfied the physical needs of these orphans; however, it did not remedy the psychological damage to children who survived the murder of their parents (e.g., such as a young girl who witnessed her parents being murdered and ran away insane; another who surrendered to her Kurdish abductor for a piece of bread to feed her orphaned younger sibling; and a girl, driven into a brothel, who was forced to dance for Turkish officers). Suren Partevian's *Hayuhin* (*The Armenian Woman*) is replete with tales of these orphans' wretched fate.

An article that appeared in *The New York Times* on April 25, 1909, reported the massacres of Armenians in Adana and surrounding towns and villages, and conservatively estimated that some 30,000 had been killed and that some 100 girls were missing. The article referred to the latter as the "victims of Turkish fanaticism in Adana vilayet."

In the immediate aftermath of the Adana massacres, the Patriarchate of Constantinople sent delegations to the disaster-stricken area to report on the damage and to plan relief work. The literary responses of Zabel Yesayan and Suren Partevian, members of two separate delegations, depict in striking detail the predicament of orphans, widows, and old men as the remnants of Adana's once thriving Armenian population. Yesayan's (2010) *Averaknerun mej* (*Among the Ruins*) provides the most dramatic landscape of misery and horror: the burnt bodies of men, women, and children piled up inside the ruins of a church which the Turks had set on fire while the Armenians were praying to God for mercy; mothers gone mad, running around and shouting, still holding the bodies of their children who had already been dead for days; others, in agony, leaving their children at the church door and running away. In a chapter on orphans, Yesayan describes her visit to the German orphanage in Izmir. There a young Armenian girl who had been a resident since the 1895 killings and who served as an aide to the Mother Superior was now receiving the orphans of yet another Turkish debauchery (Yesayan 2010, 57). Yesayan also visited Mersin where hundreds of orphans had been collected by the Patriarchate and housed in a makeshift orphanage next to the church. The goal was to move them away from the disaster area in order to help them heal faster. But as Yesayan (2010) notes, the idea of healing was farfetched; the relative care and comfort given to these children could neither expunge the horrors they had witnessed nor their longing for their murdered parents. Yesayan (2010) reports that some of the children still had stains from the blood of their dying mothers on their ragged clothes. An eight-year-old girl, the victim of an appalling rape, had been turned into a speechless creature. In the ruined city of Adana, there were orphans everywhere, wandering in the streets like wild animals. It was a great challenge to collect them since they fled when pursued, seeing a killer in any male who approached them. But these were the fortunate ones; they at least had a future before them. The tiny barely covered graves just outside the city limits belonged to children who had died of diseases spread by the putrefying unburied cadavers. As one survivor stated, "The real orphanage is beneath the earth" (Yesayan 2010, 97). Yesayan writes about a Turkish woman who had loaded wounded Armenian men and children into a carriage pretending to save their lives, only to push them into the river (Peroomian 1993, 106).

Writing his memoirs on the Cilician massacres, Hagop Terzian (2009), too, described the slaughter of Armenian men, women, and children of all ages, and the public rape of young girls and the amputation of their arms and legs with axes.

The Torturous 1915 Journey toward Death and the Agonizing Survival

After the liquidation of almost all the able-bodied men,[1] the deportation decree was the last blow to the remnants. Armenians were ordered out of their homes and given very little or no time to prepare for the journey. Some families entrusted their young children to Turkish or Greek neighbors. At one and the same time, a warning from the government asserted that anyone sheltering or hiding Armenians would be severely punished, and thus many were leery of accepting Armenian children.

Many children ended up in the street. Ultimately, most were collected and disposed of by the government. Others wandered with their mothers and others in the wilderness, hungry and miserable, begging for a crust of bread, sleeping like stray dogs, and ultimately, if not murdered, dying of starvation, and/or dehydration. Some, miraculously, survived this hardship and somehow reached freedom.

Some families, especially during the first weeks of the implementation of the deportation decree, were given the option of converting to Islam and thereby avoiding exile. But even in their case, they were forced to surrender their children to Turkish orphanages to be raised as Muslims. This practice ceased after Talaat Pasha's January 15, 1916 instruction to the Government of Aleppo not to accept Armenian children in Turkish orphanages and not to feed them, which he considered "an act completely opposite to its purpose," regarding "the survival of these children as detrimental" (Kelly 2005, 231). Some Armenian children escaped from the orphanages; others were killed according to orders from above.

Caravans of the remnants, mostly women, children, and elderly men, were put on the road toward unknown destinations. Some were liquidated on the outskirts of their towns and villages. The rest continued on foot. Gendarmes who accompanied the deportees in order to "protect" them, instead alerted Muslim villagers or criminal gangs (*chetes*) to the approaching convoy and then allowed them to loot, rape, and kill at will. They snatched away small children and sold them for a few coins, mostly to Bedouin Arabs. At night, when the deportees were ordered to stop, gendarmes or bandits would attack them and prey upon young girls, rape them and leave them to die, or take them away and sell them as slaves, or keep them for use as "helpers" around the house. Young boys were snatched away for the same purpose. They too were raped, since the pedophilic tendencies of those criminals did not differentiate between the sexes. Children who survived the experience of molestation carried the guilt and shame throughout their lives. Oral interviews conducted at the University of California at Los Angeles (UCLA) with such survivors revealed the secret these wretched men and women had tried to hide and their everlasting pain.

From April to October 1915, thousands of skeletal women and children filled the roads, prey to continuous assault, hunger, thirst, disease, and the scorching desert sun. The death march passed along circuitous country roads and through rugged mountain passes crowded with the maggot-ridden corpses left behind by previous caravans. The chosen route avoided villages so that the deportees could not beg for food, water, or help. Even when the route took them past a stream or a well, the gendarmes prevented them from approaching the water. During this torturous journey, the older boys and the men who had not been arrested prior to the deportation were rounded up and shot or bayoneted, often in front of their mothers or wives. Mothers smeared mud on their daughters' faces to make them unappealing to attackers and dressed their young sons in girls' clothing to hide their gender.

Mothers, if they had any cloth, would wrap their children's bare feet, but this ragged covering easily ripped on thorns and stones. Others begged strangers to take their infants so that at least these might yet survive. Still others taught their children the Armenian alphabets, using a stick to draw in the desert sand, in the hope that after their own certain death, their children would keep the memory of their identity. Those who still had their Bibles would read to the children to soothe the pain of hunger and thirst.

Beside the hardships of the deportation route—the hunger, thirst, typhus, and dysentery to which thousands of children fell victim— Vahakn Dadrian (2003), in a striking research paper, "Children as Victims of Genocide," cites other methods by which children were liquidated. Muslim villagers used axes, hammers, clubs, scythes, spades, and saws to kill the emaciated deportees, and especially the children (423). Based on testimonies given before the Turkish Military Tribunal in 1919, Dadrian (2003) delineates the atrocious methods used in Trebizond, for example, poisoning infants; drowning older children who resisted taking their "medicine"; subjecting infants to "the steambath" (suffocation by steam); stuffing dead children into baskets and throwing them into the sea; retaining young girls for use in the governor-general's sex orgies, passing on a few of the prettiest ten to thirteen-year-olds to his fourteen-year-old son, and killing the rest (424–25). Mass drowning was also a popular method in Trebizond province. Groups of infants and young children torn away from their parents were jammed on board a vessel which was then capsized in the Black Sea. Citing Leslie A. Davis, an American consul in Kharbert (Kharpout), Dadrian (2003) recounts that mass murder by butchering helpless women and children, mutilating their bodies and drowning them also occurred at Lake Geoljuk near the city of Kharberd (Harput) on the orders of the governor of Harput province. Dadrian (2003) also quotes US Ambassador Henry Morgenthau who reported that "at Kemach Gorge hundreds of children were bayoneted by the Turks and thrown into the Euphrates" (427). Similar acts were committed on the lower stretches of the river. Dadrian also notes that mass rape was used as a tool for the liquidation of young girls and homosexual rape was inflicted on Armenian boys, both along the deportation route and in Muslim homes where they were kept as adoptive sons or helpers. Dadrian also speaks of the mass burning alive of Armenian orphans and mentions Diyarbekir, Harput, Bitlis, and Aleppo as sites of this most ferocious act.

Foreign Relief Work and Establishment of Orphanages

In early September 1915, a cable was sent to the Department of State at Washington from Ambassador Henry Morgenthau, who was in Constantinople, stating that the annihilation of the Armenian race in Turkey was rapidly progressing (J. Barton 1930, 4). This message was transmitted to James Barton, Foreign Secretary of the American Board of Commissioners for Foreign Mission (ABCFM) in Boston, an organization that had been sending missionaries to the Middle East since the mid-nineteenth century. Members of ABCFM had many stations all over the Ottoman Empire, had established many schools, orphanages, and hospitals in the region, and had provided aid for Armenians after the Hamidian massacres of 1894–1996 as well as after Adana massacres of 1909. Beginning in October 1, 1915, the Armenian Relief Committee began to contribute relief to the latest group of Armenian victims of the Turks in the Ottoman Empire. In his book *Story of Near East Relief*, James Barton provides detailed information about the activities of the committee that evolved into the Near East Relief (NER) and was chartered by act of Congress in 1919.

Other groups of Americans also reached out to the Armenians. For example, one group of affluent people (including Cleveland H. Dodge,

President Woodrow Wilson's friend and the Chairman of the Board of Trustees of Robert College at Constantinople; James L. Barton, Foreign Secretary of the ABCFM; Charles R. Crane, President of the Board of Trustees of the Constantinople College for Women; Samuel T. Dutton, Treasurer of the Constantinople College for Women and the Secretary of World Peace Foundation, among many other prominent individuals) met in New York and also organized a committee for the purpose of raising funds for suffering Armenians and sending aid to Constantinople for relief purposes. It was to be done with the active cooperation of Ambassador Morgenthau and the missionaries who were already stationed in various parts of the Ottoman Empire.

The American relief work generally fell into four categories: general relief (organized via a fundraising campaign in which ordinary people from the United States, and later Canada and many other countries, contributed funds to help thousands of refugees and orphans in the Near East), special relief (which was coordinated by many volunteers sent to the field, and resulted in the NER building hundreds of miles of roads, repairing damaged buildings and building new ones, and establishing new industries), medical work (which was accomplished not only by sending physicians and medicine overseas but by also establishing new hospitals and training hundreds of nurses), and helping orphans. Initially, the relief workers provided clothing and bedding for the orphans, especially needed in the cold winters. At the same time they began establishing hundreds of orphanages all over the Ottoman Empire, where the Armenian orphans were not only sheltered but also were educated and trained to become self-supporting by the age of sixteen. Many of the orphans had been so badly scarred mentally and emotionally that they had forgotten their names, their language, and where they came from. The NER had child welfare professionals who were working in orphanages or clinics to treat such problems.

The committee spearheaded a nationwide publicity campaign and fundraising for the Armenians in need. From 1915 until 1930, this organization raised and donated more than $116,000,000. With these funds the NER cared for one to two million refugees, mostly women and children. The NER also actively cooperated with ABCFM, Rockefeller Foundation, American Red Cross, and with other committees established all over the world.

The Scandinavian missionaries who were already in Turkey and were running orphanages and hospitals in the interior of the Ottoman Empire also actively cooperated with American relief workers. Some of them even took over the American operated orphanages when the United States entered World War I and most of the Americans had to leave.

Turkish Orphanages as Centers of Turkification

The Convention on the Prevention and Punishment of the Crime of Genocide adopted by the United Nations General Assembly defines a number of acts that constitute genocide, including "forcibly transferring children of the group to another group." Turkish orphanages set up for Armenian children would have met this definition. Recently, the location and files of the state orphanage at Antoura (1916–1919) in Mount Lebanon were discovered, bringing to light the fate of Armenian orphans and the brutal methods and punishments meted out, such as starvation and the bastinado (the beating of the soles of the feet with a rod known as "falakha"). The transgression that merited the most severe and most frequent beatings was speaking Armenian (Fisk 2010). Karnig Panian, a survivor, noted the following in his memoir: "after cruel treatment or through physical weakness, many children died. They were buried behind the old college chapel. At night the jackals and wild dogs would dig them up and throw the bones here and there . . . At night, kids would run out to nearby the forest to get apples or any fruits they could find—and their feet would hit bones. They would take these bones back to their rooms and secretly grind them to make soup, or mix them with grain so they could eat them as there was not enough food at the orphanage. They were eating the bones of their dead friends" (quoted in Fisk 2010, n.p.).

Harutyun Alboyajian, another inmate of Antoura orphanage, remembers the day that the orphans woke up to see all Turkish guards and soldiers and officers gone. That was a day or two before Beirut was liberated. The only Turk who stayed behind, the pharmacist, spoke to the orphans, admonished them to forget the Turkish names given to them in the orphanage and return to their original names. He also confessed to the children that he was instructed to poison their last supper and kill them all before leaving the orphanage. But he did not do that (Svazlian 2011, 426–28). Another survivor, Hampartzoum Chitjian, notes that his father had been tortured and forced to turn over his four sons to a Turkish orphanage (which were euphemistically called *mekteb*, meaning school) in their hometown of Perri. In his memoirs, *A Hair's Breadth from Death*, Hampartzoum (2003) describes the hardship of life in the prison-like orphanage where 150–200 boys, aged four to fourteen, lived starving and sick. He notes that he and the other incarcerated children were sent out to pillage Armenian homes, all of which were vacant as a result of the deportations, on the behalf of the Turkish government (100–103). The Turkish *mullahs* gave the orphans Turkish names, forbade them to speak Armenian, and forced them to convert to Islam. A year later, they separated the older boys who resisted conversion and killed them all. Hampartzoum miraculously escaped. A blind Turkish beggar picked him up and took him to his shack. Hampartzoum met many Islamized boys working as servants in Turkish homes. Fortunately, for him, his master did not force him to convert.

Massis Kodjoyan (Svazlian 2011), a five-year old, was snatched by a Turk on the deportation route from Bayburt (Babert) to Sebastia (Sivaz) and was used as a shepherd. For three years, Kodjoyan lived in Turkish houses until he was taken to a Turkish orphanage in Sivaz where he lived for a year. The orphanage suffered a typhus epidemic and more than half of the orphans died. The healthy ones were transferred to another Turkish orphanage. After the war, when the search for Armenian orphans was underway, he refused to leave. He had become a true Turk. However, a surviving sister found him and forced him to leave the orphanage and flee. Massis and his sister finally reached Yerevan (Svazlian 2011, 202–4).

Armenian Children in Postwar Constantinople

In early 1919, the surviving Armenian remnants, mostly widows and children stranded in the interior, began to find their way to Constantinople, which was under Allied occupation. The French, British, and later Italian military presence in Constantinople made the city safe for Armenian survivors to return. Armenian intellectuals and community leaders who had somehow managed to avoid arrest and execution also began to return to the city. Postwar Constantinople promised to become a safe haven for the revival of the massacred nation, as schools and hospitals were reopened. Several committees and organizations were formed to attend to the needs of the refugees and to collect the Armenian orphans still wandering in the interior or held captive in Muslim households or housed in Turkish orphanages. American and European missionaries also launched an extensive search to recover Armenian orphans. In an essay titled "The League of Nations and the Reclamation of Armenian Genocide Survivors," Vahram L. Shemmassian (2003) examines the gathering of the remnants of the Armenians and discusses the work of the American Red Cross, the Armenian National Movement, the Armenian General Benevolent Movement, among others. Shemmassian (2003) writes of the *Official Journal of the League of Nations* (1921) reporting on the seizure of Turkish orphanages by the Allied police "in which the names of Christian children have been struck out and Moslem names super-imposed" (86). The same report further stated that it would be impossible to check all Turkish orphanages across the empire, unless "systematic means of examination" were devised (quoted in Shemmassian 2003, 87). And that was of course, next to impossible. Shemmassian (2003) cites Emma Coushman, who had formerly been a NER worker providing assistance to Armenian deportees during the war, as reporting that Turks had managed to bring about a change in the Armenian children's minds, not only brainwashing them, luring them with cheap toys and clothing but also threatening them, making the child believe "that he is protected by the Turks from a much worse fate" (88).

Coushman presented the following statistics to the League of Nations, which was discussed by the League's Council on August 30, 1921: "The total number of Armenian orphans reclaimed since the Mudros Armistice of October 30, 1918 was 90,819. Of these 12,480 were rescued in areas in Asia Minor that were not occupied by the Allies. 11,339 in the areas occupied by the Allies, and 67,000 in Armenia, Georgia, Egypt, and Cyprus. Still, 70,350 Armenian orphans were believed to remain in Turkish institutions and homes, with 60,750 in unoccupied areas and 12,600 in the occupied areas" (quoted in Shemmassian 2003, 88). The Council received the report favorably and made recommendations and allocations. However, with the advance of Mustafa Kemal's National Army, the entire operation was jeopardized (92). That said, the League of Nations began to change policies and approaches toward Mustafa Kemal's new Turkey but still continued to support the Commission's activities and the ongoing retrieval of women and children. The Constantinople branch of the Commission of Inquiry was shut down in 1926. The branch in Aleppo remained in operation and, in fact, continued its work into the 1930s without the help of the League.

Catholicos Zaven Der Yeghiayan's (2002) memoirs, *My Patriarchal Memoirs*, provide ample information based on reports coming to the Patriarchate on the lot of the children during and after the genocide. The Armenian Patriarch of Constantinople attests that as the deportees reached major towns along the way toward the desert, they were stopped in front of each town's main government building. There, the boys and girls were separated. That accomplished, the rest of the caravan was forced back on the road again. Then the town folk were invited to come and pick any child or children they wanted (Der Yeghiayan 2002, 88). Many of these children, especially in remote areas in the interior, remained in Turkish, Kurdish, or Arab houses and were never discovered. Some Turks, however, brought these children to Constantinople to sell to rich Turks, to turn them over to Turkish orphanages, or even to turn them over to the Patriarchate.

On his return from exile after the Armistice, Patriarch Zaven Der Yeghiayan reorganized the Patriarchate and oversaw the refugee relief work. In his memoirs, he writes about Armenian organizations, such as *Vorpaknam Engerutyun* (Orphan Care Society) and *Daragrelots Engerutyun* (Deportees' Society), two organizations which merged together in 1919 forming the *Hay Azkayin Khnamagalutyun* (Armenian National Trustship). With financial support from the NER, these organizations supervised a number of orphanages in and around Constantinople such as the Kuleli Central Orphanage with about 1,000 orphans, the Beylerbeyi orphanage with some 250 orphans, the Yedi-Kule Surp Prgich National Hospital Orphanage with 300 orphans, and another twelve orphanages or so, each with 100 to 500 orphans (Der Yeghiayan 2003, 178–79). Boys were taught trades, such as shoe making and carpentry, and girls handicraft and needlework in order to prepare them for life outside these institutions. Because of the meager means available to provide for these orphans, efforts were made to find surviving relatives who could take them into their care, to wed older girls and boys and send them off, and to marry the girls off to lonely male survivors.

Zaven Patriarch attests that some Turks, fearing that they would be punished by the Allies, voluntarily delivered the children they were keeping to Armenian churches or Armenian neighbors. Others threatened the children they were keeping that if they revealed their identity they would be murdered.

According to Zaven Patriarch, there was a close collaboration with the British authorities, represented by Commander Smith, and Arakel Chakerian, an Armenian professor of chemistry in the Turkish University in Constantinople, who had dedicated himself to reclaiming Armenian women and children from Turkish homes and orphanages. In his report presented in April of 1919, Chakerian noted that 750 orphans had been retrieved. He had also found a book entitled

Kadenlar Islam Jemiyeti in which the names of Islamized Armenian orphans were registered (Der Yeghiayan 2002, 181).

Altogether, with the help of the Allies, it had been possible to reclaim about 4,000 orphans in Constantinople and its surroundings. The task was more difficult in the interior, where even after the defeat of Turkey, the Allied armies did not penetrate. Arshaluys Mardikian, a young Armenian girl whose ordeal was recorded and published under the title *Ravished Armenia: The Story of Aurora Mardiganian, The Christian Girl Who Lived through the Great Massacres* (1918), attested that after the war, Dr. MacCallum, in Erzerum, bought thousands of young Armenian girls from their Turkish captors for an equivalent of $1 a piece. Turks preferred to sell them rather than lose them without collecting money, knowing that the Russians would liberate the girls if they found them. The money to buy the girls was supplied by the American Committee for Armenian and Syrian Relief (Mardikian 1918, 198).

With the escalation of the threat of Mustafa Kemal's nationalist movement sweeping the country and the potential for a new wave of persecutions, many orphanages, especially those established by the missionaries, were moved outside of Turkey—mostly to Syria and Lebanon, some to Greece, and a few to the United States. The Turkish government forced the missionaries to pay a price for each orphan before giving them permission to leave the country. Bertha Nakshian Ketchian (1988), who as a young girl attended the school established in an orphanage for boys in Mezireh, notes in her memoir (*In the Shadow of the Fortress: The Genocide Remembered*) that in 1922 when the American missionaries were leaving Turkey, the Turkish government made them pay "five gold pieces per person to the Turkish government for permission to allow the Armenian orphans to be taken out of the country" (123).

The Continuing Psychological Impact

The wretched orphans who survived the unspeakable hardship of the Armenian Genocide continued living with their morbid memories and unhealed wounds, the lifelong psychic imprint of their tragic childhood experience. A mental picture of the traumatic experience could be triggered unbidden by a smell, sound, sight, or touch, and the subconscious would begin to override the conscious and take the victim back to his or her traumatic experience. In their adult lives, most of the orphans never had access to psychological therapy to help them facilitate psychological reconciliation. An Armenian boy who had been deported with his mother and had witnessed her die of thirst in the wilderness told his story to Major Stephen Trowbridge in Antoura orphanage and said: "Sir, may you never see anyone die from thirst" (Trowbridge 1918, 10).

As Hagop Oshagan observed, this was the generation "released from orphanages directly into the life outside, only to become orphans once more among life's deprivations" (quoted in Peroomian 2012, 146). The orphans tried hard to forget, or as psychologists would have it, to reconcile the thoughts, images, and memories associated with their traumatic experience with the schemata of their cognitive-world models. As Mardi Jon Horowitz (1986) has established, such trauma-related memories can break through the victim's defenses and intrude into their consciousness in the form of flashbacks, nightmares, and unwanted thoughts. Donald Miller and Lorna Touryan Miller (1993) report on a female survivor telling them, "Sometimes my husband wakes me up and says 'What's wrong? What's happening?' I yell in my dreams" (157). Another woman witnessed a Turk attempting to kill her mother by pushing her into an oven: "So poor woman, until she died, she used to scream in her dreams" (Miller and Miller 1993, 157).

Mushegh Ishkhan (1974), a survivor-writer, recalled in his memoirs the nightmares he used to experience, and how he would jump up in his sleep, screaming, "The Turks, mother, Turks are coming to kill" (25). Leonardo Alishan (1992), a renowned American-Armenian writer-poet, writes about his grandmother, Gayane, who never recovered from the ordeal she experienced during the deportations. She was in and out of mental hospitals all her life. On her deathbed in a London hospital in 1977, the nightmarish scene of Turkish horsemen dashing in the night into the deportee camps and picking up young girls visited her again.

Many survivors have tried to deal with the traumatic experience by themselves, and their reactions or responses vary. Miller and Miller (1993) created a typology of the different ways survivors have struggled to deal with the trauma of genocide: "Avoidance and Repression, Outrage and Anger, Revenge and Restitution, Reconciliation and Forgiveness, Resignation and Despair, and Explanation and Rationalization" (159–60).

No matter how hard these survivors try, they are tainted for good, and life is not for them to enjoy, even if the New World provides them with opportunities and a comfortable family life. "I can feel them now, those steady cutting slashes with the whips the Turks use on convicts whom they bastinado to death" (110), commented Aurora Mardiganian (1918) (see Slide 1997). Remembering another harrowing scene of torture, rape, and murder, she adds, "I saw terrible things that night that I cannot tell. When I see them in my dreams now, I scream; so even though I am safe in America, my nights are not peaceful" (Mardiganian 1918, 110) (see Slide 1997). Antony Slide (1997), who wrote a commentary on Aurora Mardiganian's life story, attests that because of the sexual violence suffered by her, for long years she would not let a man touch her (17). Virginie (Jiji) Mesropian (2007) was so severely affected that she chose never to marry: "I wanted to be alone, to suffer alone, without fear of leaving an orphan child behind" (n.p.). She was six years old when she witnessed the brutal murder of her parents and brother. She found herself in a pile of corpses, and from her "hiding place" she saw how men were dragging the corpses and throwing them into the fire. She spotted her father and brother among them.

Critical Challenges Facing the Field

One of the nascent subfields in Armenian Genocide studies is the study of the experiences of the children of the genocide, tens of thousands of them—victims as well as survivors. As for the survivors, whether they were dispersed or continued to live in Turkey, Islamized or discreetly clung to the faith of their ancestors, they were deeply affected, as were the outlook and mentality of their offspring.

Although scholars and researchers have recently tried to unearth data on the destiny of the multitude of Armenian orphans, it is still impossible to estimate their total number. The body of evidence is incomplete in regard to how many, exactly, were killed or how many were kidnapped by Turks, Kurds, and Arabs to sell or to Islamize and retain in their own households. Those who were too young to be conscious of their origins were permanently absorbed into Turkish society.

Unlike more recent genocides whose study is facilitated by oral interviews of survivors, this is no longer possible in the case of the Armenian Genocide. The survivors are gone. The sole resource in this area consists of audiotaped interviews held at the University of California, Los Angeles, and elsewhere, and videotaped interviews held by the Zoryan Institute, almost all in Armenian. The project of digitizing and translating the brief summary of the interviews is underway at UCLA.

Avenues for New Possibilities of Progress

Overall, the increasing interest in and activism for the international recognition of the Armenian Genocide and for the exposure of Turkey's denial and distortion of the event have led the current generation of Armenians to focus more attention on the traumatic Armenian past. Indeed, with the initiative of the children or grandchildren, hitherto forgotten eyewitness accounts and memoirs of the survivors, mostly in Armenian, have been translated in English and published. Examples of these books are included in the accompanying annotated bibliography. Institutions, such as the Armenian Genocide Museum-Institute (Yerevan, Armenia), Gomidas Institute (London, UK), and the Armenian National Institute (ANI) in Washington, DC, have recently released a large number of photographs, survivors' stories, and short testimonies, and have published survivors' biographies and memoirs. They have also collected and published old diaries and eyewitness accounts of American and European missionaries and relief workers, some for the first time. Some of these titles are also included in the accompanying annotated bibliography. The Gomidas Institute has also recently prepared a list of orphans, including their name, age, birthplace, father's name, and the orphanage where they were housed.

The general progress in genocide studies has also been influential, along with the elaboration of the specificity of features particular to victims and to perpetrators of gross violations of human rights and genocide. This has drawn scholars and researchers to investigate hitherto neglected areas in the field, among them children as victims of genocide. Another impetus in this subfield is the recent change of atmosphere in Turkey, where the silence surrounding the Armenian issue has been broken by the published confessions of those who had an Armenian grandfather or grandmother who was abducted or taken in by Turks.

Conclusion

Children occupy a special place in the world's effort to protect human rights today. In its Convention on the Rights of the Child, the United Nations states that the "child, by reason of his physical and mental maturity, needs special safeguards and care, including appropriate legal protection, before as well as after birth."

Recognizing children's special need for protection, the Convention specifies basic rights that every child should enjoy. Nevertheless, throughout history, children have fallen victims of genocide, massive violations of human rights, and war crimes.

Eyewitness accounts of the survivors, testimonies, and reports of foreign witnesses, journalists, diplomatic representatives, news accounts, as well as diaries and memoirs written and published during and after the massacres and deportation of Armenians, confirm the severe persecution of Armenian children in the Ottoman Empire from the late nineteenth century to the establishment of the Republic of Turkey and beyond.

Hundreds of thousands of Armenian children were tortured, raped, slaughtered, starved to death, or absorbed into Turkish society. Thousands of them escaped the persecution, or survived the deportation and terror of genocide with the assistance of various organizations and/or individuals who sometimes had to risk their lives to do so. However, being separated from their parents and siblings and sent in caravans far from home, and standing as witnesses to all those horrors at such a young age, was an incredibly traumatic experience for the children. Even though some were sheltered in orphanages or found new families at the end, for most of them any recovery or reconciliation they experienced—if, in fact, they did so—took a very long time.

Note

1. First, there was the general conscription of the male population between the ages of twenty and forty-five, enforced on every Armenian male (August 1914), then the mass executions of the Armenian soldiers beginning in November. This was followed by the arrest of notables and their murder in the provinces (beginning in October 1914) and the sporadic murder of other men (beginning in December 1914). In January 1915, the expansion of the conscription took place, taking those aged from eighteen to fifty-two (January 1915), followed by the search for weapons and mass arrest of Armenians (beginning in March 1915), and the arrest of civic and religious leaders and intellectuals in Constantinople (April 1915).

References

Alishan, Leonardo. 1992. "An Exercise on a Genre on Genocide and Exorcism." In *The Armenian Genocide: History, Politics, Ethics.* ed. Richard G. Hovannisian, 340–54. New York: St. Martin's Press.

The Armenian Review. 1984. *"Documents: The State Department File."* The *Armenian Review* 37, no. 1: 60–145.

Azadian, Libarid. 1995. *Hay Vorpere Medz Yegherni (The Orphans of the Armenian Genocide).* Glendale, CA: Sardarabad.

Barton, Clara. 1898. *The Red Cross: A History of this Remarkable International Movement in the Interest of Humanity.* Albany, NY: J. B. Lyon Company.

Barton, James L. 1930. *Story of Near East Relief (1915–1930). An Interpretation.* New York: The Macmillan Company.

Chitjian, Hampartzoum. 2003. *A Hair's Breadth from Death: The Memoirs of Hampartzoum Mardiros Chitjian.* London: Taderon Press.

Dadrian, Vahakn N. 2003. "Children as Victims of Genocide: The Armenian Case." *Journal of Genocide Research* 5, no. 3: 421–37.

Der Yeghiayan, Zaven. 2002. *My Patriarchal Memoirs.* Barrington, RI: Mayreni.

Ehmann, Johannes. 1921. "Führugen Gotten in 25 jähriger Orientarbeit (Mezereh)." In Friedrich Schuchardt's *25 Jahre im Orient: 1896–1921. Ein Gaung durch die Arbeit des Deutschen Hülfsbundes für Christliches Liebeswerk im Orient.* Frankfurt: Verlag Orient.

Fisk, Robert. 2010. "Proof of the Armenian Genocide Can Be Found at Hilltop Orphanage." *Belfast Telegraph.* March 9. www.belfasttelegraph.co.uk/.../proof-of-the-armenian-genocide-can-.

Horowitz, Mardi Jon. 1986. *Stress Response Syndromes.* 2nd Ed. New York: Jason Aronson.

Ishkhan, Mushegh. 1974. *Mnas barov mankutiun* [*Farewell Childhood*]. Beirut: Hamazkayin.

Kelly, Michael J. 2005. *Nowhere to Hide: Defeat of the Sovereign Immunity Defense for Crimes of Genocide and the Trials of Slobodan Milosevic and Saddam Hussein,* New York: Peter Lang Publishing.

Ketchian, Bertha Nakshian. 1988. *In the Shadow of the Fortress: The Genocide Remembered.* Cambridge, MA: Zoryan Institute.

Lepsius, Johannes. 1897. "Berichte über das deutche Hilfswerk in Armenien." In *Der Christliche Orient,* ed. Johannes Lepsius, 42–49. Western-Berlin: Verlag der Akademischen Buchhandlang W. Faber & Co.

Mardiganian, Aurora. 1918. *Ravished Armenia: The Story of Aurora Mardiganian, The Christian Girl Who Lived through the Great Massacres.* New York: Kingfield.

Mesropian Virginie—Jiji. 2007. *J'avez six ans en Armenie . . . 1915* [*I Was Six Years Old in Armenia . . . 1915*]. Paris: L'inventaire.

Miller, Donald E., and Lorna Touryan Miller. 1993. *Survivors, An Oral History of the Armenian Genocide.* Berkeley and Los Angeles: University of California Press.

Morgenthau, Henry. 1975. *Ambassador Morgenthau's Story.* Memorial Edition. Plandome: New Age Publishers.

Mugrditchian, Hovhannes. 1996. *To Armenians with Love: The Memoirs of a Patriot.* Hobe Sound, FL: Paul Mart Publishing.

Peroomian, Rubina. 1993. *The Literary Responses to Catastrophe, A Comparison of the Armenian and Jewish Experience.* Atlanta, GA: Scholars Press.

———. 2006. "The Restless World of Leonardo Alishan (March 1951–January 2005): A Burnt Offering on the Altar of the Armenian Genocide." *Genocide Studies and Prevention* 1, no. 3: 289–303.

———. 2012. *The Armenian Genocide in Literature, Perceptions of those Who Lived through the Years of Calamity.* Yerevan: Armenian Genocide Museum-Institute.

Shemmassian, Vahram L. 2003. "The League of Nations and the Reclamation of Armenian Genocide Survivors." In *Looking Backward, Moving Forward:*

Confronting the Armenian Genocide, ed. Richard Hovannisian, 81–112. New Brunswick, NJ: Transaction Publishers.

Slide, Antony. (Compiler). 1997. *Ravished Armenia and the Story of Aurora Mardiganian*. Lanham, MD., and London: The Scarecrow Press, Inc.

Svazlian, Verjine. 2011. *The Armenian Genocide, Testimonies of the Eyewitness Survivors*. Yerevan: Gitutyun Publishing House of NAS RA.

Terzian, Hagop. 2009. *Cilicia 1909: the Massacre of Armenians*. London: Taderon Press by special arrangement for the Gomidas Institute.

Trowbridge, Stephen. 1918. *Antoura, the Shelter of a Thousand Tragedies*. Jerusalem: Syrian Orphanage Press.

Yesayan, Zabel. 2010. *Averaknerun mej (Among the Ruins)*. Istanbul: Sena Ofset. (First edition 1911, Constantinople: Armenian Publishing Association.)

Annotated Bibliography

Diaries

Jacobsen, Maria. *Diaries of a Danish Missionary, Harpoot, 1907–1919*. Princeton, NJ and London: Gomidas Institute Books, 2001, 266 pp.

This is an eyewitness account of the Harpoot (Kharbert) deportations and caravans of deportees that passed through the city. Maria Jacobsen tells about the Turkish families who took in Armenian children and gave them Turkish names. She speaks of the orphanage set up by the missionaries and how they were forced by the government to close the orphanage down.

Sarian, Hrant. *Le Journal de mon Pere*. 2008. http://choisy.pagesperso-orange. fr/index.htm.

This diary by Hrant Sarian was translated from Armenian into French by his daughter, Louise Kiffer, and posted online, together with the Armenian original, in 2008.

Hrant Sarian was born in 1901 in Adabazar. He provides an amazingly detailed description of the places and hardship of the family's deportation route to Arifiye, toward Birejik and on to Eskishehir and down to Hama. He ran away the night the Arab who had taken Hrant as a helper brought a mullah to circumcise him and force him to convert to Islam. He walked for weeks, begging for pieces of bread as he traveled from one village to another. All along the way, Arabs beat him. In various villages he came across many Armenian girls whom Arabs had taken as their wives. It was these girls who gave him bread and tried to help him when they found out that he was Armenian. He finally made it to Aleppo and found his brother and sister in an orphanage. After the war, Hrant reached Constantinople and was admitted to the Katekiugh orphanage. His diary stretches over the years up and until 1923.

Eyewitness Accounts

Barton, James L. *Story of Near East Relief (1915–1930). An Interpretation*, New York: The Macmillan Company, 1930, 479 pp.

James Barton was one of the founders of the Near East Relief organization and Foreign Secretary of the American Board of Commissioners for Foreign Missions. In his book, Barton tells the story of the relief work of US citizens in the Near East—work in which he was personally involved. Separate chapters of the book depict the conditions of the Armenian children, their training in orphanages and schools, and their transition from life in the orphanages to independence.

Chambers, William Nesbitt. *Yoljuluk: Random Thoughts on a Life in Imperial Turkey*. London: Simpkin Marshall, Ltd., 1928, 125 pp.

William Chambers describes the missionary activities in the Near East and three main tragedies he personally witnessed during his forty-five years of service: the 1895 massacres in Erzerum, the 1909 massacres in Adana, and the 1915 deportation of Armenians from Adana. He was a missionary with the American Board of Commissioners for Foreign Missions and was personally involved in sheltering and hiding Armenian children in his home.

Clark, Alice Keep. *Letters from Cilicia*. Chicago, IL: A. D. Weinthrop & Co., 1924, 201 pp.

Alice Clark was an American relief worker sent to the Ottoman Empire by the Near East Relief organization. Her book is comprised of excerpts from the letters written by Clark to Clark's family in the United States, and excerpts from her diary kept between February through June 1920 when the city of Hadjin was besieged by the Turks when postal and telegraphic communication with the rest of the world was cut off. She started her work in Hadjin in 1919 and sheltered and took care of many Armenian children and women—the remnants of Armenians after the genocide.

Kerr, Stanley Elphinstone. *The Lions of Marash: Personal Experiences with American Near East Relief, 1919–1922*. Albany: State University of New York, 1973, 318 pp.

Stanley Kerr was a relief worker and was sent to the Middle East by the Near East Relief organization. He worked in Aleppo, then in Marash and helped to reclaim Armenian women and children from Muslim households and to provide humanitarian assistance for hundreds in need. In his book, Kerr tells about German missionaries and their assistance to Armenian orphans during World War I, about American aid after the armistice, and the establishment of orphanages all over the Near East. He provides detailed information about German, British, and American orphanages in Marash.

Lovejoy, Esther P. *Certain Samaritans*. New York: The Macmillan Company, 1927, 302 pp.

Esther Lovejoy was a member of American Women's Hospital and also worked with Armenian orphans and refugees after the genocide. She provides information on the cooperation between members of different American organizations in assisting Armenian orphans, both in the Ottoman Empire and in the Republic of Armenia. In doing so, Lovejoy examines the experience of Armenian children during the massacres and later in the orphanages.

Knapp, Grace H. *The Tragedy of Bitlis*. London: Sterndale Classics, 2002, 109 pp.

Grace Knapp retells the accounts written down by Ms. McLaren and Ms. Shane, two American missionaries who witnessed the atrocities committed in Bitlis. Additionally, she added her own eyewitness accounts in Van. The last chapter deals with the aftermath—the surviving refugees from Bitlis and Van in the Caucasus.

Kunzler, Jakob. *In the Land of Blood and Tears, Experiences in Mesopotamia During the World War (1914–1918)*. Arlington, MA: Armenian Cultural Foundation, 2007, 187 pp.

A missionary and a medical doctor stationed in Urfa since 1899, Jakob Kunzler witnessed caravans of widows and orphans continuously arriving in Urfa on their way to the desert. He did everything possible to assist the refugees and alleviate their deplorable situation. He opened an orphanage and tried to gather Armenian children from the streets and Moslem households. After a short visit in Switzerland, Kunzler and his wife returned to Urfa in 1920 and engaged in the difficult work of transferring 8,000 orphans to the safer Syrian towns.

Lambert, Rose. *Hadjin and the Armenian Massacres*. New York: Fleming H. Revell Company, 1911, 106 pp.

The author, a missionary stationed in Hadjin, records the accounts of the 1909 massacres in the city and the Armenian defense of the city.

Parmelee, Ruth M. *A Pioneer in the Euphrates Valley*. Princeton, NJ and London: Gomidas Institute, 2002, 68 pp.

Herein, Dr. Ruth Parmelee, an American medical missionary in the Ottoman Empire during World War I, presents her testimony about the Turkish atrocities against Armenians in the region of Kharbert.

Ross, Frank A., Luther C. Fry, and Elbridge Sibley. *The Near East and American Philanthropy: A Survey Conducted under the Guidance of the General of the Near East Survey*. New York: Columbia University Press, 1929, 308 pp.

Frank Ross, Luther Fry, and Elbridge Sibley conducted this survey in the Caucasus, the Balkans, Turkey, and in Iraq, Palestine, and Syria. Essentially, they provided detailed information about the socioeconomic conditions in those regions and the conditions of orphans and refugees in need.

Memoirs and Autobiographies

Balakian, Grigoris. *Armenian Golgotha, A Memoir of the Armenian Genocide, 1915–1918* New York: Alfred A. Knopf Publishing, 2009, 509 pp.

Arrested in Constantinople and exiled on April 24, 1915, Grigoris Balakian, a priest, began a four-year ordeal on the unending road of exile. His eyewitness account is one of the most poignant testimonies of the bloodiest scenes of atrocity committed against Armenian men, women, and children.

Bedoukian, Kerop. *The Urchin: An Armenian's Escape*. London: Butler and Tanner Ltd., 1978, 186 pp. (Also published as *Some of Us Survived*. New York: Farrar Straus Giroux, 1979, 242 pp.)

Kerop Bedoukian was nine years old when the deportation of Armenians in Sivaz began. His memoir is dedicated to his mother and sister who shared his horrifying ordeal, and protected and helped him escape to freedom.

Chitjian Hambartzoum, Mardiros. *A Hair's Breadth from Death: The Memoirs of Hambartzoum Mardiros Chitjian*. London: Taderon Press, 2003, 433 pp.

Early on, as the deportation started in their hometown, Ismayil, Chitjian Hambartzoum's father returned home from his weeks of incarceration and torture with blood stains on his coat. He was virtually forced to hand his four sons over to the Turkish religious school (*mekteb*). Hambartzoum the oldest was fourteen. The boys never saw their father again. Two of them were able to escape later and reached freedom after years of hardship.

Der Yeghiayan, Zaven. *My Patriarchal Memoirs*. Barrington, RI: Mayreni Publishing, 2002, 304 pp.

This work, by Armenian Patriarch of Constantinople Zaven Der Yeghiayan is important not only in terms of the plethora of documentations on the deportation and massacres, the process of collecting and sheltering Armenian children, and the list of orphanages that were established, but also in terms of the Armenian Patriarch of Constantinople's own eyewitness accounts on the route of his exile in 1916. He served as the Armenian Patriarch of Constantinople from 1913 through 1922.

Kouymjian Highgas, Dirouhi. *Refugee Girl*, Watertown, MA: Baykar, 1985, 178 pp.

Dirouhi Kouymjian Highgas, born in Konia, was a little girl in 1915 when her father was arrested and the family was deported. As an unusual case, the family was reunited with the father and they all went through months of hardship in Arab villages until the father died of typhus. She describes the lot of the Armenian children during the deportation and how her parents tried to hide her so that the gendarmes would not take her away.

Martin, Ramela. *Out of Darkness*. Cambridge, MA: Zoryan Institute Publications, 1989, 220 pp.

Born in the Pilibisian family in Malatia, Ramela Martin was a little girl during the years of deportation and massacres of 1915–1917. She lost her mother during the deportations and struggled all alone until she found her way to an orphanage, where she witnessed children dying from hunger and illnesses.

Meymarian, Euphronia Halebian. *Housher: My Life in the Aftermath of the Armenian Genocide*. London: Taderon Press, 2004, 102 pp.

Born in 1908 in Aintab, Euphronia Halebian Meymarian survived the terrors of the Adana massacres and the genocide. Her family survived only because her father worked for the Ottoman army and knew the right people to ask for assistance. After they escaped the massacres, they settled in Lebanon in 1920. In addition to the latter, Meymarian also describes the life of Armenian children in the American orphanage in Jbeil and other orphanages founded in Beirut and the adjacent settlements.

Minassian, John. *Many Hills Yet to Climb: Memoirs of an Armenian Deportee*. Santa Barbara, CA: Jim Cook Publisher, 1986, 255 pp.

John Minassian was born in Sivas. He survived the deportation to write a detailed account of the Armenian suffering, the demise of his young siblings and the children to whom he provided care while working in different orphanages.

Muggerditchian Shipley, Alice. *We Walked Then Ran*. Phoenix, AZ: A. M. Shipley, 1983, 290 pp..

Alice Muggerditchian Shipley was born in Diyarbekir and was raised in Harpout. She was eleven years old when the deportations began. Her father was in the service of the British government and had to escape to Egypt to avoid arrest. Alice's mother and her three daughters suffered through the deportation and were on the run to avoid the government's pursuit to kill them in retaliation for their father's escape.

Muggrditchian, Hovhannes. *To Armenians with Love: The Memoirs of a Patriot*. Hobe Sound, FL: Paul Mart, 1996, 214 pp.

Hovhannes Muggrditchian was newly married and a young teacher when the deportations began. His newborn baby perished during the deportation. After great hardship, Muggrditchian reached Aleppo to find his wife whom he had lost track of for some eight months. This memoir is significant for the description of orphanages in Aleppo and the deplorable state of Armenian children who died by the hundreds of starvation and diseases.

Mardiganian, Aurora. *Ravished Armenia, The Story of Aurora Mardiganian, The Christian Girl Who Lived through the Massacres.* New York: Kingfield Press, Inc., 1918, 175 pp.

This is the story of a fourteen-year-old girl who was kidnapped and abused physically and sexually throughout her years of captivity. She relates her harrowing experiences and those of other children. A film by that same name was produced and shown in the United States and Europe. Today, only a twenty-minute section of the film survives.

Nakshian Ketchian, Bertha. *In the Shadow of the Fortress, The Genocide Remembered.* Cambridge, MA: Zoryan Institute Publications, 1988, 151 pp.

Herein, Bertha Nakshian Ketchian remembers her childhood in Husenig, in the province of Kharbert. She describes women, children, and old men during the death march, young women being kidnapped, children taken away by Arabs and Kurds, and women hurling themselves from cliffs. She remembers her grandmother trying hard to keep the family together. Bertha ended up in an orphanage after the remnants of the family returned to Kharbert.

Surmelian, Levon Z. *I Ask You Ladies and Gentlemen.* New York: E. P. Dutton & Co., Inc., 1945, 316 pp.

This autobiography is one of the first English-language works on the Armenian Genocide. The tragedy of 1915 is described through the eyes of a young boy.

Tavoukdjian, Serpouhi. *Exiled: Story of an Armenian Girl.* Takoma Park, MD: Review and Herald Publishing Association, 1933, 126 pp.

Serpouhi Tavoukdjian was born in Ovajik, a small town near Ismid. When Turkey entered World War I, Serpouhi was ten years old. Her father, Aaron, was conscripted and the rest of her family was forced into exile. She witnessed the starvation and suffering of her family members during the deportation. She was then taken into an Arab family, given a new name, and tattooed. Finally, with the assistance of the American Red Cross, Serpouhi found her father, but before long they both became refugees and were separated again. Serpouhi was first sheltered in American orphanages in Constantinople, and then in Greece.

Biography

Ahnert, Margaret Ajemian. *The Knock at the Door: A Journey through the Darkness of the Armenian Genocide.* New York: Beaufort Books, 2007, 215 pp.

Margaret Ahnert wrote this book based on the stories and recollections of her mother, Ester. Ester was from Amasia and was fifteen in 1915, and thus related stories to her daughter not only about her experiences during the massacres and deportation but also about her family and her childhood before the genocide. During the genocide, Ester was deported, taken to an orphanage, and eventually forced into an marriage (which was abusive) against her will.

Alamuddin, Ida. *Papa Kuenzler and the Armenians.* London: William Heinemann Ltd., 1970, 168 pp.

Ida Alamuddin, daughter of Jacob Kuenzler, a Swiss missionary who served in Turkey for twenty-five years, provides detailed information about the "Father of the Armenian Orphans" as Jacob Kuenzler was called in the Near East. She describes the evacuation of thousands of Armenian orphans in Turkey, their transfer to Lebanon, and the life of orphans in the orphanage in the village of Ghazir, run by Kuenzler, where the children were taught trades and prepared for their future.

Bagdasarian, Adam. *Forgotten Fire*. New York: DK Publishing, Inc., 2000, 273 pp.

Twelve-year-old Vahan's childhood abruptly ended when he watched, horror stricken, the execution of his two older brothers by gendarmes in their own garden in Bitlis. The book is based on Adam Bagdasarian's great uncle, Vahan's life story. Members of the family and fellow deportees are vividly portrayed throughout the story.

Kherdian, David. *The Road from Home: The Story of an Armenian Girl*. New York: Greenwillow Books, 1979, 238 pp.

David Kherdian tells the story of his mother, Veron, who was born in Azizia to a well-to-do family. At the age of sixteen, she was deported with her family and survived unspeakable hardship.

Kricorian, Nancy. *Zabelle*. New York: Avon Books, 1999, 241 pp.

This is the story of Zabelle Chahasbanian, from her childhood in Hadjin to her immigration to the United States, with frequent flashbacks into the darkest years of her life during the deportations.

Najarian, Peter. *Daughters of Memory* . Berkeley, CA: City Miner Books, 1986, 157 pp.

Some women survivors of the genocide living in the United States get together every so often and share their horrible experiences during the deportations of 1915. Peter Najarian's mother was one of them. These are stories that Peter overheard in his childhood years.

Soghoian, Florence M. *Portrait of a Survivor*. Hanover, MA: The Christopher Publishing House, 1997, 147 pp.

Florence Soghoian has written the story of her mother, Shnorhig, who was deported from Zeitun at the age of seven. Her father was a soldier in the Turkish army and was away. They never heard from him again. Her family members were separated from one another and died one by one, eventually leaving Soghoian to fend for herself on the streets of Marash. Ultimately, she was taken to an orphanage and later reunited with her mother, the only other survivor of their large family.

Tashjian, Alice A. *Silences: My Mother's Will to Survive*. Princeton, NJ: Blue Pansy Publishing, 1995, 98 pp.

This is the story of Iskouhi Parounagian of Sivaz, the author's mother. Still in her teens, Iskouhi lost her mother to the hardship of the death march. Orphaned and alone, she wandered for days without food until a Turkish woman picked her up and took her home. But sheltering Armenians was dangerous, and Turks who did so faced jail, if not death. Eventually, Iskouhi was put out, but the Turkish woman was kind enough to accompany her until she could join a caravan of Armenians. Then another ordeal began.

Theriault, Kim, S. *Rethinking Arshile Gorky*. University Park: The Pennsylvania University Press, 2009, 243 pp.

This biography of an orphaned boy who became a famous painter demonstrates the traumatic effects of the genocide and a lifelong psychological state that resulted in the demise of a great talent.

Secondary Material

Balakian, Peter. *The Burning Tigris: The Armenian Genocide and America's Response*, New York: Harper Collins Publishers, 2003, 475 pp.

Using archival materials and eyewitness accounts, Peter Balakian presents the history of the Armenian Genocide, motivations of perpetrators, and the suffering of victims. He provides valuable information about the Armenian children, including their experiences during the deportation and forcible conversions and absorption into Muslim families. In addition, Balakian describes the relief efforts of various American organizations and particularly the Near East Relief organization for Armenian children during and after the genocide.

Dadrian, Vahakn N. "Children as Victims of Genocide: The Armenian Case." *Journal of Genocide Research*, September 5, no. 3 (2003): 421–37.

Vahakn Dadrian raises the issue of children victims of the Armenian genocide, who are generally subsumed within the entire victim population and not treated as a separate and distinct subject of study. Based on the records of foreign representatives and eyewitnesses, as well as Armenian survivors, he delineates the various methods of liquidation used against Armenian children during the genocide: drowning, burning alive, poisoning, wholesale rapes that preceded killing, and burying alive.

Daniel, Robert L. *American Philanthropy in the Near East, 1820–1960*. Athens: Ohio University Press, 1970, 322 pp.

In exploring various relief efforts of several American philanthropic committees and organizations for people in need in the Near East, Robert Daniel describes the establishment of schools and orphanages for Armenian children by American missionaries all over the interior of the Ottoman Empire, beginning from the mid-nineteenth century. Daniel particularly zeros in on the work of the Near East Relief organization and assesses its relief and rehabilitation activities for the Armenian children in the post-genocide period.

Miller, Donald E., and Lorna Touryan Miller. "Women and Children of the Armenian Genocide." In *The Armenian Genocide, History, Politics, Ethics*, edited by Richard G. Hovannisian, 152–72. New York: St. Martin's Press, 1992.

This chapter focuses on eyewitness testimonies of two survivors of the Armenian Genocide, a young girl and a mother of two children. The authors discuss the experiences and suffering of Armenian women and children based on these two stories, and in doing so examines three categories of suffering: physical, emotional, and moral.

Moranian, Suzanne Elizabeth. *The American Missionaries and the Armenian Question: 1915–1927*. Ann Arbor, MI: UMI Dissertation Services, 1994, 609 pp.

In her dissertation, Suzanne Moranian provides detailed information about the American response to Armenian Genocide, the deportation and massacres of Armenians, and the activities of American missionaries in the Near East. In doing so, she examines: the fundraising campaigns to help hundreds of thousands of Armenian orphans and refugees in the Near East; the establishment of orphanages, kitchens, and hospitals; the relief efforts of missionaries for Armenian children; the children's experiences in orphanages; and health care and training to help the Armenian children to become self-supporting.

Moranian, Suzanne Elizabeth. "Bearing Witness: The Missionary Archives as Evidence of the Armenian Genocide." In *The Armenian Genocide, History,*

Politics, Ethics, edited by Richard G. Hovannisian, 103–28. New York: St. Martin's Press, 1992.

Moranian recounts missionary activities in the Ottoman Empire, especially during the massacres and deportations, and cites their reports. She describes how difficult it was for the missionaries to witness the deportations, knowing that the deportees "faced almost certain death." Anna Birge remembers women and children jammed into cattle cars going south without food and water: "One woman gave birth to twins in one of the cattle cars, and upon crossing a river, the woman hurled herself and her two infants into the water." Toward the end of the genocide the Turkish Government exempted the Armenian Catholics and Protestants from deportation, but most of them were already gone.

Peroomian, Rubina. *And Those Who Continued Living in Turkey after 1915.* Yerevan: Armenian Genocide Museum Institute, 2008 and 2012, 277 pp.

Based on Turkish and Turkish-Armenian literature, memoirs, eyewitness accounts, and interviews, Rubina Peroomian discusses the details of the surviving children, many of them Islamized, living in Turkish, Kurdish, and Arab households as helpers, adopted sons and daughters or concubines, and wives. In doing so, she discusses how many were beaten, tortured, or sexually abused. She also discusses the impact of the generation of captives on their offspring, the generation that constitutes a part of the Turkish society today.

Peroomian, Rubina. *The Armenian Genocide in Literature, Perceptions of Those Who Lived Through the Years of Calamity.* Yerevan: The Armenian Genocide Museum Institute, 2012, 474 pp.

Peroomian discusses the autobiographies of the child survivors of the Armenian genocide, the literature of the orphan generation, and various memoirs by survivors. It includes sources in Armenian, English, and French.

Peterson, Merrill D. *"Starving Armenians": America and the Armenian Genocide, 1915–1930 and After.* Charlottesville: University of Virginia Press, 2004, 199 pp.

Using archival materials and eyewitness accounts, Merrill Peterson presents the history of the Armenian genocide, including the plight of Armenian children during the massacres and deportation. He explores the American response to these atrocities and the unprecedented philanthropic campaign of the Near East Relief organization to help hundreds of thousands of Armenian children in distress.

Sarafian, Ara. "The Absorption of Armenian Women and Children into Muslim Households as a Structural Component of the Armenian Genocide." In *In God's Name: Genocide and Religion in the Twentieth Century,* edited by. Omer Bartov and Phyllis Mack, 209–21. New York: Berghahn Books, 2001.

Ara Sarafian examines the issue of absorption of the Armenian women and children into Turkish society and Muslim households as a genocidal act and a major element in the genocidal policy of the Ottoman Empire. As evidence for the assimilation policy of the Ottoman government, the author refers to American consular and missionary sources.

Shemmassian, Vahram L. "The League of Nations and the Reclamation of Armenian Genocide Survivors." In *Looking Backward, Moving Forward: Confronting the Armenian Genocide,* edited by Richard G. Hovannisian, 81–112. New Brunswick, NJ: Transaction Publishers, 2003.

This chapter focuses on the reclamation efforts of Armenian women and children in Syria and Lebanon during 1918–1920. Vahram Shemmassian provides estimates of the number of captive survivors, presents information about the agencies and individuals involved in rescue, and discusses the obstacles that occurred on the way to emancipation. Finally, the author estimates the quantitative accomplishment of such recovery operations.

Shirinian, George N. "The Armenian Massacres of 1894–1897: A Bibliography." *Armenian Review* 47, no. 1–2 (2001): 113–64.

This compilation of material on the historical background, documents, memoirs, and eyewitness accounts is a valuable contribution to the research and understanding of the Armenian massacres of 1894–1897.

Peterson, Merrill D. *"Starving Armenians": America and the Armenian Genocide, 1915–1930 and After.* Charlottesville: University of Virginia Press, 2004, 199 pp.

4

Children and the Holocaust

Jeffrey Blutinger

Introduction

The history of children in the Holocaust is one of paradox: no group was more vulnerable to abuse, yet at the same time, no group was more targeted for rescue. Despite the heroic efforts of parents and communities, the Nazis murdered over one million Jewish children. Both the Nazis and their victims made the survival and education of children one of their top priorities; both groups saw children as essential to their future survival. The fascist values that underlay the Nazi state robbed children of their individual value and dignity. Those deemed unworthy, whether because the Nazis labeled them non-Aryans, or determined that they were socially or biologically defective, were persecuted, expelled, incarcerated, sterilized, and ultimately murdered. Even those declared fit for Aryan society could still be sacrificed as child soldiers if their deaths could keep the Nazis in power.

Definitional Problems

One of the issues that arises when studying the experiences of children during the Holocaust is deciding who was a child. While the category certainly includes infants, toddlers, and elementary school-aged children, it becomes a bit murkier when we reach the later teen-age years. Some studies limit themselves to children up to the age of sixteen, while others included "youths" up to the age of twenty-five. Furthermore, children who were infants or toddlers when Nazi rule began, experienced the Holocaust in radically different ways than their older siblings. In almost all cases, the arrival of the Nazis marked the end of anything resembling childhood, and children were forced to grow up very quickly. And yet, the differences between a child of sixteen and one of twenty were far less than the differences between that same sixteen-year-old and the twelve-year-old brother.

Another foundational question is whose story should be included as part of the Holocaust. While few would challenge recognizing Roma, Poles, and even Aryan children subjected to either the sterilization or T-4 murder campaigns as victims of the Holocaust, what of those children who were privileged by the Nazi state, educated in Nazi schools, and made to join the *Hitler Jugend* or the *Bund Deutscher Mädel*? In this chapter, I will consider all children and youth whose lives where shaped or affected by Nazi rule and the Holocaust.

Finally, there remains the problem of numbers. Estimates for the number of children killed by the Germans or their allies during the Holocaust vary significantly. For Jewish children alone, the number varies from a low of 1 million to a high of 1.5 million. This latter number, the most frequently cited, refers to children under the age of sixteen, and comes from estimates created by researchers in 1946 and 1947 (Dwork 1991, 274 n. 27). There is even less data available for the deaths of non-Jewish children.

Children in Nazi Germany before the War (1933–1939)

Aryan Children

The Nazis saw children and their training as critical to the future of the racial state they were trying to create. Originally a voluntary movement, membership in the *Hitler Jugend* (*HJ*) (Hitler Youth) for boys and the *Bund Deutscher Mädel* (League of German Girls) for girls grew enormously even before the September 1939 decree, making membership mandatory for Aryan children between the ages of ten and eighteen. These organizations sought to inculcate Nazi values of racism and militarism; boys received paramilitary training while girls were encouraged to become wives and mothers. Some survivors of the *HJ* consider this warping of human values a form of child abuse (Heck 1985).

Concomitant with the rise of Nazi youth organizations was the suppression of rival movements. Communist and socialist youth organizations were disbanded, as were the nonpolitical Scouts and Youth Leagues. Protestant youth groups were quickly folded into the *HJ*, while Catholic youth groups faced attacks from *HJ* members. The latter were shut down between 1933 and 1939. Some Aryan youth rebelled against the new system by forming nonconforming associations. Some, like the *Edelweiss* pirates, were more working class, while others like the *Swingjugend* (Swing Youth), were more middle class in origin. All these groups attracted attention from the police and the Gestapo, and several participants were executed during the war.

Aryan children who deviated from the Nazi norm faced severe repression. While some 1,000,000 children deemed delinquent faced horrific conditions in reformatories, those deemed "hereditarily ill" or "life unworthy of life" (i.e., suffering a physical or mental disability) were either sterilized or murdered. This latter effort, known by the code phrase "T-4," for the address in Berlin where it was headquartered, began in 1939. Many children in hospitals were killed through a combination of starvation and sedatives, others through lethal injection, and still others in carbon monoxide gas chambers developed by the T-4 program. The number of Aryan children killed in this fashion is likely over 10,000.

Non-Aryan Children

When the Nazis came to power, the overwhelming majority of Jewish children attended public schools. As these schools Nazified in spring 1933, Jewish children faced intense isolation and harassment. Teachers often took a lead role in bullying and encouraged their students to do the same. Eventually, most Jewish parents pulled their children out and placed them in newly created, private Jewish schools. These were staffed with teachers who had been fired from German schools, and they sought to prepare children for emigration, while providing an education. Beyond these schools, non-Aryan children faced an increasingly hostile environment. Many coped by joining youth movements, many Zionist-oriented, which in turn helped to prepare them for emigration.

As the situation for first German and later Austrian and Czech Jews deteriorated, many sought to leave Nazi Germany. In general, the young left before the elderly, as parents tried to save the coming generation. When parents could not leave, many sent their children ahead alone. Following the Kristallnacht pogrom in November 1938, thousands of German-, Austrian-, and Czech-Jewish children left on what were called *Kindertransport*, primarily to England, where many mourned their missing parents. By 1939, over 80 percent of children and youth under twenty-four years of age had left Nazi Germany.

Invasion and Occupation (1939–1941)

Poland and Eastern Europe

The German invasion of Poland brought destruction and horror to Polish children, Jews and Christians alike. Mass bombings and strafing of civilian targets, mass executions, burnings of towns and villages, and deportations, all these directly affected children as well as their parents. At the same time, Soviet forces invaded eastern Poland, imposing Bolshevism on Polish society.

Under a policy of Germanization, thousands of Polish Christian children with "Aryan" features were abducted and forced to adopt German culture and were placed for adoption in German households. Nazi decrees restricted what could be taught in Polish schools as part of a wider process in teaching the conquered population to submit to the Germans. Millions of Poles were taken to Germany for forced labor. Since pregnancies of Polish women would interfere with their ability to work, the Nazis either subjected them to forced abortions or placed the new-born infants in "homes" where most died through deliberate malnutrition.

For Polish-Jewish children, the invasion was like a mini-*Kristallnacht*: in each conquered town or city, the Germans reenacted their earlier pogrom, looting Jewish shops, setting fire to the synagogues, abusing Jews, and in some cases, shooting large numbers of them. Shortly thereafter, the Nazis confined Jews throughout Poland to ghettos, where they slowly starved them and robbed them of all their possessions. Faced with the greatest crisis they had ever encountered, parents and communities rallied to save their future: the youngest generation. Jews established child relief agencies to try to provide food and shelter for orphans or those in refugee centers, but their resources could not meet the enormity of the need. Like their parents, most Jewish children suffered from starvation and diseases. Ghetto streets were full of young children, begging for food. After a cold night, those same streets were littered with the corpses of children frozen to death. Ghetto children played games like "going through the gate" (of the ghetto), "grave digging" (in which Hitler was symbolically buried), and "blockade" (where children pretended to avoid round ups).

In order to survive, many children went to work in the various forced-labor factories established in ghettos. Others scavenged for food, coal, or supplies, while many worked, and died, as smugglers crawling through small holes in the ghetto walls. Few had the opportunity to go to any of the many secret schools illegally established in many ghettos. As the least "productive" members of the ghetto, children were particularly vulnerable to round ups and deportation.

The Theresienstadt (Terezin) Ghetto in Czechoslovakia was unusual in that it was used by the Nazis for propaganda purposes. Behind the scenes, many inmates still died in large numbers from disease and malnutrition, and most were later shipped to Auschwitz-Birkenau where they were gassed. The ghetto leadership, however, devoted extra resources toward the preservation and education of children in the ghetto. Some 15,000 children passed through this ghetto, and many left behind a record, either through the art they created under the guidance of Friedl Dicker-Brandeis, or in the secret magazine *Vedem* (*In the Lead*) published by the boys of Home 1, or in the various artistic performances carried out in the ghetto. Only a small handful of these children survived.

As with Jews, Roma and Sinti (Gypsies) were forced into confined areas called *Zigeunerlager* or Gypsy camps. In most cases, these were separate enclosed areas, though in some cases, Roma were sent to Jewish ghettos. Thousands of Roma children were sent to the Łódź Ghetto before being murdered at Chelmno, as were a hundred Czech children from Lidice, who were held in the ghetto before they were gassed.

Western Europe

The Nazis viewed western Europeans as Aryans like themselves, so they did not subject them to the mass brutality the Germans imposed on the Slavic peoples of eastern Europe. Nonetheless, they quickly imposed anti-Jewish laws in the Netherlands, Denmark, Belgium, and France after their conquest in 1940, bringing them in line with German laws. Western European-Jewish children now faced the same exclusions and persecutions that German-Jewish children had confronted earlier.

Annihilation (1941–1945)

Death Squads and Death Camps

The invasion of the Soviet Union in June 1941 marked a radical escalation in Nazi policy. This was intended as a "war of annihilation," which would result in the elimination of millions of "useless eaters." Following behind the front lines were a variety of killing squads that shot millions of men, women, and children. Euphoric at his initial success, in the fall of 1941, Hitler expanded the genocide to the rest of Europe.

The Nazis established several extermination centers in occupied Poland: Chelmno, Belzec, Sobibor, Treblinka, Majdanek, and Auschwitz-Birkenau. The latter two camps had a mixed population, not only in terms of the kinds of victims brought there, but also in that they had significant slave-labor populations. In some cases, as ghettos were liquidated, young and healthy Jews were selected for slave labor, but in many other cases, the entire community was deported. With the exception of Majdanek and Auschwitz-Birkenau, most Jews and Roma who were sent to the death camps were murdered within hours of arrival.

Approximately 10 percent of Jews died en route in the cattle cars, with children and the elderly being the most vulnerable. Upon arrival, men and boys were separated from women, girls, and infants. The men were gassed first, followed by the women. In Auschwitz-Birkenau, where a portion of Jews were selected for extermination through labor, almost all pre-teenagers were sent directly to the gas chambers. Teenagers, or those who were able to pass as teenagers, could live a little longer as slaves. The average life span of a prisoner in Birkenau was three months.

Survival in the Camps

In addition to those older children selected for slave labor, there were four other groups of children in slave-labor camps: (1) Roma children in the "Gypsy Camp"; (2) the so-called "Family Camp"; (3) Jewish and Roma children subjected to human experimentation; and (4) Polish children sent to camps after the failure of the Warsaw Rising in October 1944.

Unlike their treatment of Jews, the Nazis did not subject the Roma to a selection upon arrival in Auschwitz-Birkenau. Roma children were permitted to stay with their families, while their parents were subjected to forced labor. Children under six were cared for by women prisoners, and the *Schutzstaffel* (SS) would sometimes play with them. According to Auschwitz records, some 6,000 children under the age of fourteen were registered in the camp, along with 363 babies born in the camp. Roma children were malnourished and particularly vulnerable to disease. In May 1944, those Roma people healthy and old enough for slave labor were removed and the remaining population, including all the children, was gassed.

In 1943, the Nazis deported 5000 Jews from Theresienstadt (Terezin) in three waves to Auschwitz-Birkenau, but housed them in a separate "family camp." There was no selection on arrival and the Jews could keep their civilian clothes and luggage. Using Theresienstadt as a model, the prisoners created a "children's house" in one of the barracks, where the 500 children received supplemental food and education.

After six months, all surviving members of the first transport were gassed. The second and third transports, however, underwent selections before gassing, and some children between the ages of twelve and seventeen were selected for slave labor.

Nazi doctors carried out several sets of human medical experimentation in Auschwitz-Birkenau. Dr. Josef Mengele experimented on Roma and Jewish twins as part of his efforts to prove Aryan racial superiority. His colleague, Dr. Kurt Heissmeyer, experimented on twenty Jewish children, seeking to understand tuberculosis. In the fall of 1944, Heissmeyer moved his experiment to the Neuengamme concentration camp, where the children were eventually murdered in April 1945 to prevent their liberation from approaching Allied troops.

One final set of children were Polish Catholics deported to Auschwitz between 1940 and 1944. The largest of these took place in August and September 1944, when at least 1,400 children under the age of seventeen were sent to the camp from Warsaw. When Auschwitz-Birkenau was liberated by Soviet troops in January 1945, there were some 435 children left alive in the camp.

Hiding, Passing, and Rescue

Most non-Aryan children who survived did so by either hiding from public view or by passing as an Aryan child. Those who passed required false papers and elaborate fictions to keep safe from the police and prying neighbors. Jewish children had to master Christian prayers and beliefs to avoid detection, and had to make sure they spoke without a noticeable accent. Children who might be recognized as Jewish, either by their appearance, speech, or who may have been known within a community had to hide from public view. This might mean living for months or years in barns, coal cellars, attics, or wardrobes. In most cases, life in hiding meant separation from one's family.

Informal networks of non-Aryan rescuers were necessary to make hiding possible. These individuals acquired the forged papers, arranged places to hide, helped move the child to safety, and then took care of the child in hiding. In addition, formal organizations were created in several countries to help Jews and Jewish children hide. These include Żegota (in Poland), the Naamloze Vennootschap (NV) and the Piet Meerburg Group (in the Netherlands), and the Oeuvre de Secours aux Enfants (OSE) and the Garel network (in France). These organizations helped to hide tens of thousands of Jewish children across Europe. Those who were caught, such as at the OSE safe house in

Izieu, France, faced deportation and murder along with the children they were sheltering.

Children in hiding remained not only vulnerable to capture (particularly boys, whose circumcision marked them publicly as Jews), but also to exploitation from their rescuers. In some cases, the people hiding them stole what little they possessed, others used them as unpaid labor, while still others faced sexual abuse. The pressures of being hidden for such a lengthy period of time could lead to open antagonism and some rescuers forced children to find new places of refuge.

Aftermath (1945 and after)

The Volkssturm

In October 1944, as Allied forces pushed toward Germany, the Nazis drafted more and more children into the *Volkssturm* (the People's Army). Children were officially drafted at age sixteen, though far younger children also served in the final defense. Some 27,000 of these youthful conscripts were killed in the final months of the war, continuing to fight to the bitter end even after other military forces surrendered.

Displaced Persons (DP) Camps

Jewish prisoners liberated from concentration camps included a handful of young children. The largest number consisted of about 1000 children in Buchenwald, where prisoners in the last months of the war created a secret children's barracks to keep as many alive as they could. After liberation, many of these children went into the displaced persons' (DP) camps established in the British and American occupation zones. By 1946, these liberated child survivors were joined by children who had either survived in hiding or in the Soviet Union and who were trying to leave the violence of eastern Europe behind. Schools and youth groups were established in the DP camps to help rehabilitate children and educate them.

Emigration

Many surviving children faced difficult situations after the war. In most cases, they had lost all immediate family members. Some of them had no memories of their families of origin or had adopted Christianity or had formed close relationships with the foster families who hid them. This created a difficult process of adjustment.

Some children, particularly orphans, were evacuated from eastern Europe and DP camps to rehabilitation centers in France and England. About a thousand came to the United States before 1948, where they faced a difficult process of adjustment. With the establishment of the State of Israel in 1948, many survivors went there.

Long-Term Consequences

In the last thirty years, there have been an increasing number of studies of former child survivors of the Holocaust. These have examined the differences between child survivors and adult survivors, while others look at how their wartime experiences have shaped child survivors' later lives.

Critical Challenges Facing the Field Today and the Probabilities of Progress

The study of children and the Holocaust is a relatively new field in Holocaust research. Few first-person accounts and historical studies were published until the 1980s and 1990s. This new research is part of a wider trend toward studying victims not just as objects of Nazi policy, but as subjects in their own right with agency. These studies have been supplemented with a flood of memoirs of former survivors who, having reached retirement age, are ready to deal with their past.

While new sources of documentation do become available through the opening of archive collections, such as the International Tracing Service records at Bad Arolsen, the major challenge facing researchers today is that there are fewer and fewer survivors to interview. Those survivors who were ten years old when the war began in 1939 turned eighty in 2009. What is true for Jewish child survivors is even more applicable to non-Jewish survivors, who have not been the focus of as much historical research. Time is running out to interview Roma, Polish, and other child survivors in order to record their oral histories.

After the war, Jewish organizations searched for hidden children to bring them back to the community, and they were able to recover most children who had been hidden through organized efforts. Some children, however, were hidden by arrangements between desperate Jewish parents and individual rescuers; not all of those adoptive parents wanted to give up their child after the war. Since the fall of communism, there have been numerous cases of adults in their fifties and sixties who are only just now learning that they were hidden children. This is a significant new opportunity for research.

Conclusion

The study of children and the Holocaust is a relatively new field, but is expanding rapidly. The rare early monograph or account has been replaced by a flood of new material, and now historians are creating synthetic accounts, trying to bring together a broader understanding of the phenomenon. As child survivors are increasingly the only remaining living witnesses, this will be the last field where Holocaust researchers will be able to obtain new first-person testimony.

Annotated Bibliography

Material by or about Children Written during the War

Boas, Jacob, ed. *We Are Witnesses: Five Diaries of Teenagers Who Died in the Holocaust.* New York, NY: Henry Holt and Company, 1995, 196 pp.

Intended for high school students, this volume contains excerpts from the diaries of David Rubinowicz, Yitzhak Rudashevski, Moshe Flinker, Éva Heyman, and Anne Frank. Each chapter begins with a brief biographical introduction. Excerpts of diary entries follow, interspersed with explanations, context, and analysis.

Frank, Anne. *Diary of a Young Girl.* Translated by B.M. Mooyaart-Doubleday. New York, NY: Bantam Books, 1993, 283 pp.

First published in 1947, and then in English translation in 1950, it remains the most influential and widely read account of a hidden child. For several decades, it represented virtually the only published source for the experiences of children written during the Holocaust. Since the 1990s, however, a series of diaries and other materials written during the war have been published, greatly expanding the available material and offering radically different perspectives. For an interesting analysis of the *Diary* and its creation and reception, see Zapruder (2002), below.

Ginz, Petr. *The Diary of Petr Ginz.* New York, NY: Atlantic Monthly Press, 2007, 161 pp.

One of the leading figures behind the magazine *Vedem*, secretly published by Jewish boys in Theresienstadt (Terezin), Petr Ginz's diary covers the year of his life in Prague, from September 1941 until August 1942, when he was deported at age fourteen to the hybrid ghetto/concentration camp. It also contains a brief excerpt from his Terezin diary describing his deportation, as well as his surviving sister's reminiscences.

Holliday, Laurel, ed. *Children in the Holocaust and World War II: Their Secret Diaries.* New York, NY: Washington Square Press, 1995, 409 pp.

A collection of diary excerpts from twenty-three children, most of whom were Jews, ranging in age from ten to eighteen. Despite the subtitle, several of these diaries had been previously published.

Korczak, Janusz. *Ghetto Diary.* New Haven, CT, and London: Yale University Press, 2003, 115 pp.

Janusz Korczak (né Henryk Goldzmidt), the renowned child advocate, began his diary in 1939 and continued working on it intermittently for the next three years. It was less a diary than an incomplete memoir of his struggles to maintain his morale and that of the orphans in his care in the Warsaw Ghetto.

Křížková, Marie Rút, Kurt Jiři Kotouč, and Zdeněk Ornest, eds. *We Are Children Just the Same: Vedem, the Secret Magazine of the Boys of Terezín.* Translated by Novak, R. Elizabeth. Philadelphia, PA, and Jerusalem, Israel: The Jewish Publication Society, 1995, 199 pp.

Excerpts of the boys' magazine *Vedem*, secretly published in the Theresienstadt (Terezin) Ghetto between 1942 and 1944. The magazine contained short stories, articles, poems, editorials, and drawings by the boys from Home One, House L 417. Originally published as "samizdat" in 1978, this new edition expands upon the original to include original drawings from the magazine.

Sierakowiak, David. *The Diary of Dawid Sierakowiak: Five Notebooks from the Łódź Ghetto.* Edited by Adelson, Alan, and Translated by Turowski, Kamil. New York, NY, and Oxford, UK: Oxford University Press, 1996, 271 pp.

Detailed account of the Łódź Ghetto, written by a teenager (fifteen when the war began) from 1939 to 1943 (some of the diary is missing).

Volavková, Hana, ed. . . . *I Never Saw Another Butterfly . . . : Children's Drawings and Poems from Terezin Concentration Camp 1942–1944.* 2nd ed. New York: Schocken Books, 1993, 106 pp.

This volume comprises art and poetry created by children in the Theresienstadt (Terezin) Ghetto, documenting their experience from the child's point of view. Originally published in 1964, the revised edition includes additional material, including poems, illustrations, and excerpts from the diary of Helga Weissová.

Weichherz, Béla. *In Her Father's Eyes: A Childhood Extinguished by the Holocaust.* Edited and translated by Magilow, Daniel H. New Brunswick, NJ, and London, UK: Rutgers University Press, 2008, 180 pp.

The diary of a father, recounting the life of his daughter, Kitty, from her birth in 1929 in Bratislava, until spring 1942, when the diary ends abruptly. Only the last 10 percent of the diary covers the period of World War II.

Zapruder, Alexandra. *Salvaged Pages: Young Writers' Diaries of the Holocaust.* New Haven, CT, and London: Yale University Press, 2002, 481 pp.

Extended excerpts from fourteen diaries, covering the period between 1938 and 1945, and documenting the experiences of the mostly teen-aged writers (they range in age from twelve to twenty-two) in Germany, western Europe, and eastern Europe. While a few of the authors survived, most did not. The scope and breadth of the collection reflects a wide variety of experiences of children during the Holocaust, including the efforts to flee, life and suffering in the ghettos, the desperate efforts to survive, and in two cases, the joy and exhaustion of liberation.

Zelkowicz, Josef. *In Those Terrible Days: Notes from the Lodz Ghetto.* Edited by Unger, Michael. Jerusalem, Israel: Yad Vashem, 2002, 381 pp.

A journalist, a writer, and a researcher for YIVO (Institute for Jewish Research), Josef Zelkowicz worked in the Łódź Ghetto archives until his deportation to Auschwitz in August 1944, where he was murdered. This book collects a small portion of the more than fifty articles, stories, and other pieces written by Zelkowicz in the ghetto between 1940 and 1942. Several sections contain descriptions of the fate and suffering of children in the ghetto.

Published Interviews with Former Child Survivors after the War

The past two decades have seen a flood of memoirs written by now-grown child survivors. Rather than attempt to list them all, the following is limited to those anthologies of interviews with survivors.

Deutschkron, Inge. . . . *den ihrer war die Hölle: Kinder in Gettos und Lagern.* Köln: Verlag Wissenschaft und Politik, 1965, 157 pp.

An early German-language collection of child survivor accounts, drawn primarily from the Eichmann Trial (1961), the Chelmno Trial (1963), the Auschwitz Trial (1964), and the Treblinka Trial (1965), supplemented with interviews, and published reports.

Glassner, Martin Ira, and Robert Krell, eds. *And Life is Changed Forever: Holocaust Childhoods Remembered.* Detroit, MI: Wayne State University Press, 2006, 356 pp.

A collection of twenty first-person narratives by survivors who were children during the Holocaust, along with an analytical introduction and three psychosocial commentaries.

Marks, Jane. *The Hidden Children: The Secret Survivors of the Holocaust.* New York, NY: Fawcett Columbine, 1993, 307 pp.

Excerpts of interviews with twenty-two former hidden children, grouping them into four categories: (1) the ordeal of how they hid; (2) liberation, which often meant discovering one was now an orphan; (3) the legacy of the hiding experience; and (4) the efforts to heal.

Stein, André. *Hidden Children: Forgotten Survivors of the Holocaust.* Toronto and New York: Penguin, 1993, 273 pp.

A cross between autobiography and biography, the author, himself a child survivor, interviewed ten child survivors and wrote up their accounts. All were under the age of sixteen during the war and survived either in hiding or in the forests.

Valent, Paul. *Child Survivors of the Holocaust.* New York and London: Brunner-Routledge, 1994, 288 pp.

Himself a child survivor and now a psychiatrist, Paul Valent interviewed ten child survivors, asking each about their experiences and studying how they coped with their traumas. Following each interview, he includes a commentary in which he analyzes the psychological effects of trauma and survival on each child.

Jewish Children and the Holocaust

Angress, Werner T. *Between Fear & Hope: Jewish Youth in the Third Reich.* New York: Columbia University Press, 1988, 187 pp.

This monograph examines the history of the non-Zionist agricultural training farm in Gross-Bressen, Germany, which was established in 1936. The author describes the early efforts to help the trainees emigrate as a group to create a new farming community outside Germany, either in Brazil or in the United States. As a result of world reaction to the *Kristallnacht* pogrom, the first and second generations of trainees were allowed to emigrate. The Nazis closed the training center in August 1941, and used its facilities for forced labor. Almost none of the third generation of trainees survived.

Baumel, Judith Tydor. "Gender and Family Studies of the Holocaust: A Historio-graphical Overview." In *Lessons and Legacies, Vol. II: Teaching the Holocaust in a Changing World*, 105–17. Evanston, IL: Northwestern University Press, 1998.

An overview of the various phases of historical research into the study of Jewish women and children in the Holocaust.

Bentwich, Norman. *They Found Refuge: An Account of British Jewry's Work for Victims of Nazi Oppression*. London: Cresset Press, 1956, 227 pp.

An early history of British efforts to rescue Jews, including a short account by the Chairman of the Refugee Children's Movement. It also includes a de-scription of British efforts to aid the agricultural training and work programs that helped Jewish youth to emigrate.

Bogner, Nahum. *At the Mercy of Strangers: The Rescue of Jewish Children with Assumed Identities in Poland*. Translated by Mandel, Ralph. Jerusalem, Israel: Yad Vashem, 2009, 368 pp.

An excellent analysis of the difficulties faced by children living with false papers in Poland. Using a wide variety of archival sources, scholarly research, and first-person testimony, the author examines in detail not only the general problems faced by children in hiding, but also such specific cases as children living in villages, on the street, or in convents. He also discusses the problem of children returning to Jewish communities after the war.

Colodner, Solomon. *Jewish Education in Germany Under the Nazis*. New York, NY: Jewish Education Committee Press, 1964, 139 pp.

An early study of Jewish education in Germany, first under the Weimar government, and then under the Nazis. In addition to including original documents and reports, the author also conducted interviews with thirty-one surviving German-Jewish leaders. The monograph offers a great deal of statis-tical data on German-Jewish schooling, as well as information on curricula, textbooks, and vocational training.

Dwork, Debórah. *Children With a Star: Jewish Youth in Nazi Europe*. New Haven, CT: Yale University Press, 1991, 354 pp.

A major study of the experiences of Jewish youth under the Nazis; Debórah Dwork interweaves historical data with her own interviews with numerous child survivors. She begins with the home lives of children and the shock of legal persecution, and moves from there to the efforts of parents to hide their children, and the experiences of children living in secret. She then looks at the lives of children in transit camps and ghettos, followed by an examination of the fate of children deported to death and slave-labor camps, the overwhelm-ing majority of whom were murdered shortly after arrival. In the epilogue, Dwork addresses the difficulties faced by child survivors and her own efforts as a historian to record their stories.

Eisen, George. *Children and Play in the Holocaust: Games Among the Shadows*. Amherst, MA: University of Massachusetts Press, 1988, 153 pp.

A fascinating monograph on the behavior of children in both ghettos and various camps as a means of coming to terms with their "Holocaust existence." As George Eisen concludes, "the games children played were a microcosm of life, reduced from its complexities to a symbolic action" (118).

Freier, Recha. *Let the Children Come: The Early History of Youth Aliyah*. London: Weidenfeld and Nicolson, 1961, 125 pp.

A memoir by the founder and primary organizer of the Youth Aliyah movement, in which she describes the idea behind it, how it operated, and the difficulties it faced in rescuing Jewish youth, mostly German, between 1932 and 1941.

Gutman, Yisrael, and Michael Berenbaum, eds. *Anatomy of the Auschwitz Death Camp.* Bloomington and Indianapolis: Indiana University Press, in association with the United States Holocaust Memorial Museum, 1994, 638 pp.

Relevant chapters include: "Children," "The Family Camp," and "The Crimes of Dr. Mengele."

Harris, Mark Jonathan, and Deborah Oppenheimer. *Into the Arms of Strangers: Stories of the Kindertransport.* New York and London: Bloomsbury Publishing, 2000, 292 pp.

The story of the *Kindertransporte* to England, as told by the now-adult children who participated, as well as by two of the rescuers. It is the companion volume to the Academy Award-winning film of the same name.

Heberer, Patricia. *Children during the Holocaust.* Lanham, MD: AltaMira Press in association with the United States Holocaust Memorial Museum, 2011, 513 pp.

This large and impressive work is an attempt to understand the story of the Holocaust as experienced by children. While following the con- tours of a general history of the Holocaust, here Patricia Heberer highlights the reactions and responses of children to persecution, war, imprisonment, starvation, forced labor, hiding, and death. Each section contains a brief narrative overview, followed by primary source documents.

Heim, Suzanne, ed. *Children and the Holocaust: Symposium Presentations.* Washington, DC: United States Holocaust Memorial Museum, 2004, 139 pp.

A collection of papers concerning children and the Holocaust. Presentation subjects include: "Heroic Acts and Missed Opportunities: The Rescue of Youth Aliyah Groups from Germany during World War II"; "'Unknown Children': The Last Train from Westerbork"; "Bergen-Belsen: The End and the Beginning"; and "Facilities for Pregnant Forced Laborers and Their Infants in Germany, 1943–1945."

Hilberg, Raul. "Children." In, *Perpetrators, Victims, Bystanders: The Jewish Catastrophe 1933–1945*, 139–49. New York, NY: HarperCollins, Inc., 1993.

This chapter briefly covers the fate of Jewish children in Nazi-occupied Europe, with particular emphasis on the Łódź and Warsaw Ghettos.

Kaplan, Marion A. "The Daily Lives of Jewish Children and Youth in the 'Third Reich.'" In *Between Dignity and Despair: Jewish Life in Nazi Germany*, 94–118. New York: Oxford University Press, 1988.

A masterful and important study of everyday life of Jews in Nazi Germany, with particular emphasis and nuance on the differing experiences of men and women. While material on children can be found throughout the book, Marion Kaplan does devote a chapter to the experiences of children between 1933 and 1939. Here she examines the experiences of children in Nazi-controlled schools, and then in the new private Jewish schools created after 1933. She also looks at Jewish children in youth movements and their experience of emigration.

Kassow, Samuel D. *Who Will Write Our History? Rediscovering a Hidden Archive from the Warsaw Ghetto.* New York: Vintage Books, 2009, 523 pp.

Samuel Kassow draws on the Oyneg Shabbes archives, organized by Emanuel Ringelblum, to document life and death in the Warsaw Ghetto. While material on the experiences of children can be found throughout the volume, Kassow highlights several texts regarding children. These include the CENTOS (the main children's relief agency) campaigns to raise money for orphanages, soup kitchens, and day-care centers, as well as the public's response to these campaigns. Kassow also includes excerpts of children's narratives from the archive collection, a report by a nurse on conditions in the children's hospital, and descriptions by teachers of their efforts to education children and maintain their morale.

Klarsfeld, Serge. *The Children of Izieu: A Human Tragedy.* Jacobson, Kenneth (trans.). New York: Harry N. Abrams, Inc., Publishers, 1985, 134 pp.

A recounting of the tragic story of forty-five Jewish children hidden in an OSE (Oeuvre de Secours aux Enfants—Children's Welfare Organization) center in Izieu who, along with six of their guardians, were arrested in April 1944 on orders of the Gestapo officer, Klaus Barbie. All but one of the older girls was murdered. The book contains detailed information on each child murdered, along with the one survivor, and the one child who escaped the raid. The remainder of the material concerns the efforts to arrest and deport Barbie from Bolivia to France to stand trial for his crimes.

Lifton, Betty Jean. *The King of the Children: A Biography of Janusz Korczak.* New York: Farrar, Straus, and Giroux, 1988, 404 pp.

The definitive biography of the leading child advocate in Poland, and one of the most important figures in the Warsaw Ghetto. The last quarter of the book describes his increasingly desperate efforts to save the lives of the children in his care.

Nachmany-Gafny, Emunah. *Dividing Hearts: The Removal of Jewish Children from Gentile Families in Poland in the Immediate Post-Holocaust Years.* Jerusalem: Yad Vashem, 2009, 389 pp.

An important study of the efforts to recover Jewish children from non-Jewish families after the war, told in detail. The author has been active as a private researcher in this area for more than two decades, tracing missing children and families.

Schwarberg, Günther. *The Murders at the Bullenhuser Damm: The SS Doctor and the Children.* Translated by Rosenfeld, Erna Baber, and Alvin H. Rosenfeld. Bloomington: Indiana University Press, 1980 and 1984, 178 pp.

A monograph on the medical experiments conducted by Dr. Kurt Heissmeyer on some twenty Jewish children in Birkenau. In November 1944, the children were transferred to Neuengamme, where they underwent additional surgeries and experiments. On April 20, 1945, with Allied forces only a few miles away, all the children were driven to the nearby town of Bullenhuser Damm, where they were sedated and then hanged. Günther Schwarberg also examines the fate of the perpetrators and the efforts to commemorate the victims.

Strauss, Herbert. "Jewish Emigration from Germany, Part I," In *Leo Baeck Institute Year Book,* Vol. 25, 1980, 313–61.

An extremely detailed and data-driven presentation of Jewish emigration from Germany during the Nazi period. It includes good demographic information on German Jewry during the twelve years of Nazi rule, and has statistical information relating to German-Jewish children.

Tec, Nechama. *When Light Pierced the Darkness: Christian Rescue of Jews in Nazi-Occupied Poland.* New York: Oxford University Press, 1986, 288 pp.

A carefully nuanced study of Polish rescuers by a former hidden child.

Vromen, Suzanne. *Hidden Children of the Holocaust: Belgian Nuns and Their Daring Rescue of Young Jews from the Nazis.* New York: Oxford University Press, 2008, 178 pp.

A monograph on the rescue of Jewish children by Catholic religious orders in Belgium. It includes interviews with the surviving children, the nuns who hid them, and two surviving escorts from the Committee for the Defense of Jews who helped ferry Jewish children to their hiding places.

Non-Jewish Children and the Holocaust

Burleigh, Michael. "'Wheels Must Roll for Victory!' Children's 'Euthanasia' and 'Aktion T-4.'" In *Death and Deliverance: "Euthanasia" in Germany, 1900–1945,* 93–129. New York: Cambridge University Press, 1994.

A detailed account of the development and implementation of the T-4 program.

Burleigh, Michael, and Wolfgang Wipperman. Youth in the Third Reich. In, *The Racial State: Germany 1933–1945,* 201–41. Cambridge, MA: Cambridge University Press, 1991.

Synthetic history drawing on the authors' earlier research, covering schools, youth movements, the experiences of Jewish children, and nonconformist groups, such as the "swing youth" and the various "pirate" groups.

Grudzińska-Gross, Irena, and Jan Tomasz Gross, eds. *War Through Children's Eyes: The Soviet Occupation of Poland and the Deportations, 1939–1941.* Stanford, CA: Hoover Institution Press, 1981, 260 pp.

A collection of 120 testimonies taken from interviews conducted with Poles who, as children, were deported to the Soviet Union between 1939 and 1941. They were collected beginning in July 1941, after the resumption of diplomatic relations between Poland and the Soviet Union. The Polish government collected this material and organized it according to the territorial divisions of eastern Poland, an organization scheme continued in this collection. The narratives describe the Russian occupation and Sovietization of eastern Poland as well as the childern's experiences after deportation to East.

Heck, Alfons. *A Child of Hitler: Germany in the Days When God Wore a Swastika.* Frederick, CO: Renaissance House, 1985, 207 pp.

A memoir of a former *Hitler Jugend* member describing his own indoctrination into Nazism, and how Hitler warped and twisted a generation of German children.

Lukas, Richard C. *Did the Children Cry? Hitler's War against Jewish and Polish Children, 1939–1945.* New York: Hippocrene Books, 1994, 263 pp.

Part of Richard Lukas's larger project to highlight the general suffering of Poles during World War II, this volume draws explicit parallels between the experiences of Polish Jews and Christians, while at the same time recognizing the differences in Nazi policies against both groups. As Lukas puts it, "while it does not relativize the unique place Jewish children had in the scale of suffering, this account does not downplay the tragedy experienced by Polish children" (10).

Kater, Michael H. *Hitler Youth*. Cambridge, MA: Harvard University Press, 2006, 355 pp.

A comprehensive survey of the history of both the *Hitler Jugend* and the *Bund Deutscher Mädel*—their organization, ideology, growth, and repercussions for those who passed through them. Michael Kater also examines the various groups that deviated, dissented, or resisted the Nazi norms. Kater carries his study through the war years, looking at the experiences of Hitler Youth in combat, and includes a brief study of the post-Nazi era.

Lagnado, Lucette Matalon, and Sheila Cohn Dekel. *Children of the Flames: Dr. Josef Mengele and the Untold Story of the Twins of Auschwitz*. New York: William Morrow and Company, Inc., 1991, 320 pp.

An account of Dr. Josef Mengele's experiments in Auschwitz with interviews of over a dozen of the surviving twins.

Mosse, George L. "The Key: Education of Youth." In *Nazi Culture: Intellectual, Cultural, and Social Life in the Third Reich*, 263–318. New York: Gross & Dunlap, 1966.

A collection of primary sources concerning the Nazified school system, including excerpts from textbooks, as well as material on Nazi youth movements.

Nicholas, Lynn H. *Cruel World: The Children of Europe in the Nazi Web*. New York: Alfred A. Knopf, 2005, 632 pp.

An attempt to create a comprehensive narrative of the lives of children in Nazi-occupied Europe, examining both the Nazi efforts to create an Aryan ideal, as well as the efforts to subjugate or eliminate all those who deviated from that ideal.

Peukert, Detlev. "Youth in the Third Reich." In *Life in the Third Reich*, edited by Bessel, Richard, 25–40. Oxford: Oxford University Press, 2001.

A brief study of the experiences of the three groups of German teenagers who passed through late adolescence (fourteen to eighteen years of age) under the Nazis. In particular, Detlev Peukert focuses on the campaign against "deviant" behavior of teenagers who created small groups outside the Hitler Youth movement, such as the "Edelweiss Pirates" and the "Swing Youth."

Rosmus, Anna. "Involuntary Abortions for Polish Forced Laborers." In *Experience and Expression: Women, the Nazis, and the Holocaust*, edited by Baer, Elizabeth R. and Myrna Goldenberg, 76–94. Detroit, MI: Wayne State University Press, 2003.

Between 1939 and 1945, some ten million foreign women and men were sent to forced labor inside Germany. Many of the women and girls became pregnant, and since these pregnancies interfered with their ability to work, they were either terminated through forced abortions, or the newborn infants were placed in "homes," where most died through deliberate malnutrition.

Stachura, Peter D. *The German Youth Movement 1900–1945: An Interpretative and Documentary History*. New York: St. Martin's Press, 1981, 246 pp.

A study of both the various youth movements in Germany prior to the Nazi period, including general, religious, and political youth organizations, as well as the Hitler Youth movement that existed between 1933 and 1945.

Stargardt, Nicholas. *Witnesses of War: Children's Lives Under the Nazis*. New York: Alfred A. Knopf, 2006, 494 pp.

Nicholas Stargardt's goal in this fascinating volume is to create a clear narrative of children's experiences of Nazi rule by using, wherever possible, sources created by the children who lived it. As Stargardt describes it: "Children's experiences deserve to be understood across the racial and national divides, not because of their similarities but because their extreme contrasts help us see the Nazi social order as a whole. Children were neither just the mute and traumatized witnesses to this war, nor merely its innocent victims. They also lived in the war, played and fell in love during the war; the war invaded their imaginations and the war raged inside them" (19).

Child Survivors after the Holocaust

Baumel, Judith Tydor. *Unfulfilled Promise: Rescue and Resettlement of Jewish Refugee Children in the United States 1934–1945*. Juneau, AK: The Denali Press, 1990, 228 pp.

An important study of the absorption of some 1000 Jewish refugee children in the United States before and during the war, based in part on surveys done in 1945 and follow-up interviews by the author.

Cohen, Beth. "'Unaccompanied Minors': The Story of the Displaced Orphans." In *Case Closed: Holocaust Survivors in Postwar America*, 94–114. New Brunswick, NJ: Rutgers University Press, 2007.

Most of Beth Cohen's book challenges the general perception that Holocaust survivors were easily absorbed into post-war American life. In this chapter, she examines the experiences of displaced orphans, almost all of whom were adolescents when they arrived. Cohen carefully examines and analyzes the reports by field agents for the European Jewish Children's Aid (EJCA) and the Jewish Family and Children's Services (JFCS) on the absorption of these immigrants, noting the difficulties these professionals faced with understanding the particular traumas of their young charges.

Dwork, Debórah. "Custody and Care of Jewish Children in the Postwar Netherlands: Ethnic Identity and Cultural Hegemony." In *Lessons and Legacies, Vol. III; Memory, Memorialization, and Denial*, 109–37. Evanston, IL: Northwestern University Press, 1999.

An analysis of the struggles over the fate of rescued Jewish children in the Netherlands and the conflict over whether they should be returned to surviving family members, the wider Jewish community or remain with their foster families.

Hemmendinger, Judith, and Robert Krell. *The Children of Buchenwald: Child Survivors and Their Post-War Lives*. Jerusalem: Gefen Publishing House, 2000, 191 pp.

A study of the one thousand children liberated at Buchenwald, through interviews with thirty-one survivors, tracing their lives over the subsequent lives in Israel, the United States, and France.

Kestenberg, Judith S., and Ira Brenner. *The Last Witness: The Child Survivor of the Holocaust*. Washington, D.C., and London: American Psychiatric Press, Inc., 1996, 238 pp.

A set of psychoanalytic studies of children and the Holocaust, based on some 1,500 interviews with survivors, as well as published documents. While it includes material about the survivors' experiences during the Holocaust, the main emphasis is on how their experiences during the Holocaust shaped their later lives.

Laqueur, Walter. *Generation Exodus: The Fate of Young Jewish Refugees from Nazi Germany.* Hanover, NH: Brandeis University Press, 2001, 345 pp.

A fascinating study of German-Jewish refugee children and youth and their differing experiences in Palestine/Israel, the United States, the Soviet Union, Britain, South America, and other locales. The author examines their acculturation to their new societies, as well as their later lives.

Moskowitz, Sarah. *Love Despite Hate: Child Survivors of the Holocaust and Their Adult Lives.* New York: Schocken Books, 1983, 245 pp.

In August 1945, a rehabilitation center for child Holocaust survivors was opened in Lingfield, England. The first quarter of this book traces the history of the center and the difficulties it faced in treating some two dozen child survivors. The remaining bulk of the book consists of one-on-one interviews with these survivors conducted thirty years later, in which they reflect on their experiences in the center and its effect on their lives.

Suedfeld, Peter. Life after the Ashes: The Postwar Pain, and Resiliance, of Young Holocaust Survivors. Washington, DC: United States Holocaust Memorial Museum. Available at: www.ushmm.org/.../op-life-after-the-ashes-the-post-war-pain-and-resilien, 2002, 26 pp.

This brief article contains the results of a research study into the different long-term reactions to the Holocaust between child (defined as people fifteen years or younger at the end of the war) and adult survivors. The researchers compared how survivors think about the Holocaust, how they understand the factors in their survival, the effects of their experience on their personal relationships, their work lives, and their personality and mental health.

5

The Fate of Mentally and Physically Disabled Children in Nazi Germany

Jeffrey Blutinger

Introduction

While the Nazis' sterilization and murder of mentally and physically disabled children was addressed by the war crimes trials at Nuremberg, particularly the so-called Doctors' Trial, until fairly recently, most research on the Holocaust focused on the persecution of Jews. Even with the growing awareness of the key role played by the Nazi eugenics campaign in transforming Germany into a racial state and laying the groundwork for the creation of death camps, little research has been conducted into the specific fate of disabled children. Instead, the sterilization and murder campaigns usually fold their accounts of child victims into the larger narratives of adult victims, while the story of children used for medical experimentation is treated as a side story to the more famous accounts of Josef Mengele and other concentration camp doctors.

In fact, the *Kinderaktion* (children's murder campaign) was organized differently than the T-4 program designed to kill mentally and physically disabled adults (among others), so much so that it was unaffected by the ostensible halt of the T-4 program in the fall of 1941. In many ways, the Holocaust began with the murder of disabled children, on a local level in the 1930s by individual doctors and hospital directors, and on a national level in 1939. While the number of adults killed by the T-4 eugenics campaign was far larger, the children's campaign lasted far longer, continued to expand in scope over time, and involved a complete transformation of how disability was understood and treated in Germany.

The persecution of disabled children differed from most other Nazi persecutions in that the victims were Aryans, not Jews or Roma (disabled Jewish and Roma children were also murdered, though generally not because of their disability). Although the persecution and murder of disabled children furthered the wider goal of a racially pure society, the perception that these Aryan children were *gemeinschaftsfremd*, strangers to the community, has its roots not in Nazi racial theory, but rather in wider utilitarian, eugenic, and fascist theories.

Theories of Persecution

Utilitarian Approaches

During the First World War, some 30 percent of patients in German psychiatric hospitals and asylums died as a result of hunger, disease, or neglect (Burleigh 1994, 11). Faced with "the terrible exigencies of war," and the food shortages ravaging German society, resources were diverted away from the sick to keep the healthy alive. In 1920, Karl Binding and Alfred Hoche published an article entitled "Permission for the Destruction of Life Unworthy of Life," in which they laid the intellectual groundwork for "involuntary euthanasia." Among the groups to be subject to this medical killing were "incurable idiots," since, by definition, they lacked any will to live. "They are a terrible, heavy burden upon their relatives and society as a whole" (Burleigh 1994, 17). Hoche (1920) added calculations estimating the costs to maintain such "ballast existences" (54–56), depriving the nation of much-needed resources for unproductive purposes.

A few years later, Ewald Meltzer, the director of the Katharinenhof asylum in Saxony, surveyed the parents of the mentally handicapped children in his hospital on their views of the appropriateness of killing their children. To his shock, some 73 percent of the parents stated that they would "agree to the painless curtailment of the life of [their] child," with only half of the remainder saying no in all circumstances (Burleigh 1994, 23). Some parents indicated they would like to be deliberately deceived about the killing of their child. These reports and writings from the 1920s, point to a widespread belief, not limited to Germany, in the utilitarian value of eliminating nonproductive burdens on society.

Eugenic Approaches

The term "eugenics" was coined by Francis Galton in 1881 and emerged out of Social Darwinism, a theory that posited that human societies engaged in a "survival of the fittest." The goal of eugenicists was to improve a society by encouraging those people with good traits to have lots of children, while discouraging those with bad traits from having any children. The United States was an early center for eugenics movement, and American scientists sought to determine which traits were inheritable. The account of the "Jukes family," published first in 1877 with an update in 1915, tried to prove that criminality and degeneracy could also be inherited, while the study of the "Kallikak family" in 1912, was intended to prove the heritability of "feeble mindedness." These studies laid the groundwork for the enactment of sterilization laws. By the 1930s, over half the United States had adopted such laws, and the US Supreme Court upheld their constitutionality in Buck v. Bell (1927).

Eugenicists in both the United States and Europe saw the First World War as a eugenics disaster: the upper and middle classes fought and died, while the criminals and degenerates stayed home and had children. German eugenicists shifted their emphasis from "positive eugenics" (encouraging middle class and educated families to have more children) and devoted themselves to negative eugenics: promoting the sterilization of those deemed unfit. This policy of negative eugenics was often combined with racist views of the inferiority of non-Aryans and the conviction that miscegenation would lead to degeneracy. Together, they formed a doctrine of "racial hygiene," which advocated using eugenics to cleanse and purify the race by removing all those who were deemed either genetically or racially inferior.

Fascist Approaches

One of the distinguishing traits of fascist ideology is its privileging of the nation over the individual; the individual only matters to the extent that he or she contributes to the benefit of the national (or racial) group. For Nazi fascists, those whose physical or mental disability made them unproductive for the nation, now became *"gemeinschaftsfremd,"* alien to the nation (a designation later extended to anyone whose behavior was seen as antisocial or criminal). The Nazi policy of first sterilization and then murder fell into the category of *"Aufartung durch Ausmerzung"*: physical regeneration through eradication (Friedlander 1995, 20).

As aliens to the nation and a threat to its productive future, the physically and mentally disabled had no rights. The Nazi state quickly moved to transform the German medical infrastructure to distinguish between two kinds of patients: those who could be healed to become productive members of the nation, and those who could not. The latter became the first targets for forced sterilization and later for murder. Under the brutalization of war, this logic moved inexorably onward, so that by 1944, elderly widows made homeless by allied bombing raids and hospitalized in shock found themselves subject to the same killing process. As unproductive individuals, they had become redundant.

The First Phase of Persecution: Sterilization

The Nazi Transformation of the Programs for Disabled Germans

Weimar Germany was in the forefront of progressive education and treatment of mentally and physically disabled children. Institutionalization was reserved for only the most disabled children; wherever possible, children were encouraged to live with their families and work in the community. Special classes accommodated more than 34,000 disabled students in the regular school system, while those with more severe developmental disorders attended one of a thousand community day schools. In addition, Germany had over one hundred schools for the deaf, and the more than 35,000 deaf Germans were represented by the Reich Union of the Deaf in Germany.

The process of *Gleichschaltung* (coordination), in which German institutions conformed to Nazi values, effectively destroyed this progressive system. The Nazis abolished most of the special classes for disabled students in regular schools, while many of the day schools were either closed or transformed into labor centers. All disabled children had to register as such with the state, and students in day schools had to pass increasingly difficult intelligence tests. Those who failed were labeled "feeble minded" and institutionalized in psychiatric hospitals; they joined those disabled who were unable to work in the new labor-oriented day schools. As part of this wider push for institutionalization, the Nazis barred disabled students from receiving medical treatment at regular pediatric hospitals, forcing parents to place them in asylums in order to receive necessary care (Rogow 1999, 75–76). Not surprisingly, these institutions soon became overcrowded, while at the same time, per patient expenditures for food were significantly reduced.

Schools for the deaf also underwent *Gleichschaltung*. The Nazis did not close these special schools, but in many of them, the administrators, the teachers, and the staff embraced the Nazi values of racial hygiene, which viewed most congenitally deaf students as "hereditarily diseased." As a result, many of the teachers and administrators actively collaborated in the persecution of their deaf students. Like other social and cultural organizations in Nazi Germany, the deaf association lost its independence and was incorporated into the Nazi social welfare program in 1933. The leaders of this organization embraced Nazism, including its negative views of the congenitally deaf, and brought the organization in line with Nazi theories and values. Some of its members collaborated in the persecution of deaf children.

The Sterilization Law and Its Implementation

On July 14, 1933, Nazi Germany adopted the Law for the Prevention of Offspring with Hereditary Diseases. It empowered physicians with the public health service and directors of hospitals and other institutions to refer disabled individuals for sterilization. The main grounds for sterilization were:

1. Congenital feeble mindedness
2. Schizophrenia
3. Manic-depressive psychosis
4. Hereditary epilepsy
5. Huntington's chorea
6. Hereditary blindness
7. Hereditary deafness
8. Severe hereditary physical deformity
9. Severe alcoholism (on a discretionary basis).

Under the law, an application to sterilize an individual would be made to a new hereditary health court, composed of one judge, one physician from the public health service, and one physician with expertise in heredity. Appeals were possible, but they went to a similarly constituted appellate health court.

The law took effect on January 1, 1934, and the new courts were overwhelmed with a massive wave of denunciations: over 388,000 in the first three years. Further exacerbating the backlog was the lack of doctors capable of performing sterilizations. Nonetheless, between 1934 and 1936, over 139,000 Germans were sterilized under this law (Friedlander 1995, 28).

The policy of institutionalizing disabled children made them particularly vulnerable for forced sterilization, as did the use of intelligence tests to label them as "congenitally feeble minded." While there has been little research on the general application of the sterilization law to children, the smaller subset of deaf children has been studied. Administrators and teachers at deaf schools played a significant role in the referral of their students for sterilization. Some directors made a policy of screening incoming students for "hereditary disease," with rates of referrals for sterilization ranging from 20 to 50 percent of deaf students (Biesold 1999, 48–49). Some children tried to resist, either through legal means or by escaping from the school, but they could be arrested and delivered by the police to the hospital for sterilization surgery.

The Second Phase of Persecution: Murder

The Organization and Implementation of the Kinderaktion

Even before the formal adoption of the "euthanasia" program in 1939, individual physicians were already killing disabled children. For example, Dr. Hermann Pfannmüller of the Egling-Haar hospital near Munich appears to have systematically starved mentally disabled children in his care on the grounds that they were a "burden for the healthy body of our *Volk*" (Gallagher 1990, 127).

The most famous case involved a blind, deformed infant from the Knauer family, who wrote Hitler and asked that their child be killed. Hitler sent his doctor, Karl Brandt, to investigate and kill the child if he confirmed the diagnosis, which he did.

Subsequently, Hitler authorized Brandt and Philipp Bouhler (the head of the Chancellery of the Führer) to establish a program to kill physically and mentally disabled children. The program to murder children was run out of Bouhler's offices, in coordination with the Health Department of the Reich Ministry of Interior. They created a cover agency, the "Reich Committee for the Scientific Registration of Severe Hereditary Ailments," behind which the Chancellery carried out the killing operation.

In August 1939, the Reich Ministry of Interior circulated a decree to all midwives and physicians requiring them to report all infants and children, up to the age of three, with certain physical and mental disabilities. The returned forms were forwarded to the Chancellery's Reich Committee, where they were evaluated by Werner Catel, Hans Heinze, and Ernst Wentzler, all enthusiasts for the "euthanasia" program, and all involved in planning the killing process. They voted in turn on whether to kill or spare a child, with each seeing how the others had voted. In order to centralize the killing process, the Reich Committee created twenty-two "children's wards" (*Kinderfachabteilung*) at state hospitals and clinics, recruiting doctors and nurses to do the killing, while the Ministry of Interior assured the collaboration of the civil service.

The Reich Committee left the details of the killing up to the individual ward. In some cases, the children were killed through starvation, but the favored method was lethal medication. Since children in hospitals regularly received either injections or took tablets, it made it easier to camouflage the killing operation. In some cases, the child was killed immediately on arrival in one of the wards; but in many cases, the child was observed, and once the attending physician issued a negative report the child was murdered. The order to kill came from the Reich Committee and was called an "authorization" to "treat" the child (Friedlander 1995, 57). Altogether some 5000 children were murdered between 1939 and 1945 under this program.

The T-4 Program and Children

In the summer of 1939, Hitler first turned to Leonardo Conti, the state secretary for health in the Ministry of Interior, to set up a program to kill disabled adults. However, as a result of the frequent power struggles in the Nazi bureaucracy, Philipp Bouhler from the Chancellery convinced Hitler that as he was already overseeing the killing of disabled children, he should also handle the killing of disabled adults. Bouhler worked with Brandt to create the program so that it would complement the *Kinderaktion*. Administratively based at 4 Tiergartenstraße in Berlin, the program was code named T-4 and was headed by Viktor Brack.

As with the *Kinderaktion*, the Ministry of Interior circulated a questionnaire to institutions asking them to register certain categories of patients, including patients with ailments, which was generally grounds for sterilization, patients who had been at the institution for more than five years, and the criminally insane. The completed forms were returned to the T-4 offices where the average reviewer examined some 3,500 forms a month. Since the number of disabled adult victims was so much larger, the T-4 program established six central killing centers where large numbers of patients could be killed at once in carbon monoxide gas chambers. Between 1940 and 1941, at least 70,000 mentally and physically disabled were murdered in these facilities.

Concerning victims, there was not a clear-cut dividing line between the *Kinderaktion* and the T-4. There are many examples of older children and even adolescents who were murdered in the children's wards; at the same time, even some very young children were sent to the T-4 gas chambers. One major difference between the programs, however, is that while the T-4 program was officially "suspended" in the fall of 1941, the *Kinderaktion* continued uninterrupted until May 1945. Although the T-4 stopped using gas chambers, disabled children and adults continued to be murdered in individual hospitals by cooperative staff through the end of the war.

The killing of the disabled appears to have mostly replaced the earlier sterilization program. As the Nazis began to kill the disabled, sterilization rates plummeted. Since the grounds for murder overlapped significantly with those for sterilization, the latter became mostly superfluous. For example, before the war, deaf students requiring remedial education were labeled "feeble minded" and sterilized; during the war, they were "remanded because of ineducability," and selected for death (Biesold 1999, 164).

Experimentation on Disabled Children

Although somewhat obscured by the more famous experiments on Jewish and Roma children at Auschwitz-Birkenau and Neuengamme, physically and mentally disabled children were also used as test subjects. Several institutions used children drawn from the children's killing wards to test tuberculosis vaccines. In some cases, vaccinated and unvaccinated children were injected with the tuberculosis bacterium in order to determine the effectiveness of the vaccine (Scharsach 2000, 93–94). Generally, these tests were done without any consideration for the intense pain and suffering inflicted on the victims.

In addition, many doctors and scientists used the bodies of murdered children for their research, harvesting organs for study. The brains of mentally disabled victims seemed particularly interesting to researchers; as late as 1955, two such scientists published their research on the brain of a Hamburg girl murdered in 1944 (Friedlander 1995, 129).

After the War

In December 1946, the Doctors' Trial began in Nuremberg, in which twenty-three participants in the T-4 program, the *Kinderaktion*, and other medical killings were indicted for war crimes and crimes against humanity. Among the defendants were Karl Brandt and Viktor Brack, who were executed, but most of the individuals who ran the day-to-day operations of the various killing centers escaped any serious punishment. For example, Pfannmüller, who had been involved with killing patients in the 1930s, and who oversaw a children's killing ward, served only five years in prison. Werner Catel, who had been involved with the murder of the Knauer baby and then went on to oversee the selection of disabled children and adults for the killing centers of T-4 and the children's wards, became a professor of pediatric medicine at the University of Kiel, though he was forced to resign in 1960 due to public outrage over his actions under the Nazis.

Support for the persecution of the disabled continued long after the Nazi period. Catel, for example, published a book after the war advocating the killing of defective infants (Burleigh 1994, 284). There was little incentive for cooperating physicians or administrators to reevaluate their actions. For example, in 1960, a deaf man who had been sterilized as a teenager sent a letter to the former director of an institution for deaf students confronting him with the pain he had suffered since his forced sterilization. The now-retired director replied a few months later saying: "The fact that you have no children should not be seen as a misfortune. Better to have no children than one who is blind or deaf or epileptic" (Biesold 1999, 58).

Critical Challenges Facing the Field Today and the Probabilities of Progress

For a variety of reasons, researchers have only recently begun to study the persecution of physically and mentally disabled persons, including children, under the Nazis. In 1947, Alexander Mitscherlich and Fred Mielke published the documentation used at the Doctors' Trial in Nuremberg and provided it to members of the West German Chambers of Physicians, but the German medical establishment pretended as if the book did not exist and Mitscherlich's career suffered as he was labeled a traitor by his colleagues (Pross 1992, 41). The role of doctors in the persecution of their patients was mostly repressed until the 1980s, when a series of conferences in West Germany called attention to Nazi medicine. An Association for Research on Nazi Health and Social Policy was established in 1983, and began to publish a periodical in 1985. Horst Beisold began his research into the persecution of deaf Germans in 1979, and over the next decade faced severe obstacles in his effort to access material from the Nazi period at various German schools for the deaf. In some cases, the files were destroyed after he requested them; in other cases, the material was quickly moved to regional archives where he was denied access for various bureaucratic reasons (Biesold 1999, 12–15).

The first scholarly works on the persecution of the disabled appeared in German in the mid-1980s, including Ernst Klee (1983 and 1985), Bruno Müller-Hill (1984 in German, 1988 in English), Gisela Bock (1986), Götz Aly and Christian Pross (mid-1980s in German, 1994 in English), and Horst Biesold (1988 in German, 1999 in English). In addition to the translation of German studies, original works in English began to appear somewhat later, including those by Robert Jay Lifton (1986), Robert Proctor (1988), Paul Weindling (1989), Hugh Gallagher (1990), Michael Burleigh (1994), and Henry Friedlander (1995).

The most significant challenge to research in this area, besides the destruction or concealment of archival sources, is that very little of this research focuses just on the persecution of disabled children. Instead, disabled children appear as a subset within the wider category of the sterilization and murder of the disabled. While there has been some limited research focusing on the experiences of disabled children, these tend to be narrowly focused articles, rather than comprehensive accounts. As a result, while we have an estimate of how many children were killed in the children's wards, we do not know how many were murdered as a part of the T-4 program. We do not know which factors determined whether a child would be sent to a children's ward or to a gas chamber. While there is evidence that the killing process was expanded over time to cover more and more disabled children, including some that earlier would merely have been sterilized, so far this has been only documented anecdotally.

Finally, only a few first-person testimonies of surviving children have been gathered and these tend to be published as a text to accompany a scholarly discussion of the subject rather than in a collected volume. It is essential that these accounts be recorded while the witnesses are still able to speak.

Conclusion

German scholars continue to take the lead in pursuing new research in this field and increasingly scholars are recognizing that the experiences of mentally and physically disabled children differed markedly from that of their adult counterparts. They were among both the first and last groups the Nazis murdered, and as child survivors will soon be the last remaining witnesses to the Nazi genocides, their testimonies will be among the last to be gathered.

References

Biesold, Horst. 1999. *Crying Hands: Eugenics and Deaf People in Nazi Germany*. Trans. William Sayers. Washington, DC: Gallaudet University Press.

Burleigh, Michael. 1994. *Death and Deliverance: "Euthanasia" in Germany, 1900–1945*. Cambridge, UK, and New York : Cambridge University Press.

Friedlander, Henry. 1995. *The Origins of Nazi Genocide: From Euthanasia to the Final Solution*. Chapel Hill, NC, and London: The University of North Carolina Press.

Gallagher, Hugh Gregory. 1990. *By Trust Betrayed: Patients, Physicians, and the License to Kill in the Third Reich*. New York: Henry Holt and Company.

Hochs, Alfred, Karl Bindung, Wolfgang Haucke. 2006. *Die Freigabe der Vernichtung lebensunwerten Lebens : ihr Maß und ihre Form* [1920]. Berlin: Berliner Wissenschaft Verlag.

Pross, Christian. 1992. "Nazi Doctors, German Medicine, and the Fight for Historical Truth." In *The Nazi Doctors and the Nuremberg Code: Human Rights and Human Experimentation*, eds. Annas, George J. and Michael A. Grodin, 32–52. New York, and Oxford, UK: Oxford University Press.

Rogow, Sally M. 1999. "Child Victims in Nazi Germany." *The Journal of Holocaust Education* 8, no. 3: 71–86.

Scharsach, Hans-Henning. 2000. *Die Ärzte der Nazis*. Vienna: Verlag Orlac im Verlag Kremayr & Scheriau.

Annotated Bibliography

Note: The experience of mentally and physically disabled children in Nazi Germany has increasingly been included in surveys of the Nazi period. To find such material, please see the annotated bibliography accompanying the chapter on Children and the Holocaust.

Books and Monographs on Nazi Eugenics and Racial Hygiene Policies

The overwhelming majority of books and articles on the experiences of disabled children appear as sections in larger works on racial hygiene, eugenics, and the Nazi persecution of disabled adults.

Aly, Götz, Peter Chroust, and Christian Pross. *Cleansing the Fatherland: Nazi Medicine and Racial Hygiene*. Baltimore, MD, and London: The Johns Hopkins University Press, 1994, 295 pp.

English translations of important German-language research into doctors in the Nazi system. Of particular interest are Aly's chapters "Pure and Tainted Progress" and "Medicine against the Useless," both of which deal in part with the children's murder campaign.

Annas, George J. and Michael A. Grodin, eds. *The Nazi Doctors and the Nuremberg Code: Human Rights and Human Experimentation*. New York: Oxford University Press, 1992, 371 pp.

A collection of essays on questions relating to Nazi medical experimentation and the development of the Nuremberg Code, which became the international model governing the ethics of human experimentation. The early essays address questions of Nazi doctors and medical experimentation, and the Doctors' Trial in Nuremberg. The bulk of the essays, however, concern the role of the

Nuremberg Code in international and US law and the applications of the code to contemporary medical situations. Christian Pross's essay, "Nazi Doctors, German Medicine, and the Fight for Historical Truth," provides an excellent historiography of the subject from 1945 to 1990.

Biesold, Horst. *Crying Hands: Eugenics and Deaf People in Nazi Germany.* Washington, DC: Gallaudet University Press, 1999, 230 pp.

A landmark study in the persecution of deaf people under the Nazis. Despite significant research hurdles (archival material from some institutions was destroyed after the author requested it), Biesold uncovers the widespread collaboration of the teachers and administrators at German schools for the deaf in the persecution of their own students. School administrators regularly evaluated their students for sterilization, reporting many of them to the authorities. This collaboration extended to the Reich Union of the Deaf in Germany, which was Nazified in 1933, and which actively supported the sterilization of the hereditarily deaf in Germany. While fewer deaf children were subjected to the murder campaign than other groups of disabled children, the author does find evidence that in some deaf schools, students who fell behind academically were not offered remedial programs but instead were selected for death.

Bock, Gisela. *Zwangssterilisation im Nationalsozialismus: Studien zur Rassenpolitik und Frauenpolitik.* Opladen, Germany: Westdeutscher Verlag, 1986, 494 pp.

A very comprehensive German-language study of the development and application of the forced sterilization policy in Nazi Germany, with particular emphasis on its connections to racial policy and "the women's question." While child victims are only mentioned occasionally in the text, one of the highlighted cases the author uses involves a seventeen-year-old girl, Anna P. As part of the evidence supporting her sterilization, the authorities cited a school report that her mother was a less-than-stellar student. As a result, she was judged hereditarily tainted on her mother's side, and forcibly sterilized in February 1937. Through careful analysis, Bock estimates the total number of victims of the Nazi sterilization policy at 375,000.

Burleigh, Michael. *Death and Deliverance: "Euthanasia" in Germany, 1900–1945.* Cambridge, UK, and New York: Cambridge University Press, 1994, 382 pp.

A detailed analysis of the origins and development of the campaign to murder disabled children and adults, including an examination of the propaganda to support sterilization and murder.

Dressen, Willi. "Die bundesrepublikanische Rechtsprechung in Sachen NS-'Euthanasie.'" In *Medizin und Verbrechen: Festschrift zum 60. Geburtstag von Walter Wuttke*, edited by Christoph Kopke, 288–99. Ulm, Germany: Verlag Klemm und Oelschäger, 2001.

An examination, in part, of the postwar careers of Dr. Werner Catel, Dr. Alfred Leu, Dr. Hans Hefelman, and several other doctors who participated in the children and adult euthanasia campaigns.

Friedl, W., and B. Poier, T. Oelschläger, and R. Danziger. "The Fate of Psychiatric Patients during the Nazi Period in Styria/Austria." *International Journal of Mental Health* 35, no. 3 (2006): 30–40.

A concise analysis of the operation of the T-4 program and the Children's Department in Feldhof Hospital under the Nazis. The experts of the children's ward undertook a survey of all children and adolescents in area hospitals and clinics in order to evaluate them for killing. While only forty-five children were deported to Hartheim (the regional killing center for the T-4 program), out of a total of 1,177 deported patients, this obscures the total number killed, since most children were killed by hospital staff. Charting out the death rates for children during the war years, the authors identify more than two hundred children who perished in Feldhof between 1942 and 1945.

Friedlander, Henry. *The Origins of Nazi Genocide: From Euthanasia to the Final Solution*. Chapel Hill: The University of North Carolina Press, 1995, 421 pp.

A ground breaking English-language account of the development and implementation of the campaign to kill mentally and physically disabled children and adults, as well as the connections between these programs and the genocides of the Roma and of the Jews. The author argues that the killing of the disabled should be understood as part of these other genocides, and that it represents the beginning of the murder process.

As part of his treatment of the larger narrative, Friedlander includes a chapter on the killing of handicapped children, tracing out the efforts to have all doctors and midwives report the births of disabled children to the set of three "experts" who evaluated these reports and decided who should live and who should die, and onto the creation of nearly two dozen child-killing wards. He also describes the process for murdering the children, and notes that this process continued until the very last days of World War II.

Gallagher, Hugh Gregory. *By Trust Betrayed: Patients, Physicians, and the License to Kill in the Third Reich*. New York: Henry Holt and Company, 1990, 342 pp.

A highly personal study of the T-4 program, its ideological roots, development, expansion, and subsequent trials, along with comparisons to antidisabled prejudices and actions in the United States. Only Chapter 6, "The Children's Program," focuses specifically on children. Appendices at the end of the book contain translations of the report by Pastor Braune from 1940, laying out the structure and operation of the T-4 program as seen and opposed by vice president of the leading German Protestant welfare agency; the sermon from Clemens August Graf von Galen, the Catholic bishop of Münster, denouncing the T-4 Program; the final plea of Karl Brandt's lawyer at Nuremberg; and Karl Brandt's final statement. Only Braune's memo mentions the murder of children, and that too only in passing.

Jockusch, Ulrich, and Lothar Scholz, eds. *Administered Killings at the Time of National Socialism: Involvement—Suppression—Responsibility of Psychiatry and Judicial System*. Regensburg, Germany: S. Roderer Verlag, 1992, 146 pp. (bound together with the German original *Verwaltetes Morden in Nationalsozialismus*).

This bilingual volume contains papers presented at a 1990 conference on psychiatry during the Nazi era. While many of the essays concern the role of psychiatrists and psychiatric institutions in the murder of the mentally disabled, few make reference to child victims.

Kater, Michael H. *Doctors Under Hitler*. Chapel Hill: The University of North Carolina Press, 1989, 426 pp.

An important study of the transformation of the German medical profession under Hitler, but with only incidental mention of child victims of the euthanasia campaign.

Kolloquium des Institutes für Zeitgeschichte. *Medizin im Nationalsozialismus.* Munich, Germany: R. Oldenbourg Verlag, 1988, 110 pp.

The proceedings of a conference held in November 1987 with several of the most prominent German-language researchers on Nazi medicine, marking the fortieth anniversary of the Doctors' Trial at Nuremberg.

Kringlen, Einar. "No Extermination of Mental Patients in Norway during the German Occupation, 1940–1945." *International Journal of Mental Health* 35, no. 3 (2007): 90–93.

A short study of the treatment of mental patients and children in Norway under the German occupation. The author notes that while German visitors encouraged the murder of patients, the local asylum directors did not carry it out.

Lifton, Robert Jay. *The Nazi Doctors: Medical Killing and the Psychology of Genocide.* New York: Basic Books, Inc., 1986, 561 pp.

Most famous for his theory of psychological "doubling" as a way of explaining how doctors could torture and kill, only a small portion of this early English-language study of Nazi doctors concerns the persecution of disabled children.

Miller, Frieda. *Life Unworthy of Life: Nazi Euthanasia Crimes at Hadamar: A Teacher's Guide.* Vancouver: Vancouver Holocaust Education Centre, 2002, 36 pp.

Although this booklet was intended as preparatory material for students planning to visit an exhibit of the same name, it does provide pedagogic material and guidance for high school teachers thinking of covering this material in the classroom.

Müller-Hill, Benno. *Murderous Science: Elimination by Scientific Selection of Jews, Gypsies, and Others, Germany 1933–1945.* Oxford, UK: Oxford University Press, 1988, 208 pp.

The first half of the book is an overview of the role of doctors, scientists, and anthropologists in the development of the campaign to sterilize and murder those who were different. The second half is a set of conversations with perpetrators or their surviving relatives and colleagues.

Proctor, Robert N. *Racial Hygiene: Medicine Under the Nazis.* Cambridge, MA, and London: Harvard University Press, 1988, 414 pp.

An early and important work on the role of the biomedical sciences under the Nazis. Unlike earlier approaches, which looked at how the Nazis corrupted medicine, Proctor shows how doctors and scientists participated in the construction and shaping of Nazi racial policy. This includes a study of the pre-Nazi development of racial hygiene doctrine in Germany with the aim of showing why the German medical profession found Nazism attractive. The bulk of the book details how German doctors helped to create and administer various Nazi racial and eugenics campaigns, with chapters that examine in details such issues as the Sterilization Law, "the woman question," the "Jewish question," and the T-4 campaign. Proctor concludes with a look at the "organic vision" of Nazi medicine and the broader moral and political questions raised by German doctors.

Ryan, Donna F., and John S. Schuchman, eds. *Deaf People in Hitler's Europe.* Washington, DC.: Gallaudet University Press in association with the United States Holocaust Memorial Museum, 2002, 233 pp.

A collection of essays growing out of an international conference of the same name, held in 1998. Among the material of particular interest to those concerned about the persecution of disabled children in Nazi Germany include the translation of a 1934 article praising the Nazi state for recognizing that the deaf "never can be full citizens, but merely German subjects"; and an article on how teachers in deaf schools collaborated with the Nazi regime in the persecution of their own students, particularly with regard to their sterilization.

Scharsach, Hans-Henning. *Die Ärzte der Nazis*. Vienna: Verlag Orlac im Verlag Kremayr & Scheriau, 2000, 256 pp.

A German-language study of the role of doctors in the Nazi state, with specific chapters devoted to the forced sterilization campaign, the killing of disabled adults, the killing of disabled children, and medical experimentation conducted on disabled children. The author discusses examples of "illegal" euthanasia carried out by individual doctors in the 1930s, prior to the establishment of the T-4 program. He also describes several specific sets of experiments carried out on disabled children, particularly at the Am Spiegelgrund Institute in Vienna, where several doctors carried out lethal medical tests on disabled children. These included Ernst Illing's study of tuberous sclerosis, which used a lethal encephalography technique, and Elmar Türk's study of tuberculosis, where he deliberately infected children with the bacterium. In Berlin, Professors Georg Bessau and Ernst Hefter carried out trials of a tuberculosis vaccine on disabled children drawn from the killing wards. In 1944, Bessau's student, Georg Hensel, carried out tests of the effectiveness of the vaccine by injecting vaccinated and unvaccinated children with the tuberculosis bacterium. Finally, the author lists the various doctors and scientists who collected brain samples from the bodies of murdered children to further their own research.

US Holocaust Memorial Museum, ed. *Deadly Medicine: Creating the Master Race*. Washington, DC: Author, 2004, 226 pp.

The printed text to accompany the museum's exhibition of the same name, the book contains a set of scholarly essays on eugenics, Nazi sterilization and reproductive policies, race science, the "euthanasia" programs, and the connections between the murder of the disabled and the "Final Solution." In addition, the book contains numerous illustrations and photographs, of both perpetrators and Nazi propaganda, as well as information about individual victims and survivors.

Weindling, Paul Julian. *Nazi Medicine and the Nuremberg Trials: From Medical War Crimes to Informed Consent*. Basingstoke, UK: Palgrave MacMillan, 2004, 482 pp.

This is a careful study of the Nuremberg Medical Trial, which ran from December 1946 to August 1947 and involved twenty-three of the leading Nazis in the murder of disabled adults and children and in medical experimentation. The author also provides historical details and context for the development of the "Nuremberg Code" which governs ethical human experimentation. The murder of children during the Holocaust is only mentioned in passing.

Primary Source Collections of Nazi Eugenics and Racial Hygiene Policies

Klee, Ernst. *"Euthanasie" im NS-Staat: Die "Vernichtung lebensunwerten Lebens."* Frankfurt am Main, Germany: S. Fischer Verlag, 1983, 502 pp.

One of the earliest published accounts of the murder campaign against disabled children and adults. The text blends historical description and analysis with a significant amount of primary source material. Part 8 (out of 10) concerns the so-called "children's euthanasia," the planning of which is described earlier in a section of Part 3. The author includes photocopies of the selection forms, bureaucratic orders, and court testimony.

Klee, Ernst. *Dokumente zur "Euthanasie."* Frankfurt am Main: Fischer Taschenbuch Verlag, 1985, 342 pp.

The most important German-language collection of primary sources related to the murder of disabled children and adults. Of the six sections of the book, only section 4 directly concerns the children's "euthanasia" campaign. Klee includes a copy of the questionnaire sent to doctors requiring them to report on the condition of disabled children, various memos and letters from the participants, and material and photographs concerning medical experimentation on disabled children.

Nowak, Klara. "Verweigerte Anerkennug als NS-Verfolgte: Zwangsterilisierte und 'Euthanasie'—Geschädigte." In *Medizin und Gewissen: 50 Jahre nach dem Nürnberger Ärzteprozeß: Kongreßdokumentation,* edited by Stephen Kolb, and Horst Seithe, 163–68. Franfurt am Main, Germany: Mabuse Verlag, 1998.

In 1941, the Nazi authorities sterilized the teenaged Klara and killed her eighteen-year-old brother, who had been hospitalized at the start of the war. She has become a leading activist for survivors of the sterilization and euthanasia campaigns.

Monographs and Articles on the Nazi Persecution of Children

Dahl, Matthias. "Die Arbeit am Thema "Kindereuthanasie in der Anstalt Am Speigelgrund." In *Medizin im Nationalsozialismus—Wege der Aufarbeitung,* edited by Sonia Horn, and Peter Malina, 288–93. Vienna: Pressestelle und Verlag der Österreichischen Ärztekammer, 2002.

A brief summary of the author's dissertation on the *"Kinderfachabteilung"*—the children's killing ward—at the Am Spiegelgrund Institute in Vienna. It also contains an overview of the available sources, a literature review of the research in the field, and reactions in Vienna to the author's research.

Rogow, Sally M. "Child Victims in Nazi Germany." *The Journal of Holocaust Education* 8, no. 3 (1999): 71–86.

A comprehensive survey of Nazi policy of killing disabled children, tracing its development from the systematic dismantling of the pre-Nazi system that encouraged a community-based approach to the disabled to one in which all disabled were institutionalized. Residential facilities were either closed with their patients transferred to institutions or they were converted into work camps. Children attending day schools were administered increasingly difficult IQ tests, and those who failed were labeled "feeble minded" or "severely mentally handicapped" and sent to institutions.

Once in these institutions, parents had little to no control over the treatment of their child. Parents were not informed when the child was moved to a different institution, parents who visited and saw starved or bruised children were told that their child was to blame, and those parents who attempted to remove their children were generally blocked. While some children were sent to the T-4 killing centers, many were killed in local wards.

Rosmus, Anna. "Involuntary Abortions for Polish Forced Laborers." In *Experience and Expression: Women, the Nazis, and the Holocaust,* edited by Elizabeth R. Baer, and Myrna Goldenberg, 76–94. Detroit, MI: Wayne State University Press, 2003.

Between 1939 and 1945, some ten million foreign women and men were sent to forced labor camps inside Germany. Many of the women and girls became pregnant, and since these pregnancies interfered with their mothers' ability to work, they were either terminated through forced abortions, or the new-born infants were placed in "homes," where most died through deliberate malnutrition. Although these children were not disabled, in many ways their murder flowed from the wider policy regarding disabled children as aliens to the nation.

Thomas, Florian P., Alana Beres, and Michael I. Shevell. "'A Cold Wind Coming: Heinrich Gross and Child Euthanasia in Vienna." *Journal of Child Neurology* 21, no. 4 (2006): 342–48.

A study of the scientific and policy origins of the children's euthanasia campaign at the Am Spiegelgrund Hospital in Vienna. After a brief overview of the development of the policy and its application in Austria after the *Anschluß,* the authors focus on the actions of Dr. Heinrich Gross, who oversaw the infants' ward where more than half of 722 children were killed as part of the euthanasia campaign. A few eyewitness accounts of child survivors are included. The authors detail the failed efforts to bring Gross to justice and comment on his successful medical and political career after the war.

Wyszynski, Diego F. "Men with White Coats and SS Boots: The Children's Euthanasia Programme during the Third Reich." *Paediatric and Perinatal Epidemiology* 14 (2000): 295–99.

A brief overview of the killing of children in Nazi Germany, noting the general complicity of the German medical and public health establishment in the program. After tracing the institutional development of the killing program, the author describes the process for selecting children for death, including one of the early forms used to register children. The killings began in October 1939 at Brandenburg-Gören, a facility to train physicians in how to kill children, and where some children were subjected to medical experimentation before they were murdered. The author also examines the expansion of the program to older children and then teenagers after the suspension of the T-4 program in the fall of 1941.

6

The Plight and Fate of Children vis-à-vis the Guatemalan Genocide

Samuel Totten

In giving testimonies about indiscriminate massacres, peasant sources often wondered what kind of "sin" (pecado) children could possibly be guilty of to justify their murder by state forces. Yet the army treated many Indian communities as uniformly hostile. Their rhetoric described all residents, even infants, as dangerous "communists," and worthy of death—Patrick Ball, Paul Kobrak, and Herbert Spirer

Introduction

The genocide of the Maya people by the Government of Guatemala did not attract the attention of many scholars of genocide studies until the last decade or so[1] Fortunately, that was not the case vis-à-vis human rights organizations, human rights activists, and a small number of scholars (anthropologists, historians, and political scientists) who had a vested interest in Guatemala (i.e., had conducted research in Guatemala and had come to know the people who were being targeted). Indeed, for well over thirty years now, various human rights organizations and activists have focused a laser-like light on the mass killings of men, women, and children by Guatemalan troops and their lackeys. In doing so, they have decried the destruction of 400 plus Mayan villages, the brutal torture and murder of Mayans of all ages, and the impunity enjoyed by the perpetrators of the crimes.

The Genocide

Beginning in the early 1980s, the Guatemalan government and its military carried out a particularly vicious state-driven counterinsurgency and scorched earth effort to combat leftist guerillas.[2] Instead of solely hunting down the guerillas, the military and its militia tortured, raped, and killed women, children, and infants as well.[3] It is estimated that some 200,000 people were murdered primarily by government forces during the so-called thirty-six-year war.

It is estimated that some 100,000 children lost one or both parents during the violence in the 1980s in Guatemala (Manz 1988, 30). Ball, Kobrak, and Spirer (1999) report that "1981 and 1982, the years with the greatest number of killings, were also the years with the highest proportion of child victims. . . . During the early 1980s, the proportion of all victims who were fourteen years old or younger rose above 12 percent. At the height of the army's counterinsurgency, approximately one in every eight victims of killing and disappearance were children" (Chapter 16, Figure 16.3, n.p.).

In 1997, the Commission for Historical Clarification (Comisión para el Esclarecimiento Histórico [CEH]) was founded for the express purpose of establishing the type and extent of human rights violations that were committed during the thirty-six-year civil war and to help preserve the memory of the victims. In 1999, the commission issued its report: It concluded, in part, the following:

- Repressive practices were perpetrated by institutions within the state, in particular the judiciary, and were not solely due to actions by the armed forces. The report stated that in the four regions most affected by the violence, "agents of the state committed acts of genocide against groups of Mayan people" (Final Report, English Version, para. 122).
- The total number of people killed was over 200,000; 83 percent of the victims were Mayan and 17 percent were Ladino.
- "State forces and related paramilitary groups were responsible for 93 percent of the violations documented" (Final Report, English Version, para. 15).
- "Insurgent actions produced 3 percent of the human rights violations and acts of violence" (Final Report, English Version, para. 21).
- The destruction of more than 400 indigenous villages and the murder of their inhabitants "came about with the knowledge, or by order, of the highest military authorities."

As Linda Green (1995) has noted, "By the Guatemalan military's own admission, it destroyed over 440 rural communities in the highlands and partially razed countless others" (1). Its "excuse" (they'd say, their "rationale") was that they were fighting a communist insurgency. "[O]ne million people—approximately half the rural population—were displaced within the country [often in the jungles along the Guatemala/Mexican border], while tens of thousands of men, women, and children fled across the Mexican border to live in exile" (Green 1995, 1). Daniel Wilkinson (2002) notes that "General Hector Gramajo summed up the history of the war like this: [I]n 1981 the army had been worried the guerillas might triumph; in 1982 they took care of the EGP [The Guerilla Army of the Poor] in the central and western highlands; in 1983 they took care of ORPA [The Revolutionary Organization of Armed People]; in 1984 they stopped worrying" (311).

The State of Affairs

The Type and Extent of Violence against the Children

The violence perpetrated against the Mayan children by the Government of Guatemala during its scorched earth policy against the Mayan people was brutal, vicious, and calculated (in other words, it served various purposes). Among the aims of the violence was to terrorize and pacify the people, to force them off their land and out of the highlands, to punish them for purportedly supporting the rebels (whether they had or not), and, sadistically, to cause incredible pain to those parents who were forced to watch their children being brutalized and to do the same to the children who were forced to watch as their parents were brutalized.

In regard to using the violence to pacify the people, Patricia Seminetta (2005) argues that terror was used to pacify the population and to warn others not to "disobey." To drive their warning home, the military carried out public torture sessions. [One survivor said,] "What we have seen has been terrible: burned corpses, women impaled and buried as if they were animals ready for the spit, all doubled up, and children massacred and carved up with machetes." Reinforcing this fear was the fact that there was no one to protect the people from these heinous acts (137–38).

Seminetta (2005) also suggests that "By exterminating the Maya, the Guatemalan elite was attempting to dictate a new social identity and provoke a collective amnesia. This served the government's purposes during the Cold War when a homogenous society that did not question the status quo was viewed favourably by some in the international political arena" (137–38). The latter, of course, includes

125

the United States—and particularly President Ronald Reagan and his administration.

Throughout this period, while many children were machine-gunned down (Montejo 1999, 49) and/or killed and dismembered (Montejo 1999, 114), others were forced into buildings and then burned alive (Wilkinson 2002, 24).

Following an attack of the village of Puente Alto on July 6, 1982, during which 250 people were killed, including babies and children, a survivor reported the following about how Guatemalan troops burned people alive:

> [A] man whose face was covered [with a hood] said, "Let's give them three minutes so that they can see what they won't ever see again." Then he said: "The firewood will serve to turn you into cooked pork rind." All the people screamed. Then he said: "Wait just a minute," and they began to machinegun. Afterward they poured gasoline and set us on fire. When a baby who was being burned woke up, it screamed . . . (Quoted in the report issued by the Commission on Historical Clarification in Guatemala 1999, 113)

During the course of another massacre at a place called Chel in April 1982, "small children were killed, beaten against rocks or tossed alive into the river . . ." (Fundacion de Antropologia Forense de Guatemala 1998, n.p.). During yet another massacre, this one in Las Dos Erres, older children and adults were forced to "kneel at the edge of a well and, with a blow of a sledge hammer to the head, were sent plunging into the mass of dead and dying bodies piling up inside [the well]" (Wilkinson 2002, 327). Many children nabbed by soldiers were flown away in helicopters never to be seen again (Montejo 1999, 114; Wilkinson 2002, 301).

Even babies were targeted. While some babies were bayoneted and killed (Montejo 1999, 43), others were tossed in rivers alive on the backs of their mothers who had been killed (Montejo 1999, 77). Still others were beaten to death by soldiers who swung them by the feet, smashing their heads against rocks and walls (Wilkinson 2002, 327).

The killers didn't stop at killing defenseless babies. Fetuses were also destroyed. Of such horrors, Almudena Bernabeu, of the US-based Center of Justice and Accountability, asserted, "rape, mutilation, sexual slavery and the killing of foetuses were all part of a plan to eliminate the Mayan people" (De Pablo, Zurita, and Tremlet 2011, 1).

An untold number of girls under the age of eighteen were raped (Wilkinson 2002, 44) and gang raped by Guatemalan soldiers (Wilkinson 2002, 327). In toto, it is estimated that some 100,000 females (women of all ages, as well as young girls and teenagers) were victims of mass rape. Following the rapes, many were killed. "To eliminate all the Mayans is a very difficult task, but if you destroy the women you make sure that the population is reduced and eventually disappears—'It's one of the cruelest ways of getting rid of an entire people,' says Paloma Soria, a lawyer. Not a few who were raped were abandoned by their husbands for having been raped" (quoted in De Pablo, Zurita, and Tremlett 2011, 1).

In a report ("State Violence in Guatemala, 1960–1996") issued by the American Association for the Advancement of Science, the authors assert that not only did the Guatemalan army set out to eliminate the Mayan people but did so in a way that constituted "overkill":

> Guatemalan security forces often went beyond simply eliminating their victims. "Overkill" we define as the practice of committing additional indignities on someone who is either in the process of being killed or who is already dead. For example, overkill includes burning or mutilating a corpse, decapitating a corpse after death, shooting bullets into a body already killed by stabbing, raping a victim before killing her, or torturing a victim to death.
>
> Overkill can serve many purposes. Disfiguring a corpse can augment the impact of a murder on survivors. It can also demonstrate to the politically active that the government's willingness to harm its opponents has no limits. When a superior officer forces troops (or police or paramilitary agents) to commit such horrors, it helps break down subordinates' aversion to violence and makes them more effective operatives for the government's campaign of violence. (Ball, Kobrak, and Spirer 1999, n.p.)

Continuing, Ball, Kobrak, and Spirer (1999) first note and then speculate:

> It is difficult to comprehend this type of official behavior, or to see its rationale. The government may have slaughtered children to avoid dealing with an even greater orphan problem than the one it had already created. Another reason may be the army's stated belief that allowing children in hostile villages to live would only lead to the growth of future generations of vengeful guerrilla fighters. In any case, the early 1980s government policy of killing unarmed civilian children shows how little it cared about the human consequences of

its fight against the insurgency. Often the Army was willing to destroy entire communities to facilitate its own survival. (n.p.)

When children, themselves, were not targeted, they often witnessed the brutality meted out by government troops. As Victor Montejo (1999) points out, "Children as young as four already knew that the army was capable of the most criminal acts. They witnessed helicopters bombing their villages and solders firing their machine guns on their parents or village elders" (114).

A woman named Maria Castro was brutally attacked and raped by three soldiers as her young daughter, alongside her baby brother, was forced to sit and watch. Speaking of her ordeal and that of her children, Maria said:

> The soldiers ambushed me. My little girl was with me. She was very frightened and she cried, but the soldier threw me to the ground. I remember there were three of them who raped me, but I don't know how many more because I lost consciousness. When I came to, I saw them pick up their guns and leave hurriedly for some other place. My daughter helped me by carrying her little brother, but she was still crying. She saw everything. (Quoted in De Pablo, Zurita, and Tremlet 2011, 2)

The Civil Patrol System: Forcing Brother against Brother

Mayan children were not only attacked, tortured, and killed much the same way adults were but many were also forced to take part in the killings. More specifically, the Guatemalan army instituted what it referred to as "civil patrols," a "continuing mandatory system of self-surveillance which began in 1982" (Green 1995, 1). Mayan boys as young as fourteen years old were forced to take part in the civil patrols, basically serving as auxiliary soldiers for the army. What this resulted in, essentially, is the implication of "indigenous men as accomplices to the violence and brutality against their own people" (Green 1995, 1).

Hardships and Nightmares as Mayan Fled into the Mountains, Distant Towns, or Refugee Camps in Mexico

The torment of the Mayan children continued as they and their families fled from the attacks on their villages. Children, like the adults, faced abject hunger, the danger of being caught and killed, and experienced terror from being tracked down by the Guatemalan military. Jacinta Guarcas was one of the tens of thousands who was forcibly displaced from her home and village. Ultimately, as she and her family attempted to eke out a meager existence in the mountains where they sought sanctuary, one of her children was killed by military troops while six others perished due to starvation. Dolefully, she commented, "First I buried my one-year-old son since I didn't have enough milk for him because we had nothing to eat" (quoted in De Pablo, Zurita, and Tremlet 2011, 2).

As refugees fled across the border into Mexico, all sorts of human rights abuses were perpetrated against them by the Mexican authorities. Adults and children were detained, often in subhuman conditions, threatened, beaten, and traumatized.

Over and above that, many children, who either had lost their parents or had been separated from them, were preyed on by Mexican nationals. "The most widely discussed case among the refugees was that of three girls (fourteen, thirteen, and twelve years of age) who were taken by a Mexican woman all the way to the city of Puebla and forced to 'work' in a house of prostitution run by this woman. Two other girls found themselves in the same situation in Tijuana" (Montejo 1999, 252–53).

Depression, Posttraumatic Stress

Based on what young people witnessed and experienced, it is not surprising that so many young survivors "have high incidences of health and psychological problems, and tend to live in precarious situations" (Comisión de Derechos Humanos de Guatemala 1986, n.p.).

In the late 1990s, the Human Rights Office of the Archdiocese of Guatemala amassed and analyzed more than 5,000 testimonies of survivors of the genocidal period, and its findings in regard to the ongoing suffering experienced by the survivors is telling. More specifically, Lopez (n.d.) reports that:

> Although it does not examine PTSD directly, they did observe many of the symptoms used in diagnosing the disorder, re-experiencing the traumatic event, avoidance, anxiety, and guilt. The study showed that 31% of the survivors still lived in fear, 29% were saddened by memories of the war, and 4% suffered from nightmares and traumatic memories. The nightmares consisted of reliving their trauma or the terrors done to their family. They [the authors of the report] report that many people re-experience their trauma and they have persistent memories of their family members being murdered. The testimonies also reveal that 12.5% of the survivors felt a sense of helplessness by not being able to defend themselves or to even be able to denounce what was being done to them. The testimonies

also revealed that there were people in the community that would not speak of what they witnessed or what they suffered, which is also one of the criteria . . . for the diagnosis of PTSD, avoidance (2004). (1)

The Government of Guatemala can speak all it wants to about reconciliation, but until those who continue to experience such trauma in their lives are provided solid counseling and other assistance, it is not likely that many will be inclined to consider reconciliation with those who have ruined their lives in so many different and profoundly hurtful ways.[4]

Other Hardships in the Post-Genocide Period

Guatemala established a national reparations program in 2003 for the express purpose of providing compensation to the victims of the genocide. Reparations were to cover the costs of homes that were destroyed, land that was stolen, and even psychological support and rehabilitation (Valladares 2012, 1). However, as Danilo Valladares (2012) has noted, "corruption, nepotism, and the use of the reparations programme for political ends has made its work an uphill task, and the majority of survivors are still waiting for compensation, while only some have received limited reparations" (1). To date, only 20 percent of the victims have received compensation, and that is largely due to the extensive red tape and corruption involved (Valladares 2012, 1).

Not only that, thus far the work put into rebuilding peoples' homes has been slipshod, incomplete, and made of cheap materials that are quick to break down and disintegrate over a short period of time due to weather and/or general/common use. Over and above that, "there has been no restitution of land, investment in production, or psychosocial reparations for the women who suffered violence, which also form part of the measures outlined by the government programme," said Sergio Castro, with the non-governmental Centre for Forensic Analysis and Applied Sciences" (quoted by Valladares 2012, 2).

As far as efforts at reconciliation go, the state, outrageously, "refuses to acknowledge those females who were raped during the period of the genocide." Over and above that, many of the rapists continue to live in the same areas as their victims and have enjoyed total impunity. "We want the state to acknowledge the truth. We have no voice, and officially the rapes during the conflict never happened," says Feliciana Macario, one of a group of women who has worked for twenty years to bring the rapes into the public arena (quoted in De Pablo, Zurita, and Tremlet 2011, 1). Patricia Yoj, a native Mayan lawyer, says that "even the representative of the National Indemnity Programme that was established to make reparations to victims of the conflict has said that he doesn't believe in the rapes" (quoted in De Pablo, Zurita, and Tremlet 2011, 1).

The issue of impunity is the proverbial elephant in the room. While a small number of individuals have been prosecuted for the atrocities perpetrated during the thirty-six-year war, the vast majority has not. That has to change, and soon, if Guatemalan society is going to move forward at all in the face of the horrors that tore asunder the nation.

Early on it appeared as if only low-level perpetrators would be tried. More specifically, in November 1998, three individuals who had served as part of the "civil patrol" were arrested and tried in what was to be the first case surrounding the genocide. Along with forty-two others, the three individuals had purportedly massacred seventy-seven women and 107 children. Many of the youngest women were gang raped and then murdered. During this attack, one ten-year-old Mayan boy, holding his baby brother, was accosted by a patroller, a man from a nearby town: "I'm taking you back home to work for me. But the baby can't come, he's too small." Then the man sliced the infant in two. The boy survived and lived to be one of the few eye-witnesses at the trial (some witnesses had been threatened with death in the previous months by other ex-patrollers still getting protection from the Army). The patrollers claimed they were elsewhere, planting trees. They were found guilty and sentenced to death. But "civil patrollers come low in the hierarchy," says a journalist working in Central America, "and perhaps their lives are expendable to protect the people who ordered the genocide" (Peace Pledge Union, n.d., n.p.).

Gradually, more arrests were made and a number of soldiers and officers were charged with various crimes related to their decisions and actions during the genocidal period. More specifically, in 2009, a former colonel and three former paramilitaries were convicted for "disappearing" indigenous people during the civil war. This conviction constituted the first successful prosecution of an army officer vis-à-vis such disappearances, which were a common element during the genocidal period. Then, in 2011, five soldiers who served with an elite Guatemalan army unit were convicted for their part in a massacre in the village of Dos Erres.

In January 2012, a Guatemalan judge ordered Efraín Ríos Montt, the former military dictator during the alleged period of genocide, to stand trial on charges of crimes against humanity and genocide. The order was a watershed event, in that for decades Ríos Montt, who served as a congressman in the years following his dictatorship, had avoided prosecution for the brutality and atrocities that were perpetrated during his bloody rule (1982–1983), claiming immunity due to a Guatemalan law that provides immunity to public officials. His immunity, however, ended when his term as a congressman came to a close in January 2012. Prosecutors drove home the fact that Ríos Montt, a former general, "had full command over his troops and knowledge of their actions" (Malkin 2012, 1), and had "turned a blind eye as soldiers used rape, torture and arson against leftist insurgents and targeted indigenous people during a 'scorched earth' military offensive that killed at least 1,771 members of the Ixil group" (McDonald 2013, 1). Prosecutors also highlighted "military documents that they said called for 'the extermination of subversive elements' in the region that includes the Indian communities. The prosecutors added that Mr. Ríos Montt was on the documents' distribution list" (Malkin 2012, 1).

In March of 2013, the trial of Ríos Montt began. On May 10, 2013, Rios Montt was found guilty of genocide and crimes against humanity. He was sentenced to fifty years imprisonment on charges of genocide and another thirty years on charges of crimes against humanity. In announcing the verdict, Judge Jazmin Barrios said, "As *de facto* president, it is logical that he had full knowledge of what was happening and he did nothing to stop it."

Almudena Bernabeu, a lawyer at the Center for Justice and Accountability, based in San Francisco, asserted, "A lot of things came together to change the aging dictator's fate: an intrepid attorney general, international pressure, and mounting evidence in the form of secret army plans and mass graves, still being unearthed to this day" (quoted in Replogle 2013, 1).

But then, on May 20, 2013, Guatemala's top court overturned the guilty verdict against Rios Montt: "The Constitutional Court is now considering whether a 1986 amnesty should apply to prevent the continued prosecution of the case, although international law makes clear that amnesties cannot be applied for genocide, crimes against humanity and war crimes, and Guatemala's 1986 amnesty law was explicitly repealed after the end of the armed conflict" (Open Society Foundations, May 31, 2013, p. 1). It now appears that the new trial of Rios Montt will not begin prior to April 2014.

While Guatemala and the rest of the world wait to see how the retrial of Rios Montt turns out, the fact remains that the vast majority of others who oversaw and carried out the torture, maiming, murder, and destruction of the 400 villages remain free.

What has complicated the situation (i.e., arresting the alleged suspects and conducting the trials, and finding those individuals, who planned and/or perpetrated the crimes, guilty) is that many survivors continue to face threats and retribution for providing evidence about what they suffered and/or witnessed. Witnesses have been threatened, beaten up, and, in some cases, killed. Many women have also been raped. Other figures—from certain clergy members to prosecutors—who have worked to uncover the crimes committed during the genocide have also faced retribution at the hands of the alleged perpetrators and/or their supporters.

Indeed, being upright and forthright about the crimes perpetrated during the genocidal period is a dangerous, and often deadly, proposition. For example, in April 1998, just fifty hours after Bishop Juan Gerardi, a highly regarded human rights activist, publicly presented the Catholic Church's report *Recuperation of Historical Memory* (*Nunca Más*)—which was not only emphatic that the vast majority of the atrocities perpetrated during the thirty-six-year war were carried out by the army, but also listed, by name, those known to have carried out the atrocities—he was murdered. Gerardi was viciously beaten to death with a large piece of concrete in a sadistic act of retribution, which undoubtedly was also meant to serve as a warning to anyone who might be thinking of testifying in any of the forthcoming court trials.

In June 2001, three officers (one of whom was the former head of military intelligence) were sentenced to forty years in prison for killing the bishop. It is believed that others involved in the killing got off free. The initial prosecutor who was trying the case received repeated death threats and subsequently resigned and went into exile. Subsequently, the man who oversaw the conviction of the three men, Guatemala's chief prosecutor, also fled the country and went into exile after facing repeated death threats.

Critical Challenges Facing the Field Today

There are a host of critical challenges facing both those who were children during the Guatemalan genocide as well as Guatemalan society as a whole. Among the key challenges for the survivors are: the need for comprehensive and sustained psychological support/counseling, return of their land, reparations for their material losses, the erection of well-constructed homes that will not literally fall down around them in a decade or less, and protection should they provide testimony in any of the forthcoming trials of the alleged perpetrators.

As for the challenges facing Guatemalan society in the aftermath of the genocide, they are: locating and establishing the fate of those who "disappeared" during the genocidal period,[5] ending impunity for those (political and military leaders) who planned and oversaw the genocide, ending impunity for at least those who ordered and oversaw the actual butchery and mass rapes of the people in the villages, providing the survivors of the genocide with reparations for their material losses,[6] providing protection for those who are providing testimony against the alleged perpetrators of the genocide, establishing a check-and-balance system to make sure that all of the survivors are protected from their former attackers, and the establishment and implementation of a rule of law that provides every citizen with his/her basic human rights.[7]

Only time will tell if such issues are addressed and addressed in the spirit of true reconciliation. All sorely need to be addressed, and the sooner the better. And, of course, they cannot, and should not, be addressed in a perfunctory manner, for the needs of the survivors are profound and the issue of reconciliation is central to addressing the deep wounds that still trouble Guatemalan society.

Conclusion

Nothing, of course, is going to bring back the dead. Nothing will wipe away the dark memories of what the young witnessed as their brothers and sisters, mothers and fathers, and other family and community members suffered while being tortured and killed. Nothing will expunge the wounds—physical and psychological—resulting from what the young themselves faced at the hands of their tormentors.

What can, and must, be done is to treat the survivors with respect, decency, and kindness; and in doing so, the Guatemalan government must end impunity for the alleged perpetrators, and provide solid protection for the survivors, making absolutely sure they are free from any type of harassment from the government and any of its entities (official and otherwise), including the former perpetrators and their supporters.

Notes

1. While it is true that such attention was better late than never, it does say something about the lack of attention to events unfolding in Central America and to the lack of a fully operational genocide early warning system—which, if one had been in operation, would have certainly raised red flags vis-à-vis the horrific actions of the Government of Guatemala in the highlands of Guatemala.

2. "The 'insurgents' label extended itself to be used by the Army, which specifically considered the Isil people to be the enemy, without establishing any distinction between the civilian population and combatants" (from CEH, quoted in Higonnet 2009, 31).

3. It is estimated that more than 100,000 females were raped during the course of Guatemala's thirty-six-year civil war. How many of those were teenagers and young girls is not known.

4. As Sergio Castro, an official with the nongovernmental Centre for Forensic Analysis and Applied Science (the latter of which provides support to those who were impacted by the thirty-six-year war) asserted, psychosocial support for victims "is essential for restoring the social fabric and bringing about peaceful coexistence," especially taking into account that "both victims and victimizers live in the [same] communities" (quoted in Valladares 2012, 1).

5. The Commission for Historical Clarification (CEH) recommended that the fate of all of those who disappeared during the conflict be investigated, and that a National Search Commission for Disappeared Children be established. A bill which would establish a commission to find victims of the estimated 45,000 enforced disappearances was finally presented in 2007, but is still awaiting approval by the Guatemalan Congress.

6. In 2005, a National Reparations Commission was established but processing the reparations has been riddled with problems, including malfeasance of all kinds, and thus the vast majority of victims have not received what they have been promised.

7. An agreement between the United Nations and the Government of Guatemala, the International Commission against Impunity in Guatemala (CICIG) was established and entered into force in September 2007. The CICIG's mandate is to conduct independent investigations, issue criminal complaints to Guatemala's Public Prosecutor, help prosecute the alleged perpetrators, and promote both legal and institutional reforms. The CICIG is working diligently but has been met with a raft of barriers by those with a vested interest in not seeing such arrests and convictions come to fruition.

References

Ball, Patrick, Paul Kobrak, and Herbert F. Spirer. 1999. "Chapter 13: Methods of Terror." In *State Violence in Guatemala, 1960–1996*. n.p. *A Quantitative Reflection*. Washington, DC.: American Association for the Advancement of Science. Accessed at: shr.aaas.org/guatemala/ciidh/qr/english/chap16.html

La Comisión de los Derechos Humanos de las Naciones Unidas 42 Periodo de Sesiones (Febrero-Marzo de 1986). *Resoluciones aprobadas por la Comisión de los Derechos Humanos de las Naciones Unidas 42 Periodo ordinario de Sesiones*. Guatemala City: Author. Available at: www.juridicas.unam.mx/publica/librev/rev/.../pr14.pdf

Commission for Historical Clarification (CEH). 1999. *Guatemala: Memory of Silence—The Report of the Commission for Historical Clarification*. Guatemala City: Author.

Fundacion de Antropologia Forense de Guatemala Website. 1998. "Masacres." Available at: www.fafg.org/

Green, Linda. 1995. "The Paradoxes of War and Its Aftermath: Mayan Widows in Rural Guatemala." *Cultural Survival Quarterly* 19, no. 1: n.p.

Lopez, Marisela. n.d. "Post Traumatic Distress Order in Guatemala." Departamento de Ciencias SocialesMaestría en Consejeria Psicológica y Salud Mental Psicodiagnostico de Desórdenes Mentales. Universidad del Valle de Guatemala. Available at: www.coedu.usf.edu/zalaquett/cic/ptsd.htm

Malkin, Elizabeth. 2012. "Accused of Atrocities, Guatemala's Ex-Dictator Chooses Silence." *The New York Times*. January 26. Available at: www.nytimes.com/.../efrain-rios-montt-accused-of-atrocities-in-guate

Manz, Beatriz. 1988. *Refugees of a Hidden War: The Aftermath of Counterinsurgency in Guatemala*. Albany, NY: State University of New York Press.

McDonald, Mike. 2013. "Guatemalan Trial of Ex-Dictator Rios Montt to Begin." *Reuters*. March 19. Available at: www.reuters.com/.../us-guatemala-riosmontt-idUSBRE92I03S20130

Open Society Foundations. 2013. "Stalemate over Guatemala's Rios Montt Genocide Trial Threatens Victims' Rights." *Open Society Justice Initiative*. Available at: www.opensocietyfoundations.org/.../legal-stalemate-over-guatemalas-rio (accessed May 31, 2013).

De Pablo, Ofelia, Javier Zurita, and Giles Tremlett. 2011. "Guatemalan War Rape Survivors: 'We Have No Voice.'" *The Guardian*. July 28. Available at: www.guardian.co.uk › World news › Guatemala

Peace Pledge Union. n.d. "Talking about Genocides—Guatemala." Available at: www.ppu.org.uk/genocide/g_guatemala.html.

Replogle, Jill. 2013. "Ríos Montt and Guatemala's Genocide Trial." *The World*. March 19. Available at: www.theworld.org/2013/.../rios-montt-asnd-guatemalas-genocide-trial

Seminetta, Patricia. 2005. "Politics, Violence, and Expression: The Role of Memory and Identity in Guatemala's War-Torn Past." In *Cultures of Violence: Papers from the 5th Global Conference 2004*, eds. Jonathan E. Lynch, and Gary Wheeler, 131–46. Oxford: Inter-Disciplinary Press.

Tomuschat, Christian. 2001. "Clarification Commission in Guatemala." *Human Rights Quarterly* 23: 2233–58.

UN News Centre. 2013. "UN Human Rights Chief Welcomes Trial for Guatemalan Genocide." March 18. *UN News*. Available at: www.un.org/apps/news/story.asp?NewsID=4441

Valladares, Danilo. 2012. "Victims of War, Victims of Oblivion." Inter Press Service News Agency, March 13. Available at: http://www.ipsnews.net/2012/03/victims-of-war-victims-of-oblivion/

Wilkinson, Daniel. 2002. *Silence on the Mountain: Stories of Terror, Betrayal, and Forgetting in Guatemala*. Boston, MA: Houghton-Mifflin.

Annotated Bibliography

Amnesty International. *Guatemala: A Government Program of Political Murder: The Amnesty Report.* London: Author, 1981, n.p.
    The introduction to this important report reads as follows:

> The human rights issue that dominates all others in the Republic of Guatemala is that people who oppose or are imagined to oppose the government are systematically seized without warrant, tortured, and murdered, and that these tortures and murders are part of a deliberate and long-standing program of the Guatemalan government.
>
> This report contains information, published for the first time, which shows how the selection of targets for detention and murder, and the deployment of official forces for extra-legal operations, can be pinpointed to secret offices in an annex of Guatemala's National Palace, under the direct control of the president of the republic.
>
> The report also includes transcripts of two unique interviews: the first is with a peasant who, as far as Amnesty International knows, is the sole survivor of political imprisonment in Guatemala in 1980; the second is with a former conscript soldier who served as a member of a plainclothes army unit and who described the abduction of civilians who were later tortured and murdered.
>
> Between January and November in 1980 alone, some 3,000 people described by government representatives as "subversives" and "criminals" were either shot on the spot in political assassinations or seized and murdered later; at least 364 others seized in this period have not yet been accounted for.

Amnesty International. *Guatemala: Justice and Impunity: Guatemala's Historical Clarification Commission 10 Years On.* London: Author, 2009, 5 pp.
    In 1999, Guatemala's Historical Classification Commission delivered its landmark report on human rights violations committed during the thirty-six-year internal armed conflict. To date, numerous recommendations by the Commission have not been implemented (and some that have, have been perfunctory at best), depriving survivors, victims, and their families of justice and reparation. In this appeal Amnesty International urges the Guatemalan authorities to release crucial military files; to allow for the exhumation of clandestine cemeteries; and to bring to justice those responsible for such crimes as extrajudicial execution and enforced disappearance.

Amnesty International. "Massive Extrajudicial Executions in Rural Areas Under the Government of General Efraín Ríos Montt." July, 1982, 20 pp.
    In this "Special Briefing Report," Amnesty International declares the following: "[A]fter studying the occurrence of '*disappearances*' and extrajudicial executions in Guatemala in detail for many years, [we have] concluded that the vast majority of such abuses in Guatemala are carried out by semi-official paramilitary '*death squads*,' operating under government control or with government complicity." The report goes on to note that such atrocities were carried out under the leadership of General Efrain Ríos Montt.

A long list of the actual atrocities committed are included in the report. Included in the latter are numerous statements concerning the fate of child victims, including but not limited to the following: "children bashed to death against rocks"; "machine-gunned an entire family, including a one-year-old boy"; "machine-gunned or hacked to death with machetes thirty or more people from the village, including fifteen women, five men and nine children between the ages of six months and one year"; and "an army patrol beheaded 9 peasants, among them a nine-year-old girl, as the family was praying."

Ball, Patrick, Paul Kobrak, and Herbert F. Spirer. *State Violence in Guatemala, 1960–1996, A Quantitative Reflection.* Washington, DC.: American Association for the Advancement of Science. 1999, n.p.

This detailed study provides a valuable quantitative analysis of numerous issues vis-à-vis the state violence carried out in Guatemala between 1960 and 1996. It is comprised of five parts and sixteen chapters, a set of appendices, and a rich bibliography. The parts and chapters are as follows: Part I. Introduction; Part II. A Narrative of Violence (Chapter 1. State Violence in Guatemala, 1960–1996; Chapter 2. The 1960s; Chapter 3. The 1970s; Chapter 4. The 1980s; and Chapter 5. The 1990s); Part III. Analytic Comparisons (Chapter 6. Terror and Regime; Chapter 7. Reporting the Violence; Chapter 8. Urban versus Rural Violence; Chapter 9. Reporting Urban versus Rural Violence; Chapter 10. Naming the Victims; Chapter 11. Selective versus Mass Killing; Chapter 12. Terror and Seasonality; and Chapter 13. Methods of Terror); Part IV. Victims and Perpetrators (Chapter 14. The Victims; Chapter 15. Gender and Violence; Chapter 16. Age and Family; Chapter 17. Ethnicity; Chapter 18. The Perpetrators; Chapter 19. Civilian against Civilian; and Chapter 20. Populations in Resistance); and Part V. Conclusion.

The book is packed with revelatory insights. Issues and facts related to the fate of Mayan children are peppered throughout the report. For example, speaking of why the Guatemalan army went from mainly fighting rebels to carrying out a scorched earth policy that entailed torturing and killing unarmed civilians, the authors state the following: "Armed guerrillas typically harassed army troops and then slipped back into the mountains. The army, frustrated by these attacks yet undeterred by any moral consideration for their civilian victims, responded by attacking entire villages. By the early 1982 peak of terror, troops regularly burned villagers' houses and crops and killed their farm animals in a 'scorched earth' policy designed to depopulate the zones of guerrilla operations (Americas Watch 1982). What had been a selective campaign against guerrilla sympathizers turned into a mass slaughter designed to eliminate any support or *potential* support for the rebels, and included widespread killing of children, women and the elderly. It was a strategy that Ríos Montt called 'draining the sea that the fish swim in.'"

Blum, William. *Killing Hope: U.S. Military and CIA Interventions Since World War II.* Washington, DC.: Common Courage Press, 2008, 470 pp.

Chapter 23 is entitled "Guatemala." It is a revealing and sickening account of the US government's activities in Guatemala and its connection and reaction to the mass killings of the Mayan communities by the Guatemalan governments and its forces.

Carmack, Robert M., ed. *Harvest of Violence: The Maya Indians and the Guatemalan Crisis.* Norman: University of Oklahoma Press, 1992, 334 pp.

This book contains twelve powerful essays on various aspects of the genocide against the Mayan people. Various chapters include facts about the killing of children, and the ways in which they were killed.

The Commission for Historical Clarification (CEH). *Guatemala: Memory of Silence*, 4 Vols. Guatemala City, Guatemala: Author, 1999.

In June 1994, via the Accord of Oslo, the Commission for Historical Clarification (CEH) was established to investigate the human rights violations committed by both sides in the thirty-six-year civil war that ripped asunder the fabric of Guatemalan life, especially those Mayans living in the highlands. In the Prologue to the Commission's Report, the three Commission Members responsible for the study and the final report (the latter of which is entitled "Guatemala: Memory of Silence"), noted that their mandate was "to clarify with objectivity, equity and impartiality, the human rights violations and acts of violence connected with the armed confrontation that caused suffering among the Guatemalan people" (CEH, 1999, 1 of the Prologue). Commenting further, the Commissioners declared that "The main purpose of the Report is to place on record Guatemala's recent, bloody past. Although many are aware that Guatemala's armed confrontation caused death and destruction, the gravity of the abuses suffered repeatedly by its people has yet to become part of the national consciousness. The massacres that eliminated entire Mayan rural communities belong to the same reality as the persecution of the urban political opposition, trade union leaders, priests and catechists. These are neither perfidious allegations, nor figments of the imagination, but an authentic chapter in Guatemala's history" (1).

In carrying out its work, the Commission's mandate was also "to provide an answer to questions that continue to be asked in peacetime: . . . Why did the violence, especially that used by the State, affect civilians and particularly the Mayan people, whose women were considered to be the spoils of war and who bore the full brunt of the institutionalized violence? Why did defenceless children suffer acts of savagery? Why, using the name of God, was there an attempt to erase from the face of the earth the sons and daughters of Xmukane', the grandmother of life and natural creation? Why did these acts of outrageous brutality, which showed no respect for the most basic rules of humanitarian law, Christian ethics and the values of Mayan spirituality, take place?" (CEH, 1999, 1 of the Prologue).

The Commission "was not established to judge—that is the function of the courts of law—but rather to clarify the history of the events of more than three decades of fratricidal war" (CEH, 1999, 1 of the Prologue). Ultimately, the CEH's members received/heard the testimony of thousands of survivors, interviewed former high level government officials/leaders and military officers, viewed the exhumations of secret graves, and sought out and read thousands of pages of documentation by various nongovernmental organizations. The CEH issued its final report, the aforementioned *Guatemala: Memory of Silence*, in February 1999.

Esparza, Marcia. "Post-War Guatemala: Long-Term Effects of Psychological and Ideological Militarization of the K'iche Mayans." *Journal of Genocide Research* 7, no. 3 (2005): 377.

In this article, the author argues that "persisting militarization [in Guatemala] continues the genocidal destruction of indigenous people's traditional communal bonds by setting army loyalists against human rights workers and the left-oriented wing of the Catholic Church." In doing so, she identifies "three interrelated post-war outcomes of the polarization and militarization among the K'iche: (i) community conflicts arising from dehumanization of the 'other'; (ii) economic breakdown; and (iii) the spreading of a perception of the army as guardian and protector." The study involved extensive field work (including in-depth interviews with army collaborator) conducted in Guatemala from 1997 through 2000.

Gall, Norman. "Guatemalan Slaughter." *New York Review of Books*, May 20, 1971, 13–17.

In this early and significant essay on the mass murder of the indigenous people of Guatemala, Norman Gall writes as follows:

One of the most gruesome slaughters of this century in Latin America has been taking place in Guatemala during the past four years, and it has increased radically in recent months. This nation of ancient Mayan highland culture and rain-soaked hills and savannas is suffering a reign of terror that has claimed several hundred lives in the past few months alone, and thousands since it began in 1967, with US support, as a counterinsurgency operation to destroy a rapidly expanding guerrilla movement. Only rarely have the victims been members of the guerrilla bands, which are based primarily in the capital and in the dry, hungry hill country of the Guatemalan Oriente. More often the victims have been peasants, students, university professors, journalists, union leaders, and congressional deputies, who have been killed for vaguely leftist political associations or because of personal grudges.

. . . In Guatemala only a part of the killing of dissidents has been done by the government's official forces. In 1967 more than twenty right-wing paramilitary terrorist groups went into action with weapons supplied to the Guatemalan army under the US military aid program. The groups used names like the White Hand, the Purple Rose, the New Anti-Communist Organization, etc. They first circulated leaflets carrying the names and sometimes the photographs of their announced victims, whose corpses—and those of many others—were later found grotesquely mutilated: dead men with their eyes gouged out, their testicles in their mouths, without hands or tongues, and female cadavers with their breasts cut off.

In early 1967 a Guatemalan army source gave me an estimate of some 2,000 persons killed by vigilante groups in the Oriente, while other estimates for the 1967–68 period have run between 3,000 and 6,000. In May, 1967, Guatemala's Catholic bishops declared: "We cannot remain indifferent while entire towns are decimated, while each day leaves new widows and orphans who are victims of mysterious struggles and vendettas, while men are seized in their houses by unknown kidnappers and detained in unknown places or are vilely murdered, their bodies appearing later horribly disfigured and profaned." But the killing continues.

Higonnet, Etelle, ed. *The Hidden Genocide: Guatemala, 1981–1983*. New Brunswick, NJ: Transaction Publishers, 2009, 237 pp.

This is a highly informative book. What makes this book especially interesting, and informative is the inclusion of large swaths of English translations of sections of the "Genocide Argument" in the Final Report of the Guatemalan

Commission for Historical Clarification's *Memory of Silence.* Such sections include excerpts from first person accounts of attacks and massacres by the Guatemalan military, as well as objective facts concerning each of the latter. Not a few include information about the slaughter of Mayan children and babies.

Lykes, M. B. "Terror, Silencing and Children: International, Multidisciplinary Collaboration with Guatemalan Maya Communities." *Social Science & Medicine* 38, no. 4 (1994):543–52.

M.B. Lykes outlines various problems faced by the Mayan children caught up in the violent environments of war and state-sponsored terrorism, and discusses the development of a program (Creative Workshops for Children, an international, interdisciplinary program organized by mental health workers from Argentina, Guatemala, and United States) to address such concerns.

Lykes notes the following about this article:

> The inadequacies of psychological theory based on a medical model that sees trauma as an intrapsychic phenomenon and conceptualizes its effects in situations of war as post-traumatic stress are described and a reconceptualization of trauma as psychosocial is proposed. The accompanying need to address the "normal abnormality" of war and state-sponsored terror through a community-based group process is presented. The model incorporates drawing, story telling, collage and dramatization in a group process that seeks to create a space and time in which the child can express him or herself, communicate experiences to others, and discharge energy and emotion connected to previous traumatic experiences. The work draws on existing cultural traditions (e.g., oral story telling and dramatization) and resources (e.g., nature, plants) of indigenous communities. . . . Through participation in the creative workshop the child survivor enhances natural means for communication that will facilitate the expression of physical and mental tensions and the development of a capacity to construct an identity that is not exclusively subject to the dehumanizing and traumatizing reality of war. The strengths of this work and the limits of psychoassistance work within a context of war are enumerated and discussed.

Melville, M. B., and M. B. Lykes. "Guatemalan Indian Children and the Sociocultural Effects of Government-Sponsored Terrorism." *Social Science & Medicine* 34, no. 5 (1992): 533–48.

The authors comment as follows about this study:

> This research is intended to elucidate selected characteristics of the psychosocial trauma of civil war as experienced by Guatemalan Mayan children, to describe some of the sociocultural effects of civil war on the children's Mayan ethnic identity and to identify those factors that helped them to survive severe trauma and loss. Specifically, during the summer of 1988, 32 children in Guatemala and 36 exiled in Mexico, between the ages of 8 and 16, participated in research designed to compare the negative effects of civil war and the adaptive capabilities of children who have experienced the trauma of the loss of immediate

family members, the witnessing of violent crimes and the displacement from their homes. In addition to a semi-structure, open-ended interview and taped personal story/testimonies, several traditional psychological instruments were used to facilitate our understanding of the overall well-being of these children who have been affected by systematic violence. The long-term effects of this trauma cannot be fully anticipated, but the results suggest that these children suffer an abiding fear and face many uncertainties. The children in the orphanages in Guatemala have few expectations for the future and those in refugee camps in Mexico see a bleak future with few opportunities besides survival. The training and preparation of community mental health workers is a realistic possibility with positive effects for the psychic health of the children.

Montejo, Victor. *Voices from Exile: Violence and Survival in Modern Maya History.* Norman: Oklahoma University Press, 1999, 287 pp.

This book presents the story of one group of Mayas from the Kuchumatan highlands in Guatemala who fled into Mexico and sought refuge there from the violence at home. It includes short sections on the plight and fate of the children in the group: children during the counterinsurgency, in flight, and the return.

REMHI. *Guatemala: Never Again! (Guatemala: Nunca Mass) The Official Report of the Human Rights Office, Archdiocese of Guatemala.* Maryknoll, NY: Orbis Books, 1999, 323 pp.

Presented to the public on April 24, 1998, this report is a product of the Recovery of Historical Memory Project, which constitutes the Catholic Church-led effort to document the atrocities perpetrated during Guatemala's thirty-six-year civil war. The report is packed with eyewitness testimony that delineates the killings perpetrated against Guatemala's indigenous population (and especially the Mayans) by the military during Guatemala's thirty-six-year civil war.

It presents a vivid and harrowing picture of the horrific effects on the indigenous people of Guatemala. This book constitutes an edited version of the massive original report. Still, it includes powerful and significant testimony that provides the reader with a solid sense of the horrific violence, the fear people lived with on a daily basis, and the ramifications of such for the indigenous people.

While many of the sections address, in part, the plight and fate of the children, the following exclusively does so: Chapter 2. Destroying the Seed (Violence against Children, Children on the Run, The Militarization of Childhood, The Children of Violence, From Adoption to Abduction, The Will to Live). (*See,* also, the annotation of Oficina de Derechos Humanos del Arzobispado de Guatemala (1988). *Guatemala: Nunca Más.* Four Volumes. Guatemala City: Recuperacion de la Memoria Historica (REMHI).)

Two days after the public presentation of this report, on April 26th, Bishop Juan Gerardi, the director of the project, was assassinated.

Rich, Victoria. "Gender Violence in Guatemala." *Third World Resurgence No. 74.* October, 1996. Accessed at: www.twnside.org.sg/title/gender-cn.htm.

The facts in this report are so disturbing, and significant, for human rights and genocide scholars to be cognizant of, a large section of the report is being included herein. Victoria Rich argues that "in Guatemala, as elsewhere, it is most probable that gender specific violence was used as a calculated strategic part of the counter-insurgency military campaigns carried out across the country in the 1980s and, to a lesser degree, in the 1990s. Testimonies of survivors and forensic evidence from mass grave exhumations provide direct proof of this additional part of the history of Guatemala's repression."

Continuing, Rich says:

> While all instances of rape may be considered politically motivated, in Guatemala the overt political sanction transforms the act from an individual, deviant transgression into a normative act of social control executed on behalf of a collective goal. That goal in . . . Guatemala is the annihilation of the political opposition, through a counter-insurgency programme of psychological warfare. . . . Sexual violence was and is so prevalent and condoned that one study found that the overwhelming fear expressed by almost all Guatemalan women refugees in 1982 was the fear of being raped. One town official commented that with all the soldiers raping Mayan girls in combat zones in the highlands, "It would be difficult to find a girl of 11 to 15 who has not been raped. Even seven-year-old girls have been raped."

Rich asserts that "The area of Rabinal in the mountainous department of Baja Verapaz is a case study of counter-insurgency tactics that included different forms of gender violence against women and girls. In July of 1982, during the massacre of the villagers of Plan de Sanchez, young girls between aged 12–14 were separated off and raped before being executed. The Guatemala Forensic Anthropology Team—EAFG—found and exhumed their bodies about 40 metres away from the main mass graves where the majority of the 130 Maya-Achi members of the Plan de Sanchez community were buried."

"Survivor Juan Manuel recounts: The soldiers went from house to house and took all the people out and brought them to the house of my. . .sister. Once they had finished bringing the people here and putting them in my sister's house, somewhere between 3:00 and 5:00 in the afternoon, one of the soldiers asked permission from the Commander to choose the prettiest girls between the ages of 12 and 14 years old. They separated them from the group and took them just over there where they raped them. They repeatedly raped the girls. . . . Of the poor young girls that were separated off and raped, three survived, or rather, they were let go. What happened is that the soldiers that came here with the patrollers were from the community of Concul. The Patrollers knew the girls. The poor girls pleaded for the soldiers to do whatever they wanted, but not to kill them. That is why they left these poor girls alive. This is how we know about what happened. . . . One of my sisters-in-law was raped, and as soon as they grabbed my actual sister from her house, they raped her there in front of her house. Both of their bodies were dug out from the mass graves. In the village of Rio Negro, the soldiers and civil patrollers made the women march to the top of the mountain. They were forced to dance with the men who asked them, 'Is this how you danced with the guerrillas?' On the march up, pregnant women were given no rest. When they could not go on, the patrollers and soldiers hit them on the legs with heavy sticks, yelling, 'Come on, cows!'"

"Once they arrived at the top of the mountain, to a place known locally as Pacoxom Portezuelo, most of the young girls and women were raped before the patrollers and soldiers killed the 177 women and children. Survivor Ana describes [what took place]:

"The soldiers and the patrollers started grabbing girls and raping us. Only two soldiers raped me because my grandmother was there and she defended me. All the girls were raped. I am the only one who was raped that survived. They forced me to lie down and when it was over they took me to Xococ with them. When we were walking they told each other how many they had killed that day."

The Rabinal area is but one example of this type of violence in Guatemala's conflict. In a testimony given to Amnesty International, a 17-year-old Maya-Kekchi girl from the village of Chirrenquiche, department of Alta Verapaz, stated: "The soldiers came (on 7 April, 1982); we went to the mountains. . . where we hid. A group of soldiers came in behind us. . . . They slashed me with the machete; they raped me, they threw me on the ground and slashed my head with the machete, my breasts, my hand."

Sanford, Victoria. "From Genocide to Feminicide: Impunity and Human Rights in Twenty-First Century Guatemala." *Journal of Human Rights* 7, no. 2 (2008): 104–22.

At one point, Victoria Sanford writes:

"Genocide is a gendered atrocity because it has the intention to destroy a cultural group. This means the destruction of the material bases of the community as well as its reproductive capacity. In this way, women and girls are primary targets of genocide. In 1981, females (including adult women and girls) comprised 14 percent of massacre victims in Rabinal [a small town in Guatemala] (Sanford 2003a, 2003b). In June 1982, three months into Ríos Montt's dictatorship, females made up to 42 percent of massacre victims. In mid-1982, the number of women and girls killed rose so sharply that the comparative percentage of male victims actually dropped. This point of intersection represents the successful implementation of a change in Guatemalan army strategy that shifts from selective massacres of men to massive massacres of all men, women, and children. This shift, located in mid-1982, is three months after Ríos Montt came to power through military coup."

Stoll, David. *Between Two Armies in the Ixil Towns of Guatemala.* New York: Columbia University Press, 1993, 283 pp.

An important book that provides critical insights into how civilians (Mayan mothers, fathers, and children) were, against their will, inexorably pulled into the conflict between the rebels and government troops. David Stoll basically argues that the Ixils, who supported Guatemalan rebels in the early 1980s, "did so because they were caught in the crossfire between the guerillas and the army, not because revolutionary violence expressed community aspirations."

Tomuschat, Christian. "Clarification Commission in Guatemala." *Human Rights Quarterly* 23 (2001): 2233–58.

Herein, Christian Tomuschat (who served as the coordinator of the Commission) discusses the findings of the Guatemalan Commission for Historical Clarification (CEH). As he notes at the outset, "The CEH constituted a centerpiece within the comprehensive peace settlement that the Government of Guatemala and the URNG had finalized on 29 December 1996 by concluding the final Agreement on a Firm and Lasting Peace. Its establishment had already been decided more than two years earlier by virtue of the so-called Oslo Agreement of 23 June 1994. This Agreement provided that the CEH shall clarify the human rights violations and acts of violence committed during the armed confrontation that affected Guatemala for thirty-five years."

Welsh, Jim. "Children and Torture." *Lancet* 356, no. 9247 (2000): 2093.

The author examines international human rights violations against children across the globe. One of the cases he touches on is that of the children who were "disappeared" during the genocidal period in Guatemala.

Zur, Judith N. *Violent Memories: Mayan War Widows in Guatemala*. Boulder, CO: Westview Press, 1998, 352 pp.

Based on extensive fieldwork in the department of El Quiche, Guatemala, and written by an independent researcher based in London, this book is basically a study of the impact of political violence on a Maya Indian village between 1988 and 1990. Essentially, "it examines the processes of fragmentation and realignment in a community undergoing rapid and violent change and relates local, social, cultural, and psychological phenomena to the impact of the war on widows' lives." In doing so, the author "combines a narrative, life-history approach with anthropological analysis, emphasizing the way people talk about and explain the violence." Among the host of issues Judith Zur discusses are "the survival strategies of widows and their attempts to reconstruct their lives, both on a physical level and in terms of meaning."

7

The Plight of Children during and following the 1994 Rwandan Genocide

Amanda Grzyb

From April to July 1994, the extremist Hutu government of Rwanda—with the aid of the Rwandan army, the Interahamwe militia, and "ordinary" Hutu civilians—massacred 500,000 to 1,000,000 Tutsi civilians and thousands of politically moderate Hutu in one hundred days. Babies, children, and youth were deliberately targeted by the genocidaires, lest they should grow into adulthood and produce another generation of Tutsis (Geltman and Stover 1997; Des Forges 1999; Straus 2006). Children were not only victims but some children and youth also participated in the genocide as perpetrators, and some were soldiers in the Uganda-based Rwandan Patriotic Front (RPF) rebel army (Des Forges 1999; Caplan 2000). This chapter focuses on the plight of children during and after the genocide, including the longer-term psychological, social, and educational consequences on child survivors and orphaned/separated children, and the role of children and youth in the reconstruction and reconciliation processes in post-genocide Rwanda.

Background

The 1994 Rwandan Genocide was swift, brutal, well-organized, and as suggested by most scholars, highly preventable (Des Forges 1999; Caplan 2000; Melvern 2000). With deep roots in the discriminatory ideologies of its former Belgian colonial ruler and the establishment by the Belgians of fixed Hutu/Tutsi/Twa ethno-racial identities marked by racial identity cards, the genocide was preceded by the growth of a "Hutu power" movement, the expulsion of Tutsis in 1959, and a series of isolated massacres targeting Tutsi civilians. The genocide was supported by vitriolic anti-Tutsi propaganda, which was broadcast on Radio Télévision Libre des Mille Collines (RTLM) and published in the *Kangura* magazine for months prior to the first massacres (Des Forges 1999; Mamdani 2001). The orchestrators of the genocide also imported machetes and other weapons into the country in enormous quantities in preparation for the large-scale killing.

The genocide began on the evening of April 6, 1994, only hours after a missile hit the Rwandan presidential plane, killing the Rwandan President Juvénal Habyarimana and the Burundian President Cyprien Ntaryamira, as they returned to Kigali following a meeting dealing with the Arusha Accords. The violence quickly spread from Kigali into the countryside, eventually enveloping the entire country. Tutsi victims often took refuge in schools or churches in such places as Ntarama, Nyamata, Nyange, and Nyarabuye, where they were massacred in massive numbers with artillery, machetes, and clubs, sometimes at the hands of their own neighbors. In addition to assassinating the politically moderate Hutu, the genocidaires also killed ten Belgian soldiers in an effort to destabilize the United Nations Assistance Mission for Rwanda (UNAMIR), a Chapter 6 mission under the command of Canadian Lieutenant-General Roméo Dallaire. UNAMIR arrived in Rwanda in 1993 with a mandate to observe the peace process between the Rwandan government and the RPF, which had come to a ceasefire agreement in 1993 after years of civil war. In the aftermath of the soldiers' deaths, Belgium withdrew its UNAMIR troops and the United Nations Security Council—of which Rwanda was a rotating member at the time—stripped down the mission to a small group of underfunded, ill-equipped soldiers without a mandate to protect civilians. With their hands tied, the UNAMIR personnel could do little but stand by and watch the genocide unfold. Members of the international community made significant efforts to remove their foreign nationals from Rwanda, but they failed to intervene and stop the genocide and offered no protection or assistance to the Tutsi men, women, and children who were in imminent danger.

Children as Victims

Gerald Caplan (2000) dedicates a special chapter to the fate of women and children in his Organization of African Unity (OAU) report, *Rwanda: The Preventable Genocide*, noting the traditionally central position of children in Rwandan culture. He writes, "According to custom, children were supposed to enjoy love, care, and the protection of family and the community. The genocide turned these values completely upside down" (section 16.54). Attacking children was, in fact, a deliberate strategy by the genocidaires to destabilize and destroy both the current and future Tutsi population of Rwanda (Des Forges 1999; Caplan 2000; Straus 2006). Paul Geltman and Eric Stover (1997) suggest that children were "particularly vulnerable" to death, maiming, and rape during the genocide (290). Thousands of children were killed, and perpetrators deliberately targeted churches, schools, orphanages, and children's homes. In their book (*Shake Hands with the Devil: The Failure of Humanity in Rwanda*) about the genocide, General Roméo Dallaire sand Major Brent Beardsley (2003), the commander of UNAMIR and his personal staff officer, respectively, describe a horrific scene in the vicinity of Gikondo Parish Church, where UNAMIR soldiers witnessed "an entire alleyway littered with the bodies of women and children," a baby that "tried to feed on the breast of its dead mother," and a pregnant woman who was "disemboweled and her fetus severed" (279–80).

In many cases, the perpetrators specifically targeted babies and children because as Caplan suggests, they "had to be wiped out before they grew into subversive adults" (section 16.1). Mahmood Mamdani (2001) writes that massacres "came to be referred to as *umuganda* (communal work), chopping up men as 'bush clearing,' and slaughtering women and children as 'pulling out the bad weeds'" (194). Children were most often killed with clubs and machetes, as opposed to the artillery or firearms used to kill young adults (Verwimp 2006). In some regions, children were spared in the first wave of massacres, but the killers returned for them a month later. Alison Des Forges (1999) describes a "mid-May slaughter" when the "women and children who had survived the first weeks of the genocide were slain." She reports that many perpetrators justified the massacre of children "by repeating a phrase about Kagame or Rwigema (the latter of whom was the original RPF commander who led the 1990 invasion but was replaced by Kagame when he died from a gunshot wound on the second day of fighting against the Habyarimana regime) having once been a baby, too" (Des Forges 1999). Scott Straus (2006) found similar justifications during post-genocide interviews with accused perpetrators, who claimed that "Kagame had left as a child," "children and women would reproduce," they could "claim the goods that had been looted," and they supported male victims by bringing "food to those who were hiding" (162–63)

Children as Perpetrators

The youth participated in the genocide as members of the Rwandan army or the Interahamwe militia. Some also joined in the killing with their families or were ordered to kill Tutsis by adults they respected or under threat of death (Geltman and Stover 1997; Caplan 2000, section 61.71). Unemployment and landlessness, frustrations about past RPF invasions, and the propagation of the anti-Tutsi ideology communicated via popular media encouraged high levels of participation in the massacres among the general Hutu population. The proliferation of perpetrators meant that the prison population in Rwanda expanded exponentially after the genocide, creating a secondary humanitarian crisis. Geltman and Stover (1997) reported in the *Journal of the American Medical Association* that more than 1,000 of the 85,000 Rwandan prisoners were minors, including 318 children under six years of age (290). In 1998, the number of children in prison rose to 3,000, although some were not convicted criminals but rather lived in the prisons with their parents, who were alleged to have taken part in the killing (Caplan 2000, 16.69). In recent years, the Rwandan government has made efforts to move children from adult prisons to rehabilitation centers, where they are educated and reintegrated back into their communities with varying degrees of success.

Orphans, Separated Children, and Youth Heads of Household

In the immediate aftermath of the genocide, there were, in toto, as many as 500,000 orphaned and separated children inside Rwanda and in refugee camps in Zaire, Burundi, and Tanzania (Geltman and Stover 1997; Caplan 2000). Children and parents who initially became separated while fleeing violence often experienced prolonged separation in the chaotic aftermath of the genocide. Ten years after the genocide, there were approximately 300,000 orphans in Rwanda, which was the result of parental deaths in the genocide, parental imprisonment as genocide perpetrators, and parental deaths from HIV/AIDS (Rose 2005). These children generally suffered extreme traumatization, and a high proportion of them continue to suffer from posttraumatic stress disorder (PTSD), anxiety, and depression (Betancourt et al. 2011). In one study of orphans in Kigali, Susanne Schaal and Thomas

Elbert (2006) found that 97 percent had seen dead bodies, 88 percent had been victims of attacks during the genocide, and 41 percent had witnessed the deaths of their own parents.

While some children were reunited with a surviving parent or another close relative after a period of separation, many were housed in children's homes, in orphanages, or with foster families. Immediately following the genocide, additional children's homes were opened across Rwanda and inside or adjacent to the refugee camps in neighboring countries. Widows who had lost their own children in the genocide often cared for ten or more orphans in these homes but lacked formal training, supplies, and psychological support (Geltman and Stover 1997; Caplan 2000). Children who were reunited with relatives or taken in by foster families found that their domestic situations were complicated by poverty, stress, and trauma, and a significant proportion of fostered or reunified children ran away from home or chose to live with peers or young siblings (Ledward and Mann 2000). Likewise, many children in their early teens living in the refugee camps married other children; although these unions usually didn't last long, adult Rwandans living in the refugee camps identified the issue of child marriages as a significant social problem (Smedt 1998), often leaving girls abandoned and bereft.

In many cases, children and youth took on the responsibility of leading youth-headed households (YHHs), caring for younger siblings, cousins, or unrelated children. Four years after the genocide, as many as 300,000 children were living in YHHs (Schaal and Elbert 2006). Youth heads of household were often socially isolated and encountered significant barriers to community support and education (Ledward and Mann 2000; Boris et al. 2006; Thurman et al. 2008; Boris, Thurman, Snider, Spencer & Brown, 2006; Ledward & Mann, 2000). They exhibited high rates of depression (Boris et al. 2006), engaged in risky sexual activity (Ntaganira et al. Hass, Hosner, Brown & Mock, 2012), and were vulnerable to sexual and labor exploitation by adults (Geltman and Stover 1997). Children living in the care of a youth head of household generally experienced poorer health and less access to education than their peers who are parented by adults (Boris et al. 2006). Food security and economic stability were fleeting for the members of YHHs. In Gikongoro, for example, 77 percent of youth heads of household were subsistence farmers and survived on only one meal a day (Boris et al. 2006).

Psychological Consequences

The genocide wrought unfathomable psychological trauma for individual survivors, but it also produced a deep collective wound for the entire Rwandan nation. With blood on the hands of so many Rwandans and more than 500 memorial sites dotted across the country, the recollection of the genocide is always present.

A study of children conducted thirteen months after the genocide determined that children had experienced particularly high exposures to violence during the genocide, and that 15 percent of the 3,030 children interviewed had to hide under dead bodies to survive (Dyregrov et al. 2000). Many girls were not only survivors of genocide but also survivors of rape (Nagarajan 2012). In some cases, genocidal rape resulted in HIV infection, chronic physical injuries, and thousands of pregnancies that bore thousands of "children of bad memories" or "little Interahamwe" (Nagarajan 2012, 115). Many child survivors also suffer from prolonged grief disorder, a condition related to depression, anxiety, and PTSD, which are also widespread in the population (Dyregrov et al. 2000). Studies show higher rates of PTSD and depression in youth-headed households than in orphanages or children's homes (Dyregrov et al. 2000; Boris et al. 2012; Schaal and Elbert 2012), even in cases where the latter had experienced more trauma. While Rwandans clearly suffer from psychological damage, some scholars, physicians, and therapists question the rationale for providing care using a Western model and Western definitions (Betancourt et al. 2011). They suggest that traumatized children need "community-based care" (Thurman et al. 2008) and can continue to heal through local initiatives dealing with memory, testimony, justice, and reconciliation.

Social Consequences

The genocide had a profound and lasting impact on community cohesion and social supports, affecting almost every aspect of Rwandan children's basic security: economic stability, access to food, physical health and access to medical care, psychological needs, connectedness to family, safe housing, and education (Betancourt et al. 2012). Combined with high rates of HIV and AIDS, the genocide has had "devastating consequences for families" and the basic needs of children (Betancourt et al. 2011). Under-five mortality was predictably high in 1994, but there was another peak in 1998 related to post-genocide social instability, a lack of doctors and medical infrastructure, and a drought in the eastern part of the country (Gakusi and Garenne 2007).

Many Rwandan children continue to feel marginalized, owing to their traumatic experiences in 1994 and their post-genocide struggles with poverty, HIV, and social exclusion. Timothy Williams, Agnes Binagwaho, and Theresa Betancourt (2012) report that many children, mostly girls, have resorted to transactional sex "as a survival strategy in response to situations of adversity including economic deprivation, difficulty accessing school, and social pressure" (354). Likewise, Rwanda has a significant population of street children, and there are as many as 6,000 homeless children in Kigali. Veale and Dona (2003) found that street children were mostly boys, and a large number were orphans who lost one or both parents during the genocide. On the other hand, children who own land are often cheated out of their inheritance by guardians or community members who refuse to honor Rwandan laws respecting children's land rights (Rose 2005).

In his book-length study of youth in post-genocide Rwanda, *Stuck*, Marc Sommers (2012) examines the longer-term consequences of genocide and poverty, particularly among children and youth. He finds that poverty, overpopulation, and government restrictions about house construction have put limits on young people's ability to transition from youth to adults. Without steady work in Kigali or the ability to build a house in rural Rwanda, young men cannot marry and start a family. The gap for boys also affects the development of girls, who rely on their male counterparts to meet the requirements for adulthood. Sommers refers to the current generation of youth and young adults as "stuck" between childhood and adulthood.

Education in Post-Genocide Rwanda

Another serious social consequence of the genocide was the near complete destruction of the educational infrastructure in Rwanda (Hirano et al. 2011, 31). Seventy-five percent of Rwandan teachers were either killed during the genocide or imprisoned shortly after, leaving the education system bereft of its backbone and producing a chronic shortage of educational staff (Hodgkin 2006, 200). While the country strives to meet medium-term educational goals with an eye toward the development of a knowledge-based economy, the education sector "faces many challenges and needs, such as increasing adequate teacher training, improving girls' education, improving special needs education, and developing science, technology, and infrastructure" (Hirano et al. 2011).

Of particular note is the failure of the education sector to develop a new post-genocide history curriculum (King 2005; Freedman et al. 2011). The history textbooks that once instructed students in the ideologies of "ethnic divisions" between Hutu and Tutsi were understandably discarded after the genocide, and there were no immediate resources to replace them (King 2005; Hodgkin 2006). Without a new history curriculum, new history textbooks, or teachers trained to deal with "politically sensitive material," the subject of history "has not been taught in Rwanda's schools since the genocide" (King 2005, 912). Some scholars worry that the exclusion of history instruction—along with the exclusion of open discussions about the colonial construction of historical ethnic differences and the tensions that led to the genocide—are ultimately detrimental to the country's reconciliation process.

Conclusion: Reconstruction, Reconciliation, and Hope

More than eighteen years have passed since the genocide, meaning that every Rwandan who was alive in 1994 is now an adult. Young survivors, orphans, and separated children have grown, but the legacy of the genocide and its aftermath continue to impact the current population of children and youth from social structures to education to second-generation-survivor trauma. The Rwandan government has made many strides in its approach to fulfilling the needs of children and youth, including the Ministry of Family and Gender Promotion's "Strategic Plan for Orphans and Other Vulnerable Children, 2007–2011" and the Ministry of Education's 2011 "Early Childhood Development Policy." As the reconstruction of post-genocide Rwanda continues apace and the country brings genocide perpetrators to justice through international tribunals and national courts of countries other than Rwanda, children also have feelings of resilience (Pells 2011), hope, and reconciliation in the midst of deep trauma and grief. Children may bear the scars of Rwanda's genocide, but they are also the country's hope for the future.

Annotated Bibliography

Betancourt, T. S., J. E. Rubin-Smith, W. R. Beardslee, S. N. Stulac, I. Fayida, and S. Safren. "Understanding Locally, Culturally, and Contextually Relevant Mental Health Problems among Rwandan Children and Adolescents Affected by HIV/AIDS." *Aids Care* 23, no. 4 (2011): 401–12.

    The authors suggest that using mental health measures developed in other settings, particularly Western models, may not provide appropriate measures for mental health problems in Sub-Saharan Africa. Using Rwanda as a case study, this study focuses on local Rwandan perceptions of mental health syndromes and suggests that these local measures must be consulted when developing assessments or planning interventions for Rwandan children and adolescents affected by HIV/AIDS.

Betancourt, T. S., T. P. Williams, S. E. Kellner, J. Gebre-Medhin, K. Hann, and Y. Kayiteshonga. "Interrelatedness of Child Health, Protection, and Well-Being: An Application of the SAFE Model in Rwanda." *Social Science and Medicine* 74 (2012): 1504–11.

On the basis of fifteen focus groups with adults, seven focus groups with children aged ten to seventeen, and interviews with child-protection stakeholders, the authors identify components of child security and well-being with the goal of better attending to issues of child protection in Rwanda. The results identified three important themes: deterioration of community after the genocide, poverty, and caregiver illness and death. The authors suggest that child security is integrally tied to other basic security needs, and any approach to improving child security should recognize this interrelatedness.

Boris, N., L. Brown, T. Thurman, J. Rice, L. Snider, J. Ntaganira, and L. Nyira-zinyoye. "Depressive Symptoms in Youth Heads of Household in Rwanda: Correlates and Implications for Intervention." *Archives of Pediatrics and Adolescent Medicine*, September 162, no. 9 (2008): 836–43.

In this article, the authors examine the level of depressive symptoms and their predictors in 539 youth heads of household (twenty-four years old or younger) in four adjoining districts in Gikongoro, Rwanda. They found that 77 percent were subsistence farmers, few attended school longer than six years, half only ate one meal a day in the last week, and 80 percent rated their own health as fair or poor. They found that orphaned youth who function as heads of households in rural western Rwanda have high rates of depressive symptoms. Beyond efforts to improve food security and household assets, the authors conclude that it may be necessary to reduce social isolation and depression.

Boris, N., T. Thurman, L. Snider, E. Spencer, and L. Brown. "Infants and Young Children Living in Youth-Headed Households in Rwanda: Implications of Emerging Data." *Infant Mental Health Journal* 27, no. 6 (2006): 584–602.

The authors examine the social trend of households headed by Rwandan youth, aged 13–24, in the aftermath of the genocide and the HIV/AIDS pandemic. Prior to this study, there were no studies looking at the health and socioemotional functioning of children who are five and younger in youth-headed households (YHHs). The authors conducted a study of YHHs with at least one child under age five and found that a majority of young children in YHHs are in fair or poor health. The youth heading the households had high levels of depressive symptoms and this correlated with higher rates of emotional distress among the young children in their care.

Buckley-Zistel, S. "Nation, Narration Unification? The Politics of History Teaching after the Rwandan Genocide." *Journal of Genocide Research* 11, no. 1 (2009): 31–53.

This article examines the way history is taught in post-genocide Rwanda under the auspices of the Rwandan government's goals of national unity and reconciliation. The author argues that the interpretation of Rwandan history that excludes the narrative of ethnic identity or ethnic strife, combined with government censorship and the scars of the genocide, contribute to continued "division and resentment" in the Rwandan population. This article explores both education of children in schools and *ingandos* (education camps) for released prisoners charged as genocidaires.

Caplan, G. "Chapter 16: The Plight of Women and Children." In *Rwanda: The Preventable Genocide*. Organization of African Unity (OAU), 2000, 145–63. Available at: http://www.africa-union.org/official_documents/reports/report_rowanda_genocide.pdf.

Written by Canadian independent scholar, Gerald Caplan, this 2000 OAU report about the 1994 Rwandan genocide cites documents by UNICEF, the UNDP, the UN, World Vision, the World Bank, the Government of Rwanda, and the Coalition to Stop the Use of Child Soldiers. In a chapter dedicated to the fate of women and children during the genocide, Caplan explains that women and children are often the forgotten victims of war and genocide. He outlines the important role of children in traditional Rwandan society; and provides examples of anti-Tutsi propaganda (such as the notorious "Hutu Ten Commandments") targeting Tutsi girls and women (for example: 1. "Each Hutu man must know that the Tutsi woman, no matter whom, works in solidarity with her Tutsi ethnicity. In consequence, every Hutu man is a traitor who marries a Tutsi woman, who makes a Tutsi woman his concubine, who makes a Tutsi woman his secretary or protegee" and 2. "Every Hutu man must know that our Hutu girls are more dignified and more conscientious in their roles as woman, wife, and mother"); the staggering number of children killed, orphaned, and separated from their families in the genocide; the psychosocial trauma and acute anxiety experienced by children who witnessed acts of violence during the genocide; the plight of child-headed households and street children; child perpetrators, children in detention, and rehabilitation programs; child soldiers; and the state of schools and educational programs in post-genocide Rwanda.

Dallaire, R., and B. Beardsley. *Shake Hands with the Devil: The Failure of Humanity in Rwanda*. Toronto: Random House Canada, 2003, 592.

In their memoir about commanding the United Nations Assistance Mission in Rwanda (UNAMIR), Lieutenant-General (Ret.) Romeo Dallaire and Major (Ret.) Brent Beardsley describe the genocide from their eye-witness perspective. The authors provide graphic descriptions of acts of genocide they witnessed, including the massacre of infants, children, and pregnant women.

Des Forges, A. *Leave None to Tell the Story: Genocide in Rwanda*. New York: Human Rights Watch, 1999, 789.

In her seminal and authoritative account of the genocide, Alison Des Forges cites multiple stories about the massacre of children in Tutsi families and groups of Tutsi orphans. In a section entitled "Mid-May Slaughter: Women and Children as Victims," Des Forges reports that women and children who were spared during the initial killings in April and early May were specifically targeted by the genocidaires in mid-May as part of the "final phase" of the genocide. She also cites cases of the "popular participation" of child perpetrators and the participation of Tutsi children (along with women and the elderly) in resistance against the genocidaires in the hilltops of southern and western Rwanda.

Donovan, P. "Rape and HIV/AIDS in Rwanda." *The Lancet Supplement* 360 (2002): s17–s18.

Paula Donovan provides an overview of the convergence of HIV/AIDS in Rwanda, and the rape of women and girls during the 1994 genocide. She posits that the perpetrators used deliberate HIV infection as a tool for genocidal violence. She mentions the 2,000–2,500 babies born to women who were raped, and notes that every Tutsi woman who survived the genocide either experienced or witnessed sexual violence. She suggests that we must recognize the prevalence of rape in war and genocide and employ legal mechanisms to punish perpetrators who raped women and children.

Dyregrov, A., L. Gupta, R. Gjestad, and E. Mukanoheli. "Trauma Exposure and Psychological Reactions Among Rwandan Children." *Journal of Traumatic Stress* 13, no. 1, (2000): 3–21.

Thirteen months after the genocide, the authors interviewed 3,030 children aged eight to nineteen about their experiences during the genocide. They found that more than two-thirds of the children witnessed killing, 78 percent lost an immediate family member, 90 percent believed they might die during the genocide, and most had to hide in order to survive almost certain death (16 percent of the children interviewed hid under dead bodies of genocide victims). The authors conclude that a majority of Rwandan children experience "high levels of distress," including daily intrusions, avoidance reactions, and other posttraumatic issues.

Englehard, F. "Child Health in Rwanda." *The Lancet* 346, no. 8977 (1995): 777.

In a letter to *The Lancet*, physician Frank Engelhard summarizes the results of a study of child health at Remera Hospital, in Remera, the South Province in Rwanda, in February–March 1995. Engelhard reports that 30.5 percent of the children were too small or too light for their age, with 4.1 percent of the children suffering from wasting (severe malnutrition).

Freedman, S. W., H. M. Weinstein, K. L. Murphy, and T. Longman. "Teaching History in Post-Genocide Rwanda." In *Remaking Rwanda: State Building and Human Rights after Mass Violence*, edited by S. Straus, and L. Waldorf, 297–315. Madison: University of Wisconsin Press, 2011.

In this chapter, the authors examine the history curriculum in Rwandan secondary schools and the development of a new collective national identity in a post-genocide context. In particular, they cite the tensions between the government's official historical narrative, curricular reform, and democratic teaching styles. They conclude that there are significant barriers—the inability to discuss ethnicity, the government's "distortion of historical fact," constraints that do not allow teachers to encourage critical thinking, and the pervasive "fear of productive conflict"—that prevent significant forms of curricular reform.

Gakusi, A.-E., and M. Garenne. "Socio-Political and Economic Context of Child Survival in Rwanda over the 1950–2000 Period." *European Journal of Development Research* 19, no. 3 (2007): 412–32.

This paper surveys the history of under-five mortality in Rwanda from 1950 to 2000, examining periods of declining and increasing rates of child deaths in relation to sociopolitical and economic factors. The authors suggest that increases in child mortality were related to independence from the Belgian rule, the departure of Belgian expatriates, international isolation, declining international aid, Tutsi exile, and possibly the departure of herders and cattle following Hutu-Tutsi conflicts between 1959 and 1966. Peaks in under-five mortality in 1994 and 1998 were related to the genocide and its aftermath.

Geltman, P., and E. Stover. "Genocide and the Plight of Children in Rwanda." *Journal of the American Medical Association* 277, no. 4 (1997): 289–94.

Paul Geltman and Eric Stover report on three visits to Rwanda between August 1994 and February 1996 under the auspices of Medecins du Monde and Physicians for Human Rights to examine the scope of the genocide and its impact on children and to assess how Rwanda's medical and social services were responding to the needs of traumatized children. They suggest that children were particularly vulnerable during the genocide and were often the target of slaughter and rape, and that some were forced to participate as perpetrators of violence. Child survivors were often traumatized by witnessing violence, losing family members, or suffering from malnutrition and diseases in refugee and internally displaced people (IDP) camps. They also cite deep concerns about psychological trauma, the problem of family reunification, and the effect of orphanages and group care facilities on orphaned and displaced children. They conclude that more must be done to understand the impact of genocide and displacement on children, and what sorts of culturally appropriate social services and education programs will help Rwandan children recover.

Hilker, L. M. "Young Rwandans' Narratives of the Past (and Present)." In *Remaking Rwanda: State Building and Human Rights after Mass Violence*, edited by S. Straus, and L. Waldorf, 316–30. Madison: University of Wisconsin Press, 2011.

This chapter examines the differences between the government's official account of history in the public sphere and the unofficial narratives about the past that circulate amongst ordinary Rwandans in the private sphere. On the basis of field interviews with young people in 2004–2005, Lyndsay Hilker optimistically concludes that there is a diversity of understanding about Rwandan history and ethnicity, and that there should be more efforts to permit an environment of open, critical debate.

Hirano, S., E. Kayumba, A. Grafweg, and I. Kelman. "Developing Rwanda's Schools Infrastructure Standards and Guidelines." *International Journal of Disaster Resilience in the Built Environment* 2, no. 1 (2011): 30–46.

The authors outline the field experiences and knowledge of the people who created the "new national school infrastructure standards and guidelines for Rwanda." The authors offer a positive assessment of Rwanda's progress in education standards and infrastructure despite a history of genocide, underdevelopment, and a lack of resources, and suggest that the Rwanda case study can provide a useful example for other countries grappling with the development of national education programs. While the authors laud the government for improving educational standards, they do not address the problems addressed by other authors regarding the lack of a history curriculum or the inability to productively discuss the history of ethnic identities and ethnic divisions that led to the genocide, among other issues/concerns.

Hodgkin, M. "Reconciliation in Rwanda: Education, History, and the State." *Journal of International Affairs* 60, no. 1 (2006): 199–210.

Marian Hodgkin discusses the difficult task of teaching history in post-genocide Rwanda, particularly when the historical narratives are in dispute. She explains that the Rwandan government has removed formal national history from the school curriculum, arguing that precolonial unity and reconciliation must be taught in place of a contested and divisive history. Hodgkin argues that regardless of the noble intent of the government's policy, the difficult moments in Rwandan history must be taught or risk creating "a new dynamics of social exclusion."

King, E. "Educating for Conflict or Peace: Challenges and Dilemmas in Post-Conflict Rwanda." *International Journal* 60, no. 4 (2005): 904–18.

This article explores the "relationship between education, ethnic conflict, and peacebuilding" in post-genocide Rwanda, suggesting that schools are important sites for the construction of ethnic conflict and the recovery from it. She explains the ways that history curriculum was historically manipulated depending on the group in power and the efforts of the RPF government to produce a single "Rwandan" identity in the post-genocide environment. King states that while the old education system could not be reinstated after 1994, it is notable that history has not been taught in Rwandan schools since the genocide. She concludes by suggesting that scholars must conduct additional research about "education's role in conflict and its possibilities for contributing to post-conflict peace building and conflict prevention."

Kritz, B. "International Legal Protection for Women and Female Children: Rwanda—A Case Study." *Suffolk Transnational Law Review* 33 (2010): 1–34.

Situating the case of Rwanda in the broader context of African military and civil conflict, Kritz addresses the "endemic victimization of African women and female children" and suggests a number of international legal reforms to offer them protection. Kritz examines historical factors related to the problems facing women and girls in Rwanda, international legal mechanisms available for improving protection for women and girls, and regional legal mechanisms that can also be used to provide better protection during times of conflict.

Ledward, A., and G. Mann. "The Best Interests of 'Separated' Children in Rwanda." *Cultural Survival Quarterly* 24, no. 2 (2000): 59–61.

The authors trace the plight of children in the aftermath of the 1994 Rwandan genocide and question the logic that only adults can be adequate caregivers for orphaned or separated children, either at children's centres or in foster families. The authors also cite evidence that a considerable number of children who have been reunited with their families chose to run away and live in other contexts. They conclude by suggesting that the 300,000 children living in 85,000 child-headed households often provide significant emotional and protective support for children recovering from the trauma of the genocide.

Lopez, H., and Q. Wodon. "The Economic Impact of Armed Conflict in Rwanda." *Journal of African Economies* 14, no. 4 (2005): 586–602.

In this article by researchers at the World Bank, the authors acknowledge the devastating impact of the genocide and the long road of healing ahead. They also laud Rwanda's current progress in terms of basic education and reducing child mortality. They conclude that the per capita GDP of Rwanda would be 25–30 percent higher if the genocide had not happened.

Mamdani, M. *When Victims Become Killers: Colonialism, Nativism, and the Genocide in Rwanda.* Princeton, NJ: Princeton University Press, 2001, 384.

Mahmood Mamdani offers a theoretical explanation of the 1994 genocide in Rwanda as a result of native/settler ideologies tied to the Belgian colonial rule. The genocide is, he claims, a "testimony to the crisis of citizenship in postcolonial Africa." In his descriptive overview of the genocide, Mamdani makes reference to women and children as a particular subset of victims.

Nagarajan, C. "An Appraisal of Rwanda's Response to Survivors Who Experienced Sexual Violence in 1994." *Wagadu* 10 (2012): 108–31.

Chitra Nagarajan writes about women who were raped during the Rwandan genocide, and who now experience trauma, shame, illness, and social exclusion in the aftermath of the genocide. She focuses, in particular, on women who contracted HIV, and the approximately 30,000 pregnancies (the "children of bad memories") that resulted from the genocidal rapes. She suggests that the government "has been slow to offer redress" and treatment for these women, who live with survivor guilt and often encounter neighbors who were perpetrators in every day life.

Ntaganira, J., L. Hass, S. Hosner, L. Brown, and N. Mock. "Sexual Risk Behaviors Among Youth Heads of Household in Gikongoro, South Province of Rwanda." *BMC Public Health* 12, no. 225 (2012): 1–13.

This article examines sexual behaviors among 692 Rwandan youth heads of household, aged 12–24, who were orphaned by genocide and AIDS. The study found that 41 percent of the youth became sexually active before age 15, and rates were higher for those youth who experienced less social connectedness and who used drugs. There was very little knowledge of the "ABC" prevention program implemented by the Rwandan government, and the youth viewed themselves as low risk for HIV infection.

Pells, K. "Building a Rwanda 'Fit for Children.'" In *Remaking Rwanda: State Building and Human Rights after Mass Violence*, edited by S. Straus, and L. Waldorf, 79–86. Madison: University of Wisconsin Press, 2011.

Kirrily Pells' chapter about post-genocide Rwanda posits childhood as a "political space" that is critical to the country's nation-building efforts and its "metanarrative of national rebirth." She suggests that Rwandan children reframe these narratives and indicate how government rhetoric intersects with lived experience. She uses two primary sources: the work of the Ministry of Gender and Promotion of Child and Family Rights and their annual National Summit for Children and Young People, and the results of Pells' focus groups on the everyday lives of children and youth.

Pells, K. "'Keep Going Despite Everything': Legacies of Genocide for Rwanda's Children and Youth." *International Journal of Sociology and Social Policy* 31, no. 9, (2011): 594–606.

Using focus groups and ethnographic research, Kirrily Pells combines studies of "the everyday" and social studies of childhood to understand the impact of the genocide on children and youth. Pells suggests that we should think beyond the dominant trauma paradigm in an effort to gain a more holistic understanding of how recovery, resiliency, post-genocide resources, and hope for the future impact children and youth in post-genocide Rwanda.

Perrier, F., and J. B. Nsengiyumva. "Active Science as a Contribution to the Trauma Recovery Process: Preliminary Indications with Orphans from the 1994 Genocide in Rwanda." *International Journal of Science Education* 25, no. 9 (2003): 1111–28.

In this article, Frédéric Perrier and Jean-Baptiste Nsengiyumva question the limitations of Western-oriented treatment programs, clinical interventions, and concepts of suffering and posttraumatic stress disorder in the post-genocide Rwandan cultural context. They suggest that one alternative approach to trauma could be "to apply constructivist science education methods" as a means of therapeutic practice. They present the results of a study at an Un-Accompanied Children Centre (UACC), where experimental science activities showed that children found pleasure in hands-on exploration, developing affective connections with the authors, and the sound expression of feelings, all of which could set the stage for psychiatric therapists to begin to do their work with the children.

Republic of Rwanda. *Early Childhood Development Policy. Ministry of Education.* Kigali, Rwanda: Author, 2011, 26.

This report by the Rwandan Ministry of Education focuses on early childhood development policies and programs, with a particular emphasis on children with economic disadvantages. The Early Childhood Development Policy supports a reduction in infant and maternal mortality, improved parent/guardian knowledge of child development, ensuring nurturing care for infants and toddlers of working mothers, ensuring that all children are ready to begin school at the proper age, addressing child malnutrition, a reduction in under-five mortality, a reduction in childhood diseases, and ensuring that child rights are respected.

Republic of Rwanda. *Strategic Plan for Orphans and Other Vulnerable Children. Minister in the Prime Minister's Office in Charge of Family and Gender Promotion.* Kigali, Rwanda: Author, 2007, 43.

This report focuses on the 1.26 million orphans and other vulnerable children in Rwanda who are affected by HIV/AIDS, the genocide, and poverty. The plan prioritizes local households and communities as the main providers of material and emotional support for orphans, thus decentralizing resources and services for those who need it. The report suggests that the plight of orphans and vulnerable children does not belong to one government ministry, but to all government sectors, nongovernmental organizations, civil society organizations, communities, the international community, and the children themselves.

Ron-Balsera, M. "Does the Human Capital Discourse Promote or Hinder the Right to Education? The Case of Girls, Orphans, and Vulnerable Children in Rwanda." *Journal of International Development* 23 (2011): 274–87.

Maria Ron-Balsera explores the status of post-genocide education in Rwanda through the theoretical lenses of human capital discourse, decommodification, and governmentality. Using government and civil society organization reports and interviews, she suggests that characterizing education as an "investment" tied to economic growth might conflict with the notion of education as a right. In particular, she focuses on how the education policy in Rwanda affects girls, orphans, and vulnerable children.

Rose, L. "Orphan's Land Rights in Post-War Rwanda: The Problem of Guardianship." *Development and Change* 36, no. 5 (2005): 911–36.

On the basis of field research between 1995 and 2004, Laurel Rose writes that the genocide and HIV/AIDS have produced a population of 300,000 orphans in Rwanda, some of whom head households of other children. This article explores the complications of guardianship and the problem of orphans' land rights. Rose focuses, in particular, on cases where orphans have attempted to deal with land rights independently, and suggests that the government should "re-examine their ideas about guardianship and grant orphans urgent attention as individuals and as a special interest group."

Schaal, S., J. P. Dusingizemungu, N. Jacob, F. Neuner, and T. Elbert. "Associations Between Prolonged Grief Disorder, Depression, Posttraumatic Stress Disorder, and Anxiety in Rwandan Genocide Survivors." *Death Studies* 36 (2012): 97–117.

The authors interviewed a total of 400 orphaned and widowed survivors of the genocide, and assessed the associations between prolonged grief disorder (PGD) and depression, anxiety, and PTSD. As in other similar studies, they found significant overlap between PGD and the other three diagnoses.

Schaal, S., and T. Elbert. "Ten Years after the Genocide: Trauma Confrontation and Posttraumatic Stress in Rwandan Adolescents." *Journal of Traumatic Stress* 19, no. 1 (2006): 95–105.

This article is based on interviews with sixty-eight Rwandan orphans living in orphanages or child-headed households about their experiences during the genocide and PTSD symptoms ten years after the genocide. The authors found that 41 percent had seen one of their parents murdered and all the children had witnessed intense violence. Of the sixty-eight orphans interviewed, 44 percent had PTSD; the prevalence was higher for children who were aged eight to thirteen during the genocide, and lower for those who were aged three to seven.

Sezibera, V., N. Van Broeck, and P. Philippot. "Intervening on Persistent Posttraumatic Stress Disorder: Rumination-Focused Cognitive and Behavioral Therapy in a Population of Young Survivors of the 1994 Genocide in Rwanda." *Journal of Cognitive Psychotherapy: An International Quarterly* 23, no. 2 (2009): 107–13.

This article reflects on the outcome of "brief rumination-focused cognitive and behavioral intervention in treating posttraumatic stress disorder (PTSD) symptoms" among adolescent (aged 15–18) survivors of the 1994 genocide. The authors obtained data eleven years after the genocide (as a baseline measure), thirteen years after the genocide (pretreatment), two weeks after treatment, and two months after the initial posttreatment visit. They found that PTSD symptoms rose in the two-year period between baseline and pretreatment, that the symptoms were reduced two weeks after treatment, and that these gains were maintained during the follow-up period. The authors conclude by suggesting that longer interventions in treatment may "decrease depressive symptoms in the present population."

De Smedt, J. "Child Marriages in Rwandan Refugee Camps." *Africa: Journal of the International African Institute* 68, no. 2 (1998): 211–37.

In this article, Johan de Smedt focuses on the phenomenon of child marriages of genocide survivors residing in Tanzanian refugee camps in the aftermath of the genocide, often between girls aged thirteen to fourteen and boys aged fourteen to fifteen. He observes that many of the marriages only lasted a few months and usually ended when the boys left the girls. The article focuses on the impact of civil war and genocide, the resulting poverty and displacement, and the way behavior and social structures can change radically in the aftermath.

Sommers, M. "In the Shadow of Genocide: Rwanda's Youth Challenge." In *Trouble-makers or Peacemakers: Youth and Post-Accord Peace Buildingm*, edited by S. McEvoy-Levy, 81–97, Notre Dame: University of Notre Dame Press, 2006.

Cognizant of the youth who filled the ranks of the *Interahamwe* militia during the genocide, Marc Sommers summarizes the results of interviews with rural Rwandan youth in a village in the then Byumba Province of northeastern Rwanda. In particular, he addresses the ways in which youth and women are marginalized and speculates about the "potential for renewed youth violence in Rwanda."

Sommers, M. *Stuck: Rwandan Youth and the Struggle for Adulthood.* Athens: University of Georgia Press, 2012, 288.

Sommers's book on ethnographic research in Rwanda explores the plight of urban and rural youth in post-genocide Rwanda, where poverty, over-population, and government restrictions on house construction have limited the ability of many youth to meet the cultural requirements of adulthood. Sommers focuses, in particular, on the Rwandan construction of masculinity and the ways in which both male and female youth get "stuck" at the margins between youth and adult identities. He also differentiates between rural and urban struggles, with rural males focused on earning enough money to buy a house and get married and urban males focused on making enough money for day-to-day sustenance and survival in Kigali, the capital of Rwanda.

Straus, S. *The Order of Genocide: Race, Power, and War in Rwanda.* Ithaca and London: Cornell University Press, 2006, 273.

Scott Straus' empirical study and analysis of the 1994 Rwandan genocide uses a combination of interviews and statistics to explore how and why the genocide happened. He focuses, in particular, on the "local dynamics" of the genocide and, through his interviews, asks perpetrators why Tutsi women and children were massacred.

Sydor, G., and Philippot, P. "Conséquences Psychologiques des Massacres de 1994 au Rwanda." *Santé Mental au Québec* 21, no. 1 (1996): 229–45.

French scholars Guy Sydor and Pierre Philippot present the results of a study of the psychological effects of massacres on unaccompanied Rwandan children, a small group of Belgians present during the genocide, and a group of soldiers and civilians present during the genocide. The study of children and adolescents between the ages of nine and seventeen found that 71 percent did not appear to have significant psychological problems, 18 percent suffered from posttraumatic stress disorder (PTSD), 6 percent suffered from PTSD and depression, and 5 percent suffered from depression.

Taton V., C. Nabongo, I. Chiejine, and A. Kamuragiye. "Investing in Rwanda: Effective Choices for Orphans and Girls in Primary Education." New York: UNICEF, Division of Policy and Planning Working Papers. 2007, 40.

This 2007 UNCIEF report reflects on the gaps left by the Rwandan government's Vision 2020, which includes a "Fee Free Education Policy" adopted in 2003. In particular, the report recognizes the need for school uniforms, materials, food, and child care, which present significant barriers for poor families. Focusing on orphaned children, the report recommends increased government subsidies, better resource management, cash transfers for families caring for orphans, improving policy implementation, and providing a head-start program to ensure affirmative action.

Thomas, K. J. A. "Family Contexts and Schooling Disruption Among Orphans in Post-Genocide Rwanda." *Population Research and Policy Review* 29 (2010): 819–42.

In this article, Kevin Thomas studies the relationship between post-genocide orphans and the disruption of study in school. Thomas finds that paternal orphans—those living with a single mother—have better educational outcomes than maternal orphans and non-orphans. Paternal orphans fare worse than non-orphans, and double-orphans living with non-related heads of household fare the worst.

Thurman, T., L. Snider, N. Boris, E. Kalisa, L. Nyirazinyoye, and L. Brown. "Barriers to the Community Support of Orphans and Vulnerable Youth in Rwanda." *Social Science & Medicine* 66 (2008): 1557–67.

This study explores the sociocultural factors and "community-level barriers to care for orphans and vulnerable youth in Rwanda." The authors examine data from a survey of young heads of household, a survey of adults who mentored the youth, and focus groups with both youth and adults in the communities. They suggest that three factors play a key role in orphan youth marginalization: poverty, cause of parental death, and "community perceptions of orphan behavior." They also find that international aid specifically targeting orphaned youth may, inadvertently, decrease the amount of support they get from the community and further marginalize them.

Totten, S. and Rafiki Ubaldo. *We Cannot Forget: Interviews with Survivors of the 1994 Genocide in Rwanda.* New Brunswick, NJ: Rutgers University Press, 2011. 205 pp.

A large number of the interviews herein are with individuals who were children during the period of the genocide. What the young people (now in their mid- to late-20's) witnessed, experienced and relate in their interviews is harrowing.

Veale, A., and D. Giorgia. "Street Children and Political Violence: A Socio-Demographic Analysis of Street Children in Rwanda." *Child Abuse & Neglect* 27 (2002): 253–69.

Angela Veale and Donà Giorgia used observational mapping, structured interviews, and focus groups to determine background, well-being, and street involvement of Rwandan street children with an aim of examining the links between street children and political violence, the causal factors of street children in Rwanda, and the "socio-cultural and political impact of the genocide." The authors found that the majority of street children were adolescent boys and 42 percent were homeless; contributing factors included the death of at least one parent, the imprisonment of parents, poverty, and issues of repatriation.

Verwimp, P. "Machetes and Firearms: The Organization of Massacres in Rwanda." *Journal of Peace Research* 43, no. 1 (2006): 5–22.

Philip Verwimp presents the results of a quantitative study about the use of machetes and firearms in the Kibuye Prefecture during the Rwandan genocide as a way of understanding the latter's structural organization. The data was based on the deaths of 59,050 victims and the information was collected between 1996 and 1999; of these victims, 13,955 were pupils in school and 8,925 were under the age of seven. The author found that that type of weapon depended on the location and scale of the massacres, the date the victim was killed, and his/her age. In particular, he found that children were much less likely to be killed by a modern weapon (firearm) than young adults.

De Walque, D. "Parental Education and Children's Schooling Outcomes: Evidence from Recomposed Families in Rwanda." *Economic Development and Cultural Change* 57, no. 4 (2009): 723–46.

In this article, Damien de Walque suggests that owing to the genocide and the prevalence of HIV/AIDS Rwanda has one of the highest rates of orphaned children in the world. His study assesses the school performance of orphaned children in relation to the educational levels of the adoptive parents. He finds that the education of the female adoptive parent has a "significant effect" on the education of the adopted child if that child is related to the members of the new household. He suggests that it is best for orphaned children to remain with relatives to transmit "human capital."

Williams, T. P., A. Binagwaho, and T. S. Betancourt. "Transactional Sex as a Form of Child Sexual Exploitation and Abuse in Rwanda: Implications for Child Security and Protection." *Child Abuse & Neglect* 36 (2012): 354–61.

On the basis of focus groups with thirty-nine adults and fifty-two children, this article describes transactional sexual exploitation and abuse of Rwandan children in an effort to motivate appropriate responses by government and local communities. The authors conclude that children—most of them girls—use transactional sex as a "survival strategy" in cases of poverty, lack of access to school, and "social pressure," and policies and programs should seek to secure these basic needs.

8

The Darfur Genocide: The Plight and Fate of the Black African Children

Samuel Totten

Introduction

It is a simple but profound fact that genocidaires do not discriminate when it comes to the age of their victims. Infants, young children and late adolescents are, more often than not, all targeted along with their parents and other adults in their group. This was certainly the case in regard to the youngest of the young through those in their late teens, at the height of the killing process during the Darfur genocide.[1]

This chapter examines the plight and fate of such young people in Darfur during the period of the genocide and, in doing so, addresses the following: an overview of the type and extent of violence that black African children were subjected to in Darfur; the rape of girls by the *Janjaweed* and Government of Sudan (GoS) soldiers; the abduction of children, after which they were forced to work as slaves; the use of boys as rebel fighters; and life in the internally displaced persons (IDPs) and refugee camps.

The State of Affairs

The Type and Extent of Violence against the Black African Children of Darfur

Just like the black African adults (primarily members of the Fur, Massalit, and Zaghawa tribes) in Darfur, the children were subjected to horrific treatment at the hands of Government of Sudan troops and the *Janjaweed*, the ethnic militia that fought alongside the GoS troops in Darfur. More specifically, the children were tortured, mutilated, raped (some as young as seven years old), and murdered.[2] Even infants, some only months old, were brutalized and killed. In an interview with the US government's Atrocities Documentation Team, a Masalit woman from West Darfur (near El Geneina), reported that "in February 2004 I saw GoS soldiers catch sixteen women with babies. They broke baby boys' necks in front of their mothers and beat mothers with their own babies like whips until the babies died" (Askin 2006, 146). Another Masalit woman "in West Darfur (near El Geneina) saw Arabs take eight male babies by their feet and slam them into the ground until they died; the Janjaweed told women being raped, 'We rape you to make a free baby, not a slave like you'" (Askin 2006, 147).

As a result of being forced out into hostile deserts and mountainous areas, away from water sources, adequate food, and medical care, untold numbers of children also perished due to severe dehydration, various diseases, wounds that were not attended to, and other horrific injuries, including those incurred from gang rape. Undoubtedly, many suffered trauma from what they experienced and/or witnessed.

And the suffering did not end once the children, either alone or with family members who survived, made it to internally displaced persons (IDPs) or refugee camps. In the early years of the genocide, the United Nations International Children's Emergency Fund (UNICEF) (2004) reported that:

> Thousands of children are dying every month from diseases that are usually preventable and easily treatable. These are the stark findings of a survey just completed by the World Health Organization and Sudan's Ministry of Health in North and West Darfur. Diarrhoea is linked to 75 per cent of deaths among children under the age of five. Fever, respiratory diseases and injuries inflicted during violent attacks on villagers are other major causes of death. Mortality rates in these areas far surpass the mark that aid agencies use to define a humanitarian crisis—which is one death per 10,000 people per day. In North Darfur, the rate is 1.4 deaths per 10,000 people per day, and in West Darfur it is 2.9. Children are succumbing to a deadly array of threats: Extreme overcrowding in camps for displaced people, shortage of clean water, inadequate latrines and appalling sanitary conditions in which rain-soaked mud mingles with human excreta. Many families have no shelter other than small, tarpaulin-covered huts which are highly vulnerable to the season's heavy rains and winds. (1)

In April 2008, as part of its action campaign, Amnesty International issued a report, *Dafur's Children of Conflict*, in which it stated,

"A generation of Darfuris is growing up in extreme fear and insecurity. Of the four million people affected by the conflict in Darfur, 1.8 million are children under 18" (1). Sadly, the only thing that has changed in the past five years is that the aforementioned children have gotten five years older, and more babies have been born.

To this day (late-2013), the young black Africans from Darfur still face what Amnesty International correctly refers to "an uncertain future," as they grow up and reside in either IDP or refugee camps. They are largely uneducated beyond elementary school and have few, if any, prospects for employment with which to support themselves, and family members (current or future).

Rape of Girls by the Janjaweed and GoS Soldiers

The rape of black African girls and women is well-documented (see, for example, Amnesty International 2004a; Human Rights Watch 2005; Kristoff 2005; Totten 2009, 2010). During the height of the genocide, girls as young as eight years old were raped by GoS soldiers. Scores of girls between eight and nineteen years of age were also gang raped (and continue to be). In a single event, some girls have reported being raped sixteen times (Polgreen 2005, 1). Many of the latter were impregnated and bore babies as a result of the rapes. In 2006, the Secretary General of the UN reported girls in Darfur "being attacked late at night and rendered unconscious through the use of neck piercing, strangulation and/or drugs before being raped. Many of these attacks are reportedly carried out by uniformed men" (UN Security Council 2006, 11).

Rape not only took place during the initial attacks on the black African villages by GoS soldiers and the *Janjaweed* but also up in the mountains and out in the deserts as the girls and their families and fellow villagers sought sanctuary in IDP or refugee camps. In IDP and refugee camps in Chad, girls and women have been raped as they searched for firewood and/or lugged water. Many have also been raped by members of rebel groups and male citizens of Chad.

The gang rapes of the girls (and women) in the early to mid years of the Darfur crisis, which was systematic and widespread across the three states of Darfur, often involved more than ten to twenty men. When the men were through brutalizing the girls, they left them in the desert to their own devices. Not a few ended up with horrific injuries and/or were killed in the process.

During the course of the sexual attacks, various black African girls were subjected to piercing racial epithets. Still, others were told by the rapists that their, i.e., the rapists', intent was to make Arab babies.

In an article entitled "A Policy of Rape," a Pulitzer-Prize winning columnist for the *New York Times*, Nicholas Kristof (2005) wrote, "All countries have rapes, of course. But here in the refugee shantytowns of Darfur, the horrific stories that young women whisper are not of random criminality but of a systematic campaign of rape to terrorize civilians and drive them from 'Arab lands'—a policy of rape" (n.p.).

Continuing, Kristof (2005) reported, "The attacks are sometimes purely about humiliation. Some women[3] are raped with sticks that tear apart their insides, leaving them constantly trickling urine. One Sudanese woman working for a European aid organization was raped with a bayonet" (1).

Each and every account of the rape of young children and adolescent girls is horrific. The following statement, which was told to Human Rights Watch researchers in a displaced persons camp in South Darfur in February 2005, speaks to and typifies the brutality to which many girls have been subjected to over the years at the hands of the GoS military forces and their *Janjaweed* allies. The words are those of a sixteen-year-old girl who was raped while enroute from her village to Nyala, the capital of South Darfur:

> [I was with] a group of girls traveling from our village to Nyala. . . . Some of us were traveling on donkeys and others were walking. Suddenly the *Janjaweed* attacked us; they took our money and our donkeys. The majority [of the girls] managed to escape; me, my cousin and my sister were captured. They took all our *topes* and veils, they left us only with our dresses. We were screaming. I was taken with my younger cousin to the woods; I don't know where they took my sister. One of them forced me on the ground and all the time I was resisting them. . . . All the time one of the Janjaweed kept his gun pointed at my head. They started raping me. I was bleeding heavily but could do nothing. It was so painful, but fear was even more than pain. Four of them raped me. (Human Rights Watch 2005, 6)

Nightmarishly, even prior to their birth the babies of black African girls and women were targets of GoS troops and the *Janjaweed*. As Amnesty International (2004a) noted: "The violence of the *Janjawid* extends beyond women and children to the most vulnerable of all: unborn children. But why? According to one witness: 'I was with another woman, Aziza, aged 18, who had her stomach slit on the night we were abducted. She was pregnant and was killed as they said: 'It is the child of an enemy.' (A woman of Irena ethnicity from the village of Gabrila)" (11). In another situation, in "western Darfur (near Beida) in June 2003, a Massalit man saw the *Janjaweed* cut out the stomachs of pregnant women. If the fetus was male, the *Janjaweed* hit the fetus against a tree; if female, the fetus was left in the dirt" (Askin 2006, 146). If allowed to live, the male fetuses were seen as future enemies that the GoS and Janjaweed might meet years later on the battlefield. Thus, male fetuses had to be destroyed.

Over and above the horrific dehumanization, brutality, and injuries to which they were subjected, young girls faced a host of other problems as a direct result of the sexual attacks and rape. One of the most disturbing is that many ended up being ostracized by their own families. Sexual contact of any kind, including rape, outside marriage is perceived as an unforgivable transgression against the family and rest of society. As a result, female rape victims are rejected and forced from their homes and villages by their neighbors and often by their very own family members (mothers, fathers, brothers, and sisters). In an article about a young girl who was raped, a journalist reported the following: ". . . in this traditional society, [girls who are raped] are marked for life. A young mum (Fatma, a fifteen year old black African girl from Darfur who was raped and impregnated and had the baby) tells how neighbors whisper about her. 'They say I'm a bad girl—that I had this *Janjaweed* baby. They say that I should be sent away,' she says. [An older woman] curses the child as if she were a bad omen. 'She is calling the baby 'a dirty girl,' says Unicef's Eman el-Tigani. 'Fatma has no future here'" (Matheson 2004, 1).

Being rejected by one's family and community is, obviously, emotionally devastating. But as Amnesty International (2004b) has pointed out, "When a woman is rejected by her community because of the shame of rape, she faces far more than stigma. Her community is her social support. It is the source of her survival and economic well-being. A woman without a family, without community, must fend for herself. She has no other support. So, beyond the torture of rape, beyond her own shame and her rejection by her community, she faces starvation and the starvation of her children" (n.p.).

Not all families, fortunately, expel their daughters and sisters, but life for the rape victims often remains nightmarish. For example, the mother of a sixteen-year-old girl who had been raped and whose family arranged a marriage with her cousin in order to protect her honor, commented as follows:

> My daughter screams at night. She is not happy as she used to be before, she cannot sit in one place; she is *mashautana* (possessed). She is always worried and in continuous movement, I never talk to her about what happened, although she knows that I know what happened to her. Of course she does: I cleaned her wounds after her return every day, but still, talking about it is very difficult. Her father became very ill since that time. He never goes out with the rest of the men and he does nothing but staying inside the room. I feel very bad about the whole situation but there is nothing we can do, God only can help us. Now my daughter is married to her cousin, but where is he? He does not communicate with her or with us. (Human Rights Watch 2005, 10)

Rape victims also face potential imprisonment and other punishments for having so-called "extramarital" affairs with their rapists. Indeed, many have not only been arrested but imprisoned and beaten for their "wayward ways" (Médecins Sans Frontières 2005, 6). One young woman who was raped, impregnated as a result of the rape, and then arrested for being raped reported the following:

> I am 16 years old. On day, in March 2004, I was collecting firewood for my family when three armed men on camels came and surrounded me. They held me down, tied my hands and raped me one after the other. When I arrived home, I told my family what happened. They threw me out of home and I had to build my own hut away from them. I was engaged to a man and I was so much looking forward to getting married. After I got raped, he did not want to marry me and broke off the engagement because he said that I was now disgraced and spoilt. It is the worse thing for me.
> ... When I was eight months pregnant from the rape, the police came to my hut and forced me with their guns to go to the police station. They asked me questions, so I told them that I had been raped. They told me that as I was not married, I will deliver this baby illegally. They beat me with a whip on the chest and back and put me in jail. There were other women in jail, who had the same story. During the day, we had to walk to the well four times a day to get the policemen water, clean and cook for them. At night, I was in a small cell with 23 other women. I had no other food than what I could find during my work during the day. And the only water was what I drank at the well. I stayed 10 days in jail and now I still have to pay the fine, 20,000 Sudanese Dinars (65 USD) they asked me. My child is now 2 months old. (Quoted in Médecins Sans Frontières 2005, 6)

And, of course, in the aftermath of the rape, girls must deal with injuries that occurred during the rape and any diseases as well. As the World Health Organization has reported, "Forced or coerced sex creates a risk of trauma: when the vagina or anus is dry and force is used genital and anal injury are more likely, increasing the risk of injury. Rape by multiple attackers both increases the likelihood of injury, as well as the risk of exposure to an HIV-positive attacker" (quoted in Human Rights Watch 2005, 14).

As Amnesty International (2004b) points out as well: "Young women and girls who are raped are prone to developing a fistula (a rupture between the vagina and the bladder or bowel). The risks of infection and permanent physical effects (including incontinence) are dire. In the first world, this trauma can be easily repaired with surgery. However, when basic hygiene and medical services are unavailable (as in the IDP camps) women are at particular risk" (n.p.).

Furthermore, there are culturally specific practices in Western Sudan (where Darfur is located) that exacerbate an already terrible situation. More specifically, "in Western Sudan infibulation (a form of female genital mutilation where the vagina is sewn almost entirely shut) is a common practice. The tearing and trauma that result from rape in this situation put the woman at increased risk for HIV/AIDS" (Amnesty International 2004b, n.p.).

Finally, those girls who have been raped face the possibility of remaining unmarried their entire lives. The stigma is such that very few males are willling to be associated with a woman who has been raped and has purportedly "brought" such dishonor to her family and community. A young woman from South Darfur spoke to Human Rights Watch researchers about this very issue—the fact that her twelve-year-old sister had been abducted and raped repeatedly over a two-day period: "My sister is very upset now, she likes to live in isolation and she suffers a great deal of humiliation in her heart. She believes she cannot marry now because she is *khasrana* (damaged)."

Fate of the Babies Born as a Result of Rape

Those babies born as a result of their mothers being raped by GoS soldiers or the *Janjaweed* often face prejudice and discrimination at the hands of their own mothers, not to mention their mothers' immediate family members (i.e., father and mother, brothers and sisters, aunts and uncles), and the larger community. Indeed, it is not unusual for black African girls who have conceived and given birth to babies as a result of being raped by GoS soldiers or the *Janjaweed* to refer to their own babies and youngsters as *"Janjaweed"* or *"Janjaweed* babies." In an article entitled "Darfur Babies of Rape Are on Trial from Birth," journalist Lydia Polgreen (2005) quoted a sixteen-year-old rape victim as saying the following about her newborn child: "'She is a *Janjaweed*,' Fatouma said softly, referring to the fearsome Arab militiamen who have terrorized this region. 'When people see her light skin and her soft hair, they will know she is a *Janjaweed*'" (1).

In a report entitled *Sudan, Darfur: Rape as a Weapon of War: Sexual Violence and Its Consequences*, Amnesty International (2004b) addresses how even the babies conceived as a result of the rape are ostracized for life. As one refugee from Kenyu says

> We believe that nobody can become pregnant when raped because this is unwanted sex and you cannot have a child from unwanted sex. For those who are in the camps in Darfur, those whom they rape day and night, they might become pregnant. Then only Allah can help the child to look like the mother. If an Arab child is born, this cannot be accepted. So, even if the woman is accepted back in the community after rape, the child will not be. Again, the woman is faced with a terrible choice. Reject her child or be rejected by her community. (1)

Quite obviously, such babies are destined to lead lives of discrimination and prejudice. To borrow a term, they virtually become "untouchables." And just like their mothers who suffered the rape, the babies are often shunned by family members and kicked out of their mothers' village along with their mothers.

Children Kidnapped and Enslaved

Large numbers of black African children were kidnapped by GoS troops and the *Janjaweed* during the course of the Darfur genocide. Young males (boys and teenagers) who were kidnapped were frequently forced to serve as domestic help and farm hands, either for those GoS soldiers or *Janjaweed* who kidnapped them or for those individuals who bought them from the kidnappers. One boy who was forced to work as an agricultural worker but managed to escape his captors told the BBC (2008), "They were treating me and the other boys very badly, they kept telling us that we are not human beings and we are here to serve them" (1).

There are also reports that some black African "girls have been trafficked within and out of Sudan to serve as commercial sexual workers, while others have been trafficked to work as domestic servants" (CBS News 2009, 1).

A Sudanese government official readily admitted that black African children from Darfur had been kidnapped throughout the crisis, and this was still taking place as late as 2008. The BBC News reported that the Sudanese politician who admitted as much, but did not want to be named, said: "'The army captured many children and women hiding in the bush outside burnt villages . . . They were transported by plane to Khartoum at night and divided up among soldiers as domestic workers and, in some cases, wives'" (1).

Young Boys Forced to Join Government of Sudan Military and Various Rebel Groups

Thousands of black African boys were kidnapped by GoS troops and *Janjaweed* and forced to take up weapons and fight against their own people. This is in direct contravention of both the United Nations Convention on the Rights of the Child (1989) and Article 8(2)(b)(xxvi) of the Rome Statute of the International Criminal Court. More specifically, Article 37 of the United Nations Convention on the Rights of the Child (1989) proclaims the following: "State parties shall take all feasible measures to ensure that persons who have not attained the age of fifteen years do not take a direct part in hostilities." The Optional Protocol (2002) to the Convention on the Rights of the Child in relation to the use of children in armed conflict further asserts that its State Parties "shall take all feasible measures to ensure that persons below the age of eighteen do not take a direct part in hostilities and that they are not compulsorily recruited into their armed forces." Article 4 of the Optional Protocol asserts that states must "take all feasible measures to prevent such recruitment and use, including the adoption of legal measures necessary to prohibit and criminalize such practices." Concomitantly, Article 6(3) of the Optional Protocol asserts that states are required to demobilize children within their jurisdiction who have been recruited or used in hostilities, and provide assistance vis-à-vis their physical and psychological recovery and social reintegration into society (Art. 6[3] Optional Protocol).

Perhaps, most strikingly, under Article 8(2)(b)(xxvi) of the Rome Statute of the International Criminal Court, which was adopted in July 1998 and entered into force on July 1, 2002, the following is spelled out: "Conscripting or enlisting children under the age of fifteen years into the national armed forces or using them to participate actively in hostilities" is a war crime.

Both during the height of the Darfur genocide and in its aftermath (through today, late 2013), young boys have been forced to join both the GoS military, the *Janjaweed*, as well as various rebel groups. This, of course, is in direct contravention of the Geneva Accords.

In most cases, the children are between fifteen and seventeen years of age, but there were also children eleven years and younger who had been abducted from their families and forced into roles as child soldiers. In other cases, "there are reports that students in Darfur towns are obliged to carry out military service in the Sudanese Armed Forces in order to sit for secondary school examinations" (UN Security Council 2006, 7).

As late as 2009, the United Nations Children Fund estimated that some 6,000 child soldiers were, in one way or another, involved in the war in Darfur. Both the GoS and the rebels actively recruited, if not outright forced, many of the children to join the effort.

A glimmer of hope appeared on the horizon in July 2010. More specifically, on July 21, 2010, the Justice and Equality Movement, one of the main rebel groups in Darfur committed, at least on paper, to doing its all to protect the children in Darfur from abuse, ranging from the recruitment and use of child soldiers, rape, sexual violence, and the maiming and killing of children. It also committed to "the release of all boys and girls associated with JEM, allow for UN and UNICEF access to all 'persons, places and documents' of JEM, ensure accountability for perpetrators, provide support from JEM for child victims and designate a JEM official to the United Nations to oversee the agreement's implementation" (United Nations Office of the Special Representative of the Secretary General for Children an Armed Conflict 2010, 1).

As of May 2012, five of the rebel groups in Darfur had signed the commitment. The remaining twenty-five plus rebel groups did not sign the action plan.

Posttraumatic Stress

Not surprisingly, many children who suffered violence, including severe beatings, gunshot wounds, and rape, have suffered posttraumatic stress. Likewise, those who witnessed the torture, rape, and/or murder of loved ones and/or community members, and/or the destruction of their homes and villages, were potentially susceptible to suffering posttraumatic stress. Tellingly, as early as July 5, 2004, the United Nation's Children's Fund, UNICEF (2004) reported that "at least a half-a-million children [had] been traumatized by the violence and brutality of the war in Sudan's western region of Darfur" (1).

As of this writing (late 2013), some two million people remain in IDP camps in Darfur, and another 250,000 to 300,000 remain in refugee camps in Chad. Many of them have been totally bereft for up to ten years now.

With virtually no counselors or counseling programs available in the IDP and refugee camps, individuals who have experienced and/or witnessed the most horrific scenes, lost loved ones, are destitute and/or without many opportunities in life, and greatly desire to return to their land but have no sense as to whether such a wish will ever come to fruition, one has to wonder how the survivors of the genocide manage to get through each and every day. This is particularly so in light of the fact that the world has largely forgotten about the plight and fate of the survivors and given little to no thought to the violence that continues unabated throughout Darfur.

Life in IDP and Refugee Camps

Life in the IDP and refugee camps is, to say the least, extremely difficult. For many, it is disheartening, and for not a few, it is dangerous. This author knows this for a fact, for he has conducted dozens of interviews in both IDP camps in Sudan and in refugee camps along the Chad/Sudan border in Chad.

For many, if not most, the lives of people in the IDP and refugee camps are bereft of much hope that their lives are going to get better any time soon. One can readily understand this in light of the following: paid work is largely unavailable; families constantly struggle to have enough food;[4] females (girls and women) face the ongoing threat of being raped by one group or another (be it Sudanese military troops, former *Janjaweed*, members of rebel groups, or bandits) when out foraging for wood, or simply traveling from one IDP or refugee camp to another; schooling for children often only goes up to the sixth grade, resulting in young adolescents and teenagers with little to no hope of acquiring a sound high school, let alone a university, education; young males are increasingly carrying firearms, which makes the camps just that more dangerous for everyone; and more and more young males are being recruited, or forced into serving, as fighters with rebel groups.

In 2012, IRIN[5] interviewed refugees about the conditions in the refugee camps in Chad. What they discovered was revelatory: "Before, in Darfur [Sudan], both men and women used to work, but virtually no one has a job here," Achtar Abubakr Ibrahim, a women's refugee leader in Djabal, told IRIN. "The men found themselves jobless, the women became dependent on the jobless men and this created frustration and anger, so the men started battering the women" (1). Such a situation, of course, impacts the entire family (and larger community) in highly negative and destructive ways.

Fortunately, over the years, various UN agencies (such as UNICEF, the World Health Organization [WHO], the World Food Program [WFP], and the United Nations High Commissioner for Refugees [UNHCR]), national organizations (such as USAID), and a host of nongovernmental organizations (including but not limited to Doctors without Borders/Médecins Sans Frontières, Oxfam, International Medical Corps, Hebrew Immigrant Aid Society, CARE, the International Committee of the Red Cross, Save the Children) have had a presence in the IDP and/or refugee camps. Collectively, they have helped to provide essential, if limited, foodstuff, water, and medical supplies. Various organizations have also worked on hygiene and sanitation projects (including digging and erecting simple public toilets, and water chlorination), erecting temporary elementary schools, and establishing small medical facilities.

Organizations such as UNICEF have supplied hundreds of tons of emergency supplies (nutritional supplements), water-treatment materials, and educational materials. UNICEF has also created a Hygiene Education Campaign, which supports the training of hundreds of Darfurians and supplies them with educational information and basic tools (shovels, rakes, and wheelbarrows). It has also distributed tons of soap. Likewise, UNICEF has vaccinated children against polio and measles and provided hundreds of thousands of doses of vaccines.

At one and the same time, some of the actions of the refugees remind one of an adage about being one's own worst enemy. For example, in 2012, IRIN "reported that in some cases [adult] males in the family (generally husbands/fathers) have traded or sold monthly food rations "'in exchange for alcohol or a mobile phone, so on food aid distribution day the woman has to secretly take along the ration card,' said an official [in the camp], recalling a case in which a man had sold the family's food ration to buy a phone. 'The woman was screaming, saying we are going to eat a mobile phone for a month.'" (1).

IRIN (2012) also cited a June 2011 report by the US Cultural Orientation Centre that asserted, "Despite efforts to promote self-sufficiency, Darfuri refugees in Chad continue to depend almost entirely on humanitarian assistance for their basic needs" (1).

Critical Challenges Facing the Field Today

There are a host of critical challenges facing both those who were children during the Darfur genocide and the Darfur society as a whole. Some key challenges are ending the ongoing violence (rape, killing, and massive dislocation of people from internally displaced camps and villages); creating effective ways to protect females from being attacked as they search for firewood and lug water back to their camps — and sooner than later, otherwise the brutal attacks (including rape) will continue unabated; providing comprehensive and sustained psychological support/counseling for the children, adolescents, and young adults who are suffering depression and PTSD; providing much more food aid so that children, as well as adults, are not constantly hungry; developing sound educational programs for secondary level students (grades seven through twelve) in both refugee camps and IDP camps; arranging to return people's land and for reparation of people's material losses.

Once the ongoing violence has been quelled (and unfortunately, based on the record of the past several years, that won't be anytime soon), the international community needs to work more arduously to help the black Africans return to their land with their families, or the remnants of their family, so that they can carry on with their lives. Currently, the people feel they are caught in a spider-like web from which they cannot extricate themselves and fear that they will grow old and perish in the IDP or refugee camp in which they sought sanctuary from the violence a decade ago. Being bereft of their own land, the black Africans are condemned to destitution with few, if any, opportunities for work in order to earn a decent wage.

The Real Probabilities of Progress in the Field

With the Darfur crisis now more than a decade old and the international community much more focused on other crises across the globe (including the civil war in Syria, North Korea's denotation and testing of nuclear bombs, Iran's suspected push for the development of a nuclear arsenal, the ongoing violent conflict in Iraq, and the war in Afghanistan), there does not seem to be a lot of hope that any of the issues/problems faced by the refugees and IDPs in Darfur are going to be addressed in a satisfactory manner any time soon. The fact that the GoS is also engaged in violent conflicts with the people of the Nuba Mountains and the Blue Nile in Sudan suggests that the GoS is not likely to place the ongoing problems in Darfur at the top of its agenda, not that it ever did. These are bleak words, but the situation merits them. As mentioned previously, many refugees and IDPs fear they will end up living their lives out in refugee and IDP camps. Many also fear that without their own land, they will have little to no opportunities to carve out a better life for themselves and their families. And the lack of higher-level educational programs (high school courses) in the camps just exacerbate matters. All of these frustrations, and more, readily lend themselves to more violence against girls between and amongst the men in the camps. It also leads many young males to leave the camps, pick up arms, and head back to Darfur where the situation is chaotic and something resembling the Wild West, with various groups (including different rebel factions) attacking each other at will and hijackers and bandits roaming the area causing even more havoc.

Speaking to the latter, Eric Reeves, the indefatigable chronicler and analyst of the genocide and the ongoing crisis in Darfur, reported the following in December 2012:

> [R]ape, widespread murder, violence in the camps and towns, and the ongoing appropriation of arable land by Arab militia groups, often by violent means [continue]. Events have finally compelled the UN and the UN/African Union Mission in Darfur (UNAMID) to acknowledge that violence is escalating in Darfur, a sharp reversal of the self-congratulatory statements by the likes of former heads of UNAMID Rodolphe Adada and Ibrahim Gambari. For example, Gambari recently celebrated his retirement as UNAMID Joint Special Representative (JSR) by declaring that he was "gratified to note that barely 31 months on, all the objectives I set out to meet have largely been met." But of course this is despicably dishonest and self-serving, given the dramatic increase in the level of violence, vast human displacement, and the deterioration of humanitarian access and resources that accelerated under Gambari's tenure. UNAMID—with an unforgiveable belatedness—now acknowledges some of these realities, although with a deeply disingenuous timeline. UNAMID leaders and spokespersons would have us believe that this sharp upswing in violence is quite recent; in fact, it has been accelerating dramatically since late 2010. (Reeves 2012, 1)[6]

Conclusion

An entire generation of young black Africans has been subjected to horrors no children should ever have to witness or experience. To this day, they live with their memories and their losses. Many children are orphans and scratching out a meagre existence on their own in IDP and refugee camps. Those girls who were raped, impregnated, and gave birth face a life of potential ostracism, isolation, and extreme hardship in a very harsh part of the world. So do their offspring.

Once genocide is brought to an end, the world, more often than not, largely forgets about those who have survived. Yes, scholars study the genocide and relief agencies continue to provide housing, food, and water, but the survivors are largely left to their own devices to cope with their despair, nightmares, desolation, and destitution. In many cases, those forced from their homes end up in IDP or refugee camps for years on end, if not their entire lives. This is certainly true of the hundreds of thousands of young people black Africans leading largely dead-end lives in internally displaced camps in Sudan and refugees camps in Chad.

More often than not, the monthly allotment of food provided to the people in the camps is inadequate to feed a family. This not only results in empty stomachs and people constantly craving food but also bodies much less resistant to diseases. It also leads to anger and a sense that no one in the international community truly cares about their fate.

Also, due to the fact that few, if any, of the refugee camps provide educational opportunities for the young beyond grade six, an entire generation of young black Africans have already had their educations cut short, leaving them with little to no hope of gainful employment, let alone a university education.

Girls and young women in IDP and refugee camps continue to be preyed upon and raped as they forage for wood and carry water back to their encampments. Nothing, to date, has been done to substantially curtail such horrific brutality.

As the years pass by, those in the IDP and refugee camps not only lose hope, but also see the young, especially the males, become increasingly frustrated, angry, and prone to violence. While many cause problems within the camps, particularly as they begin to use alcohol and acquire weapons, many others pick up arms and return to the chaos that is now Darfur. Other males, who have no interest in joining the fighting, are frequently preyed upon by both GoS troops and rebel groups and are forced to join in the fight. Not only does this result in endless numbers always available to fight but it also creates yet another generation of individuals who know little more than violence as a way of life.

Basically, the nightmare for the black Africans of Darfur continues; yes, in a different context from that of a decade ago but a nightmare nevertheless.

Notes

1. For thorough discussions of the Darfur genocide, see: Samuel Totten's *An Oral and Documentary History of the Darfur Genocide* (Santa Barbara, CA: Praeger Security International Press, 2011); *Genocide in Darfur: Investigating Atrocities in the Sudan* edited by Samuel Totten and Eric Markusen (New York: Routledge, 2006); *and Darfur and the Crimes of Genocide* by John Hagan and Wenona Rymond-Richmoond (New York: Cambridge University Press, 2009).

2. It should be duly noted that Government of Sudan troops continue to attack black African villages through today, even though much more sporadically, and as a result, the young continue to face horrific injury, gang rape, torture, and death.

3. Here, it would be more accurate to say "girls," "young women," and women well into their fifties and sixties.

4. IRIN (2012) reported that "access to arable land remains generally nonexistent for the refugees" (1).

5. Integrated Regional Information Networks (IRIN) is a humanitarian news and analysis service based with the UN Office for the Coordination of Humanitarian Affairs.

6. On February 10, 2013, Eric Reeves reported the following: Violence continues to rage throughout Darfur, indeed has dramatically accelerated in recent weeks. This has created an insecurity that endangers not only millions of civilians—within and outside the camps for displaced persons—but humanitarian personnel. Most transportation corridors are unsafe without the heaviest of escorts. Whole sections of Darfur—for example, Jebel Marra—remain subject to Khartoum's humanitarian embargo. The National Islamic Front/National Congress Party regime relentlessly obstructs not only humanitarian personnel and operations but any meaningful investigations of atrocity crimes attempted by the UN/African Union Mission in Darfur (UNAMID).

   UN silence, misrepresentation, and inaction come even as the avalanche of rape continues to roll through Darfur, threatening girls and women everywhere (see http://www.sudanreeves.org/?p=2884).

   It is incumbent upon the UN Secretary-General to provide a fuller account of sexual violence and its nature in Darfur; in particular, he should identify those most responsible, as well as the racial animus that works to define nearly all instances of rape . . . At the same time, large-scale violence against those within the camps is continuous, despite the numerous "patrols" that UNAMID boasts of (1, 2).

References

Amnesty International. 2004a. *Rape as a Weapon of War*. London: Author.

———. 2004b. *Sudan, Darfur: Rape as a Weapon of War: Sexual Violence and Its Consequences*. London: Author.

———. 2008. "Children of Conflict." London: Author. Accessed at: www.amnesty.org/en/appeals-for-action/darfurs-children-conflict

BBC News. 2008. "Thousands Made Slaves in Darfur." *BBC News*, December 17. Available at http://news.bbc.co.uk/2/hi/7786612.stm.

CBS News. 2009. "Report: Children in Darfur Tortured, Raped." *CBS News*, February 11. Available at www.cbsnews.com/2100-202_162-2704000.html

Human Rights Watch. 2005. "Sexual Violence and Its Consequences Among Displaced Persons in Darfur and Chad." *A Human Rights Watch Briefing Paper*. April 12. New York: Author.

IRIN. 2012. "Sudan-Chad: The Strains of Long-Term Displacement." July 13. Available at: www.irinnews.org/printreport.aspx?reportid=95863.

Kristof, Nicholas D. 2005. "A Policy of Rape." *The New York Times*, June 5. Available at: www.nytimes.com/2005/06/05/opinion/05kristof.html.

Matheson, Ishbel. 2004. "Darfur Breeds 'Dirty Babies'." *BBC News*, November 24. Available at: http://news.bbc.co.uk/2/hi/africa/4099601.stm.

Médecins Sans Frontières. 2005. *The Crushing Burden of Rape: Sexual Violence in Darfur—A Briefing Paper by Médecins Sans Frontières*. Amsterdam: Author.

Polgreen, Lydia. 2005. "Darfur Babies of Rape Are on Trial from Birth." *The New York Times*, February 11. Available at: www.nytimes.com › International › Africa.

Reeves, Eric. 2012. "South Sudan: Growing Violence in Darfur Deserves Honest Reporting, Not More Flatulent UN Nonsense." *South Sudan News Agency*, December 1, 1.

——— 2013. "Humanitarian Conditions in Darfur: The Most Recent Reports Reveal a Relentless Deterioration." *South Sudan News Agency*. Accessed at: www.southsudannewsagency.com › Opinion › Analyses.

UNICEF. 2004. "Thousands of Children Traumatized in Darfur." July 5. Accessed at: www.voanews.com/content/a-13-a-2004-07-04-6.../283000.html

———. 2004. "UNICEF—Sudan—Death Rate Soars for Darfur's Children." September 27. Available at: www.unicef.org/infobycountry/sudan_23313.html.

———. 2005. "Child Alert-Darfur." December 20, Available at: www.unicef.org/childalert/darfur/Child%20Alert%20Darfur.pdf

United Nations Office of the Special Representative of the Secretary General for Children and Armed Conflict. 2010. "Hope for Children in Darfur." July 21. New York: United Nations.

Annotated Bibliography

Amnesty International. *Darfur: Rape as a Weapon of War: Sexual Violence and Its Consequences*. New York: Author, 2004, 35 pp.

A major and detailed report. It provides ample evidence that both black African female children, along with women, faced rape at the hands of the *Janjaweed*, the Arab militia hired by the Government of Sudan. While the plight of children is mentioned throughout the report, one section in particular is entitled "Children as Victims of the Conflict and the Effects on Women."

Askin, Kelly. "Prosecuting Gender Crimes Committed in Darfur: Holding Leaders Accountable for Sexual Violence." In *Genocide in Darfur: Investigating Atrocities in the Sudan*, edited by Samuel Totten, and Eric Markusen, 141–60. New York: Routledge, 2006.

A detailed and disturbing account that addresses, in part, the sexual assaults faced by young black African girls in Darfur at the hands of Government of Sudan troops and the *Janjaweed*. Among some of the most disturbing information (all of which came from the interviews conducted by the State Department's group of investigators with the Atrocities Documentation Project in refugee camps in eastern Chad during July and August 2004) in regard to the way black African children were treated is as follows: "In western Darfur (near Foro Borunga in June 2003, a Fur man said his wife was raped by seven GoS soldiers, and thirteen other women were also raped during the attack. He saw horsemen [the so-called *Janjaweed*] take a baby from a woman's back, tear off its clothes and slice its stomach; another woman's baby daughter was smashed against a tree and killed. He witnessed approximately twenty male and seven female babies being killed" (14); "A Fur woman fled an attack on her village in Darfur (near Bendesi) in August 2003. She witnessed a twelve-year-old girl being gang raped by five men; the girl died soon after the attack" (146); "A Massalit woman in West Darfur (near Senena) in December 2003 said twenty girls were captured by GoS soldiers and gang-raped (vaginally and anally) for three days. Three girls had nails put in their vaginas (one of whom died); two other girls had their vaginas sewn up; and five became pregnant from the rapes. All were unmarried" (146); "In Northern Darfur (near Karnoi) in January 2004, a pregnant Zaghawa woman and four girls (ages 12, 13, 15, and 16) were abducted and raped by five to six soldiers each night, until their release five days later" (146–47); "A Fur male reported that in December 2003, a few months before his village in West Darfur (near El Geneina) was attacked, *Janjaweed* raped his daughter and two other girls" (ages 14, 15, and 16) and said, "We will take your women and make them ours. We will change the race" (147); "During an attack on her village in western Darfur (near Misterei) in January 2004, a Massalit woman reported that she was one of sixteen women caught and raped by four soldiers during an aerial/ground attack. Three other rapes she witnessed included girls having their breasts slashed, two girls died from the gang rapes" (147–48); and, "A Zaghawa woman in North Darfur (near Kotum) in March 2004 stated that sixteen girls from her village were abducted and gang raped. A perpetrator said, 'From now and for twenty years, we will kill all the blacks and all of the Zaghawa tribe'" (148).

Bashir, Halima, and Damien Lewis. *Tears of the Desert: A Memoir of Survival in Darfur*. New York: One World/Ballantine, 2008, 336 pp.

An extremely powerful memoir by a black African Darfuri woman, now a doctor residing in London, which provides a harrowing view of the Government of Sudan attacks on the black Africans of Darfur. Not only was the author's village utterly destroyed but she was also brutalized by the *Janjaweed*.

Halima Bashir describes growing up in Darfur in a wonderful family, how her father supported her love of learning, and how she became a physician. She then goes on to describe the relentless and brutal attacks on the black Africans of Darfur by the Government of Sudan. In part, she describes an attack on her family's village in Darfur, during which forty-two school girls (some as young as eight years old) and their teachers were raped. She tells of treating the traumatized girls who had been mutilated.

BBC News, "Thousands Made Slaves in Darfur," *BBC News*, December 17, 2008. Available at: http://news.bbc.co.uk/2/hi/7786612.stm

In part, this BBC News report asserted that "strong evidence has emerged of children and adults being used as slaves in Sudan's Darfur region. . . . Eyewitnesses also say the Sudanese army has been involved in abducting women and children to be sex slaves and domestic staff for troops in Khartoum" (1).

Borger, Julian, "Darfur's Child Refugees Being Sold to Militias," *The Guardian*, June 6, 2008. Available at: www.guardian.co.uk › News › World news › Sudan.

Julian Borger notes that Waging Peace, a British Human Rights organization, reported that "thousands of child refugees from Darfur, some as young as nine, are being abducted and sold to warring militias as child soldiers" (1). The organization, which conducted and filmed interviews in refugee camps in eastern Chad, noted that boys between nine and fifteen years of age had been abducted by camp leaders who are basically selling them to rebel groups, including the Justice and Equality Movement.

Louise Roland-Gosselin, the head of Waging Peace, noted that "it was impossible to know how many children were being abducted, but the UN estimated that [in 2007] between 7,000 and 10,000 child soldiers had been forcibly recruited in Chad, where more than 250,000 refugees from Darfur are in camps. She said the problem had worsened since then, despite attempts by UN agencies and aid groups to negotiate an end to trafficking" (1).

Human Rights Watch. *Five Years On: No Justice for Sexual Violence in Darfur.* New York: Author, 2008, 44 pp.

A well-documented report on the horrors that girls and woman continued to face as a result of sexual violence perpetrated against them in Darfur. It particularly focuses on the period from 2007 to 2008.

In addition to discussing the methodology of the study, the report includes, in part, the following: Background to the Conflict, Sexual Violence in Darfur in 2007–2008 (Patterns of Abuse and Obstacles to Justice for Sexual Violence Survivors); The Sudanese Government's Response to the Sexual Violence; International Response to the Sexual Violence; and Sudan's Obligation to Prevent, Investigate, and Punish Sexual Violence. It concludes with a set of recommendations.

Human Rights Watch. "Sexual Violence and Its Consequences Among Displaced Persons in Darfur and Chad." *A Human Rights Watch Briefing Paper.* April 12. New York: Author, 2005a, 17 pp.

This report includes information about, and testimony by, girls who had been raped by Government of Sudan soldiers, the *Janjaweed*, among others, during the period of the Darfur genocide. It is comprised of the following sections: Background; Rape and Sexual Violence during Attacks by Government Forces and Militias; No Protection: Rape and Sexual Violence following Displacement; Social and Psychological Results of Sexual Violence; Medical Consequences of Sexual Violence, including HIV/AIDS; Standards for Response to Sexual and Gender-Based Violence; and Recommendations.

Human Rights Watch. *Smallest Witnesses.* New York: Author, n.p., 2005b. Available at: www.hrw.org/sites/default/files/features/darfur/.../intro.html Spring 2005.

In February 2005, a team of Human Rights Watch investigators conducted an investigation into the consequences of sexual violence that girls and women were subjected to in Darfur. In order to keep the women's children occupied during the interviews, the investigators presented the children with crayons and paper. The first child to use the crayon and paper drew "without any instruction" pictures of the *Janjaweed* militia on camels and horseback shooting black African villagers in Darfur, Anotnovs dropping bombs on villages, and an army tank shooting at civilians fleeing their village. "Over the following weeks of the investigation, these violent scenes were repeated in hundreds of drawings given to Human Rights Watch, depicting the attacks by ground and by air. Children drew the *Janjaweed* over-running and burning their villages and Sudanese forces attacking with Antonovs, military helicopters, MIG planes and tanks. With great detail, children drew the artillery and guns they had seen used, including Kalashnikovs, machine guns, bombs, and rockets. They also drew the attacks as they had seen them in action: huts and villages burning, the shooting of men, women and children, and the rape of women and girls."

Human Rights Watch reports that it "had been documenting these crimes against humanity since the conflict began in 2003. On multiple missions to Darfur and Chad, investigators spoke with hundreds of victims, and documented these crimes of war. But there were rarely eyewitnesses other than the villagers who were attacked. This 'ethnic cleansing' was always meant to be out of the public view. There are virtually no publicly available photographs and little footage of *Janjaweed* militias or Sudanese soldiers attacking villages. . . . However, because of these drawings by the children of Darfur, we now have graphic representations of the atrocities. The drawings corroborate unerringly what we know of the crimes. From the point of view of humanitarian law, the drawings illustrate a compelling case against the government of Sudan as the architects of this man-made crisis in Darfur."

Human Rights Watch. *Sudan—Darfur in Flames: Atrocities in Western Sudan.* vol. 16, no. 5(1). New York: Author, 2004, 47 pp.

This report includes two sections that specifically address the plight and fate of children in Darfur during the height of the killing: Rape and Other Forms of Sexual Violence, and Abductions of Children and Adults. Many of the other sections also reference the plight of the children, including the indiscriminate killing of children and the fact that many children on the run and/or in living in makeshift internally displaced camps (and refugee camps) suffered from malnutrition.

Kristof, Nicholas, "A Policy of Rape," *New York Times*, June 5, 2005. Available at: www.nytimes.com/2005/06/05/opinion/05kristof.html

In this piece, Nicholas Kristof discusses how the rape of girls and women in Darfur by the Government of Sudan troops and the *Janjaweed* constitutes "a systematic campaign of rape to terrorize civilians and drive them from 'Arab lands'" (1).

Malchiodi, Cathy, "When Trauma Happens, Children Draw. Part II," *Psychology Today*, May 15, 2008. Available at: http://www.psychologytoday.com/blog/the-healing-arts/200805/when-trauma-happens-children-draw-part-ii

In this extremely brief article, a licensed therapist and professor discusses how two Human Rights Watch researchers provided crayons and paper to children in refugee camps in Chad, and how the children created drawings depicting what they had experienced and suffered during the genocide in Darfur. In her introduction to her piece, Cathy Malchiodi says, "Words tell our stories, but art makes it possible to bear witness to them. For the children of Darfur, art became the unexpected vehicle for exposing the atrocities of violence, oppression, and genocide, breaking the silence through a visual vocabulary of war." Speaking of the drawings, Malchiodi says: "They drew, often with frightening accuracy, pictures of murder, torture, and destruction, images few photojournalists had ever been able to capture on film. The images were so precise that they were submitted to the International Criminal Court last year to corroborate the attacks by *Janjaweed* militia against the Dafuri people" (Part I of this article provided a more general view of the use of art in helping children deal with the trauma they've experienced in both natural and man-made disasters—wars, crimes against humanity, genocide, etc.).

Matheson, Ishbel, "Darfur Breeds 'Dirty Babies,'" *BBC News*, November 24, 2006. Available at: http://news.bbc.co.uk/2/hi/africa/4099601.stm

Discusses the systematic rape of girls and women in Darfur by the *Janjaweed*, and focuses on the horrible ramifications (i.e., ostracism, isolation, etc.) for the impregnated girls and their babies.

Médecins Sans Frontières. *The Crushing Burden of Rape: Sexual Violence in Darfur*. Amsterdam: Author, 2005, 8 pp.

This report provides horrific evidence of the fact that young black African girls, thirteen and younger, faced rape at the hands of the Government of Sudan troops and the *Janjaweed*. Includes excerpts from interviews with the victims.

Morgos, D., J. W. Worden, and L. Gupta. "Psychosocial Effects of War Experiences Among Displaced Children in Southern Darfur." *Omega* 56, no. 3 (2007–2008): 229–53.

Herein, the authors discuss the psychosocial effects of the long standing, high intensity, and guerrilla-style of warfare among displaced children in Southern Darfur. The goal was to better understand the etiology, prognosis, and treatment implications for traumatic reactions, depression, and grief symptoms in this population.

"Three hundred thirty-one children aged six to seventeen from three IDP Camps were selected using a quota-sampling approach and were administered a Demographic Questionnaire, Child Post Traumatic Stress Reaction Index, Child Depression Inventory, and the Expanded Grief Inventory. Forty-three percent were girls and 57% were boys. The mean age of the children was twelve years. Results found that children were exposed to a very large number of war experiences with no significant differences between genders for types of exposure, including rape, but with older children (13–17 years) facing a larger number of exposures than younger children (6–12 years). . . . Seventy-five percent of the children met the DSM-IV criteria for PTSD, and 38% exhibited clinical symptoms of depression. The percentage of children endorsing significant levels of grief symptoms was 20%. Increased exposure to war experiences led to higher levels of: (1) traumatic reactions; (2) depression; and (3) grief symptoms. Of the war experiences, abduction, hiding to protect oneself, being raped, and being forced to kill or hurt family members were most predictive of traumatic reactions. Being raped, seeing others raped, the death of a parent/s, being forced to fight, and having to hide to protect oneself were the strongest predictors of depressive symptoms. War experiences such as abduction, death of one's parent/s, being forced to fight, and having to hide to protect oneself were the most associated with the child's experience of grief.

In addition to Total Grief, Traumatic Grief, Existential Grief, and Continuing Bonds were measured in these children. . . . This study is the first of its kind to assess the psychosocial effects of war experiences among children currently living in war zone areas within Sudan. . . . Implications for planning mental health interventions are discussed."

Physicians for Human Rights. *Nowhere to Turn: Failure to Protect, Support and Assure Justice for Darfuri Women*. May, 2009, 65 pp.

While the title of this report suggests that its focus is Darfuri women, many of the individuals interviewed were raped when they were under the age of eighteen years old. In that regard, this is a key report vis-à-vis the sexual assaults faced by black African girls and women in Darfur prior to 2009. Highly detailed, the report includes both quantitative and qualitative data (i.e., excerpts from interviews with the victims). The "n" for the study was eighty-eight black African "women" from Darfur who resided in the Farchana refugee camp in eastern Chad. "Of the thirty-two instances of confirmed and highly probable rape, seventeen occurred in Darfur" (17 of the 88 respondents) (3).

Among some of the many striking findings are as follows: "Women who experienced rape (confirmed or highly probable) were three times more likely to report suicidal thoughts than were women who did not report sexual violence" (p.6); "Women with confirmed rapes were six times more likely to be divorced or separated than those who were not raped and some women described community rejection and physical violence by family members" (6); and of the "21 women examined on the basis of the Istanbul Protocol, all 21 women experienced one or more of the following conditions: Major Depressive Disorder (MDD), Depressive Disorder Not Otherwise Specified (DD-NOS), Post Traumatic Stress Disorder (PTSD), or some symptoms of PTSD" (5).

The excerpts from the interviews, which are incorporated into the report to highlight and illustrate key findings, are heartrending. For example, "One woman described being raped during the attack on her village (Zaghawa Hills, Darfur). She was [12 or] 13 at the time: 'One of the *Janjaweed* pushed me to the ground. He forced my clothes off and they raped me one by one vaginally. . . . When they shot my father, they saw I was a little girl. I did not have any energy or force against them. They used me. I started bleeding. It was so painful. I could not stand up . . . I was sick for seven days. No one helped me . . .'" (3).

Another woman who was thirteen when Government troops and the *Janjaweed* attacked Gokor, where she resided in Darfur, reported the following: "'Early in the morning, on a Wednesday, the *Janjaweed* came into the village riding horses. Many men (wearing green Sudanese army uniforms) entered our house . . . They shot my father with a gun in front of us in our house and he died. We ran away. They (the *Janjaweed*) caught me and beat me. They used sticks and horsewhips. . . . They grabbed me and pulled my clothes . . . They raped me, many men, one by one.' She could not quantify how many. 'I was bleeding. I was sick for four days, all of my body was sick.' She reported that she saw more than 20 young girls being raped and more than 20 people killed, by gunshot" (27).

Polgreen, Lydia, "Darfur Babies of Rape Are on Trial from Birth," *New York Times*, February 11, 2005. Available at: www.nytimes.com › International › Africa.

A powerful piece on the rape and gang rape of young black African girls in Darfur and the ramifications of such incidents for both themselves and their babies. At one point, Lydia Polgreen quotes a sixteen-year-old black African who had a baby as a result of being raped by a member of the *Janjaweed*: "'She is a *Janjaweed*,'" Fatouma [a sixteen-year-old black African girl who had a baby as a result of being raped by the *Janjaweed*] said softly, referring to the fearsome Arab militiamen who have terrorized this region. 'When people see her light skin and her soft hair, they will know she is a *Janjaweed*.'"

Polgreen also reports that, "A recent United Nations investigation into war crimes in Darfur laid out, in page after graphic page, evidence of widespread and systematic rape in the two-year conflict. In one incident, a woman in Wadi Tina was raped 14 times by different men in January 2003. In March 2004, 150 soldiers and *Janjaweed* abducted and raped 16 girls in Kutum, the report said. In Kailek, it said girls as young as 10 were raped by militants."

Reeves, Eric, "Children Within Darfur's Holocaust: An Overview of Vulnerabilities Particular to Genocide's Youngest Victims," *Sudan Tribune*, December 23, 2005. Available at: www.sudantribune.com/Children-within-Darfur-s-Holocaust,13197.

A very detailed report on the attacks on and suffering of the black African children of Darfur as a result of the actions of Government of Sudan troops and the *Janjaweed*. The piece, by Eric Reeves, an indefatigable researcher of the Darfur genocide, addresses the following issues/concerns: the deliberate destruction of black African children by the Government of Sudan simply due to their ethnicity; the type and extent of violence children of Darfur suffered; "the vulnerabilities of the children from Darfur (including various diseases attenuated as a result of the attacks against the villages in Darfur) and the need for families to flee into the wilds and huge, sprawling internally displaced camps (IDPs)"; the type of existences the children experience in the IDP camps; and what the future may hold for such children.

Robertson, Nic, "Sudan Soldier: 'They Told Me to Kill, to Rape Children,'" *CNN. com*, March 5, 2009. Available at: http://edition.cnn.com/2009/WORLD/africa/03/04/darfur.rape/.

A man who had been forced to join the Sudanese Army relates how soldiers, including himself, were forced by "the [Sudanese] government" to rape young girls in Darfur. In introducing his article, journalist Nic Robertson reports that:

> "Last year in Darfur, aid workers told me children as young as five were being raped in the huge displacement camps that are home to several million Darfuris. In some camps, they told me, rape had become so common that as many as 20 babies a month born from rape were being abandoned." Robertson concludes by noting that "Aid workers say millions of women in Darfur not only have trouble sleeping at nights, but live in fear of rape 24 hours a day."

Totten, Samuel. "The Darfur Genocide: The Mass Rape of Black African Girls and Women," In *Plight and Fate of Women during and following Genocide. Volume*

Seven of Genocide: A Critical Bibliographic Review, edited by Samuel Totten, 137–68. New Brunswick, NJ: Transaction Publishers, 2009.

Provides a detailed account of what the girls and women of Darfur suffered (and continue to suffer) in the way of sexual assault at the hands of Government of Sudan troops and the *Janjaweed*. Includes a fairly lengthy annotated bibliography of key articles, book chapters, and books.

Totten, Samuel. *An Oral and Documentary History of the Darfur Genocide*. Santa Barbara, CA: ABC Clio, 2010, 556 pp.

In addition to the complete set of findings of three major reports on the Darfur crisis (one each conducted by the US Government, the United Nations, and the International Criminal Court), each of which comments on children as victims in Darfur, various first-person accounts address the atrocities and horrors faced by young black Africans in Darfur.

United Nations Children's Fund. UNICEF. *Child Alert Darfur*. New York: UNICEF. Author, 2005, 20 pp.

In its introduction, UNICEF reports that "While more than 1.5 million children living in and around camps for the displaced now have access to some of the most complete social services in Darfur's history, a daily reality of insecurity and economic paralysis dominates the lives of Darfur's children—both those in and around the camps and the nearly 1.25 million who live beyond. With little prospect of immediate change on the horizon, these factors suggest a bleak future for an entire generation" (1). The report addresses the following: the background to the crisis, the state of the Darfur crisis as of December 2005, the state of insecurity in Darfur and its impact on children, life in the camp and host communities, and the continuing violence and how it has engulfed children's lives in Darfur.

In their conclusion, the authors state that:

> Darfur's 3 million children have borne the brunt of this crisis and their long-term prospects appear bleaker with every day that passes without a lasting solution. Tens of thousands have already died as a consequence of the conflict. More than 1.75 million children live in and around camps where, despite receiving unprecedented social services, camp inhabitants live in a state of siege, traumatized by past events, continuing fear and a loss of hope for the future.
>
> Another 1.25 million children live in areas only now becoming accessible, places where food and water are scarce and services almost non-existent. With the economy in freefall, fields fallow and livestock plundered, many families have no way to feed their children. Hunger, thirst and extreme hardship loom for those currently beyond the reach of humanitarian relief.
>
> To ensure the immediate survival of Darfur's children and minimize the impact of the conflict, increased international assistance will be required at least through 2006, and probably for a further five years beyond. Though essential to preserving life in the short term, humanitarian aid is not sufficient, as has been illustrated clearly during the decades-long conflict in the South [i.e., the twenty-year civil war between the North and South in Sudan]. There must be a negotiated solution to prevent the humanitarian operations from turning into exhaustive

"care and maintenance" operations which maintain an unacceptable status quo.

The longer aid is used in place of real solutions, such as new agreements on security, shared land use and a functioning network of social services, the more dependent Darfur's people become on the fleeting solution of international relief.

Meanwhile, the children of Darfur have little prospect of a decent, independent future for themselves. The household-level economic outlook for families both in and out of the camps is precarious, and powerful entrenched forces are undermining the traditional systems for generating income, food, and trade. The majority of Darfurian children live beyond the reach of current international relief efforts, leaving them exposed to malnutrition, illness, violence, and fear. (20)

United Nations Security Council. "Report of the Secretary-General on Children and Armed Conflict in Sudan." New York: United Nations, 2006, 18 pp.

The UN Secretary General asserts that this report, which covers the period from May to July 2006, "specifies incidents of grave child rights abuses, indicative of the nature and trend of systematic violations in the Sudan. The report focuses specifically on the killing and maiming of children, their recruitment and use as soldiers, grave sexual violence, abductions and denial of humanitarian access to children, and indicates that these violations continue in the Sudan largely unabated" (1). While the latter applies to various areas in Sudan, all such incidents were taking place on a regular basis in Darfur. The report noted that in Darfur both Sudanese Armed Forces and rebel groups were responsible for various criminal acts against children.

United Nations Security Council. "Report of the Secretary-General on Children and Armed Conflict in Sudan." New York: United Nations, 2007, 21 pp.

This report asserts that "the level of grave violations against children in the Sudan remains high, including their recruitment and use by armed forces and rebel groups and rape and sexual violence, especially in Darfur" (1). Furthermore, it states that "In Darfur, rape is widespread and used as a weapon of war" (7), and, "[i]ncreasingly, the trend in Darfur seems to indicate that younger girls are being specifically targeted for rape. There were also five boys among 62 confirmed reports of rape during the year" (8).

Ward, Jeanne, and Mendy Marsh. "Sexual Violence against Women and Girls in War and Its Aftermath: Realities, Responses, and Required Resources: A Briefing Paper." Brussels: UNFPA, 2006, 31 pp.

This report addresses various conflicts, including Darfur. It is comprised of three parts: Part I: The Nature and Scope of Violence against Women and Children in Armed Conflict and Its Aftermath; Part II: Rising to the Challenge: Combating Violence against Woman and Girls during War and Its Aftermath; and Part III. Where Are We Now? Assessing Progress (the latter of which addresses the issue of ending impunity).

Watchlist on Children and Armed Conflict. *Sudan's Children at a Crossroads: An Urgent Need for Action.* New York: Women's Commission for Refugees Women and Children, 2007, 69 pp.

While this report examines the status (and plight and fate) of children throughout Sudan, a good part of it focuses specifically on the situation vis-à-vis the children in Darfur as of 2007. In their introduction, the authors report that children ". . . in Darfur and other areas of Sudan are enduring unspeakable acts of violence and abuse" (1). Among the violations against children in Darfur that this report details are as follows: forced displacement, torture, killing and maiming, rape and other forms of sexual violence, abduction, denial of humanitarian assistance, attacks on schools and hospitals, and recruitment and use of children by armed forces and groups. Furthermore, the report notes that girls had been kidnapped and forced to serve as sexual workers/slaves and/or as domestic servants. Young boys, the report continues, had also been kidnapped, some as young as four years old, and forced to serve as domestic servants and to do manual labor. Not a few were victims of both physical and sexual abuse. Shockingly, the report notes that those who sexually abused the children came from all groups involved in the Darfur crisis: Government of Sudan troops, the *Janjaweed*, rebel groups, and even members of humanitarian groups and the peace forces on the ground.

Other issues the report addresses are as follows: the context of the conflict, the status of the refugees and IDPs, health, HIV/AIDS, education, gender-based violence, trafficking and exploitation, landmines, small arms, child soldiers, UN Security Council actions, and urgent recommendations.

Films

The Children of Darfur (2006, 24 minutes, Arabic, English, Danish) is a documentary by Camilla Nielsson, an anthroplogist from Denmark, that tells "the children's version of what is happening in Darfur. Some of the strongest testimonies are related by the children and etched in drawings made in the support centres that have opened throughout Darfur."

Guisma's Story (Three Part Series. Produced by Stop Genocide Now's i-Act team. Available on-line at thisisdarfur.com/).

This is the story of one of the children the i-ACT team met in a refugee camp: Guisma, a six-year-old girl who dreams of returning to a peaceful Sudan one day. It includes anecdotes by refugees from Darfur. The illustrations are inspired by drawings by Darfuri refugee children. "The videos encapsulate the resiliency and hope of the Darfuris, despite nearly a decade of hardship living in refugee camps in eastern Chad." Ideal for use at the secondary and college levels.

"Smallest Witnesses: The Crisis in Darfur Through Children's Eyes." (Produced in 2005 by the US Holocaust Memorial Museum. 5 minutes, 51 seconds, Color.). Available at www.youtube.com/watch?v=uMdyhFaxTKE

This incredibly powerful and moving documentary features Dr. Annie Sparrow and the drawings by children from Darfur, now residing in refugee camps in Chad, who drew about their experiences during the genocidal actions carried out by the Sudanese troops and the *Janjaweed*. In introducing the film, the United States Holocaust Memorial Museum notes the following: "On a recent mission to Darfurian refugee camps in Chad, two Human Rights Watch researchers gave children paper and crayons while their families were being interviewed. Unprompted, the children drew scenes of devastation: pictures of their villages being attacked by *Janjaweed*, bombings by Sudanese government forces, the shootings, the rapes, the burning of entire villages, and the flight to Chad."

"Women and Children in Sudan." (Produced by *60 Minutes in 2004*. 6 minutes. Color. On-line. Available at: www.jewishworldwatch.org/blog/videos/news-reports/507.

A segment from "60 Minutes" on the plight of women and children in Darfur.

9

Sexual and Gender-Based Violence against Children during Genocide

Elisa von Joeden–Forgey

One of the central characteristics of the crime of genocide is widespread sexualized and gender-based violence. Not limited to rape, sexualized and gender-based violence characterizes the vast majority of crimes committed by perpetrators, so much so that we can characterize genocide as a pornographic process. More and more research is demonstrating that it is difficult to understand the crime without taking gender-based violence into consideration: biological sex and cultural beliefs about gender roles determine much about perpetrator ideology, patterns of attack, responses of victim communities, and the consequences of genocidal violence over the long term. Sexualized violence (violence that involves sexual organs and what are commonly considered to be sex acts and sexual behaviors) during genocide is, therefore, part of a much broader pattern of gender-based strategies employed by perpetrators to destroy a group. Post-genocide societies must struggle with the consequences of widespread sexualized violence in a social context (loss, displacement, poverty) that itself exacerbates gender-based violence.

Since the intent of genocide goes beyond the political, military, and territorial goals that define more conventional conflicts, the types of people specifically to be targeted also exceed traditional notions of the military opponent. Some of the least threatening groups during conventional conflicts (for example, pregnant women and small children) become intentional targets of particularly cruel violence during genocide. This is because perpetrators of genocide view reproduction to be just as threatening as any potential military opponent. Women, children, and the elderly are, therefore, the specific targets of genocidal violence rather than either the victims of indiscriminate bombing campaigns or the collateral damage of targeted attacks on opposing armies and military infrastructure. In Rwanda, for example, children were largely spared the violence of smaller-scale massacres of Tutsis that occurred between 1959 and 1993, and it was only with the outbreak of genocide in 1994 that children lost this protected status.[1]

The vulnerability of children to various forms of sexualized and gender-based violence during peacetime further intensifies their vulnerability to sexual exploitation and abuse during genocide. Children are subjected to every imaginable form of sexualized violence during genocide, some of it the consequence of the insecure conditions and the breakdown of moral codes caused by conflict in general and some of it the result of the intentional genocidal tactics employed by perpetrators. Children are raped, molested, mutilated, sexually enslaved, tortured, forced to witness the rape of loved ones, forced to commit rapes, and trafficked into the international sex trade. In instances of genocide that involve the cooptation of children into armed forces, children of both sexes face sexual exploitation by older soldiers. They also are more vulnerable to rape after the genocide: in their families, in their communities, in refugee camps, or, in cases where children participated as perpetrators, in prison. Despite the frequency of crimes committed against children, we unfortunately do not have reliable statistics regarding the incidence of sexual violence committed *specifically against them* during times of war and genocide.[2] The ages of victims of sexualized violence is rarely reflected in the data, except perhaps narratively in instances where a victim was very young or very old. What we do know about child victims of sexual violence during genocide comes from the testimony of survivors, both child and adult, who report the abuses of minors during conflict. In a few cases, human rights groups have broken data down according to adult and child victims, but such instances are rare. This subject is, thus, overdue for further research into its nature and its scope.

The systematic abuse of minors is one of the strongest indicators and a core characteristic of genocide. Children are arguably the most treasured members of a family and a community. They represent a group's future and are also sacred carriers of its past. They symbolize the totality of a group's existence, its past, present, and future, its hope and its meaning. They are, additionally, one of the most vulnerable groups within society and, as a consequence, during peacetime are

196

subject to numerous protective institutions and social norms. Indeed, the effective social protection of children is an important and universal marker of social health and wellbeing. Their defilement then—through murder, torture, sexual exploitation, mutilation, and disappearance—is one of the most potent weapons a perpetrating state and army has when committing genocide. Because children are such important symbols—to the victim group and to the perpetrators—their treatment by armed forces/genocidaires can tell us a great deal about the nature and possible development of the conflict as it is underway. If a state or armed group appears to be targeting children deliberately—through shelling campaigns or door-to-door atrocities—there is a strong chance that what we are witnessing is, or will soon be, genocide.

It is, therefore, in the interest of the international community to begin to better document the fate of children during conflict by developing reporting strategies that treat them as separate categories of victims, rather than simply including them within gender categories (as in "women and girls" and "men and boys"). Some important headway is being made in this respect with recent reports on Syria by War Child International and Save the Children that specifically focus on crimes, including sexual violence, committed against children.[3]

Psychological studies have suggested that the experience of childhood sexual violence, particularly as a very young child and particularly when it is attended by numerous other atrocities and traumata, can have much more severe effects on the long-term psychological development of the person than would be the case with an adolescent or an adult. They have shown that the age at which the abuse occurred is critical in determining the intensity of its long-term impact on the individual. Sexual terrorization at a very young age is particularly traumatic. Younger children who have experienced sexual abuse are more likely than older children to experience severe post-traumatic stress disorder (PTSD) as a consequence. Child survivors of sexual violence are also more likely to experience severe PTSD than children who experienced other forms of physical abuse. They, therefore, require special interventions and programs that recognize children's special needs.

Definitions of sexual violence vary. One of the preeminent international bodies working on sexual violence in conflict, the Inter-Agency Standing Committee (IASC) Task Force on Gender and Humanitarian Assistance, defines sexual violence as ". . . any sexual act, attempt to obtain a sexual act, unwanted sexual comments or advances, or acts to traffic a person's sexuality, using coercion, threats of harm or physical force, by any person regardless of relationship to the victim, in any setting, including but not limited to home and work."[4] Forms of sexual abuse during genocide include, but are not limited to, rape, gang rape, penetration of body orifices with foreign objects, enforced nakedness, unwanted touching and exhibitionism, enforced participation in "sex acts" for show, sexual slavery, sexual mutilation, forced prostitution, forced maternity, forced marriages, and the exchange of sex for food or safety. By most definitions, the threat of sexualized violence is enough to qualify as sexualized violence. Thus, the sadistic games that perpetrators often play with child victims, which often include threats to sexually abuse them and their loved ones, or threats to force them to commit sexual abuse against loved ones, also qualify as sexual violence.

The concept of gender-based violence includes sexualized violence but is more broadly defined to cover forms of violence that are meted out because of a child's sexual ascription. The IASC's definition of gender-based violence is ". . . any harmful act that is perpetrated against a person's will and that is based on socially ascribed (gender) differences between males and females."[5] During peacetime, common forms of gender-based violence include mutilation of the sexual organs (such as female genital mutilation and male circumcision), selective abortions of fetuses based on sex, traditions of childhood marriage, gender-based differences in access to food, shelter, medical care, and education, sex trafficking and related institutions promoting adult sex with children (such as the traditional practice in Afghanistan of using young boys for adult male sexual pleasure and entertainment), forced recruitment, and various forms of domestic violence. Gender-based violence committed against children during genocide can include mass rape of women and girls, the forced conscription of male children for use as soldiers, the kidnapping and use of girls as sex slaves and domestic servants, forced maternity, gender-based forms of sexual torture, and sex-selective massacres including the disproportionate killing of a child of a particular sex (such as male infants). While both boys and girls are victimized by sexualized violence during genocide, girls appear to be targeted in greater numbers than boys. Boys, on the other hand, may be singled out for more lethal gender-based violence in the form of sex-selective massacre alongside adult men. Sexualized violence is a core thread in the larger web of gender-based forms of destruction that go into the commission of genocide.

Sexualized Violence in Peacetime, War, and Genocide

The incidence of childhood sexual violence in peacetime varies from country to country. The first comprehensive, global study of violence against children conducted by the UN found that 150 million girls and seventy-three million boys under the age of eighteen had experienced forced sexual intercourse or other forms of sexual violence in 2002.[6] In the United States, a report by the Office of Juvenile Justice and Delinquency Prevention of the US Department of Justice estimated that in 1999, 285,400 children in the United States were sexually assaulted and 35,000 were victims of some other sexual offense. Of these, 85 percent were girls and 81 percent were between the ages of twelve and seventeen. The majority of children assaulted sexually were in fact girls between the ages of fifteen and seventeen (54 percent). A majority of the perpetrators were men, most of whom (71 percent) were an acquaintance of the child or known to him or her by sight.

Some of the peacetime patterns (as observed in the data for the United States) extend themselves into genocide. It appears that the majority of children sexually exploited during genocide are pre-adolescent and adolescent girls. The majority of perpetrators of sexual violence, though by no means all, are men. But the similarities end there. There is evidence from some conflicts that when dealing with child victims, the gap between male and female victimization narrows during genocide. Furthermore, whereas the majority of peacetime sexual victimization occurs in spaces we would call private (such as peoples' homes), the number of public and intentionally high-profile rapes and other forms of sexual violence and humiliation increases substantially during conflict. Genocidal violence is known for its use of sexual violence to destroy sacred ties within families in communities. Girls are frequently raped in front of fathers and brothers, wives in front of husbands, mothers in front of children, and members of high-profile families in front of the wider community. The level of brutality and the incidence of serious physical injury resulting from rape also increase during conflict and genocide. And during genocide, rape and sexual violation are often used as methods of murder.

Children suffer from the same violence and deprivation as their parents and other adults in the community, including injury and death during military assaults on their villages, towns and cities, malnourishment and starvation during sieges and displacements, sickness, lack of medical care, and vulnerability to criminal activity associated with prevalent insecurity and the breakdown of social mores. Infants and smaller children, like the elderly, are the most vulnerable to the consequences of the breakdown of the social order and the consequent displacement and lack of social services, food, and shelter. Since sexualized violence against civilians usually (although not always) accompanies armed conflict and its aftermath, children also frequently become its victims. Two harmful patterns thus converge during conflict to make children vulnerable to sexual victimization at every juncture: peacetime vulnerability, which is institutionalized in family, religious, penal, and educational structures and systems, and the goals and tactics practiced by armed groups engaging in hostilities. These two patterns are not only distinct but also interrelated: practices and beliefs involving the sexual violation of minors during peacetime can feed into their sexual violation in war.

Sexual violence is endemic to warfare, but it is not unavoidable. Certain conflicts, such as the Israeli/Palestinian conflict, have been characterized by remarkably low incidences of sexual violence. Certain armed forces are also known to have officially discouraged sexual violence, such as the insurgent groups in El Salvador and Sri Lanka (though sexual violence was used extensively by the states they were challenging). The Viet Cong also effectively discouraged sexual violence in a war where it was common for South Vietnamese and American troops to commit rape. Elisabeth Jean Wood has found that rape and other forms of sexual violence are most pronounced during wars in which these crimes are either encouraged or approved by the top of the military hierarchy or initiated at the bottom with permission from the top in the absence of an effective leadership hierarchy. In genocidal situations, it is no wonder that mass rape is so prevalent, since it is often used as an official tool by the architects or is indirectly allowed by a leadership interested in the total destruction of the group it is targeting.[7]

As in peacetime, the group of children at the highest risk of sexualized violence during warfare is girls over twelve, and especially girls between the ages of fifteen and eighteen. It is these girls who are most likely to get ensnared in rape campaigns by armed forces during wars of occupation and extermination. In these situations, soldiers frequently commit rape to express total conquest of the enemy territory, to humiliate enemy forces, and to enact fantasies of revenge. Young girls become prime targets because their bodies and their sexual purity are highly prized, and they are, therefore, the most highly guarded members of patriarchal societies. Girls also symbolize the group's reproductive future. By committing acts aimed at defiling adolescent girls, perpetrators attempt simultaneously to compromise the group's reproductive future and assault the core foundation of patriarchal society within the victim group: the control over female bodies, which is believed to be the cornerstone organizing and guaranteeing the group's reproduction.

Children become systematically targeted for sexualized and gender-based violence during genocide in many ways, because perpetrators of genocide instrumentalize children for a host of atrocities as part of their overarching attempts to destroy communities in whole or in part. During the genocide in Darfur, very young black African girls were frequently raped and gang raped and otherwise tortured during attacks by Government of Sudan troops and the Janjaweed, during flight, and in both internally displaced persons camps and refugee camps. They were also kidnapped and used as sexual slaves by the Janjaweed and government troops (Amnesty International 2004).

Children are both the direct and indirect victims of sexualized violence; they can be subjected to the same crimes as adult men and women, and they also suffer long-term harm from having witnessed sexualized violence against family members and from having been forced to commit sexual violence as child soldiers. Stories of very young children who witnessed, and in some cases were the only surviving witnesses of, the sexual violation and murder of their family members are common in genocide. The "ripple effects" and "secondary trauma" caused by sexual assault and other forms of violence during genocide are severe and require much more attention than they have been given in the literature up to this point.[8] Frequently, children are victimized—as direct victims and as witnesses—by sexualized violence in several different ways and at several different times over the course of a single conflict—in their homes, in hiding, during military assaults, during captivity, and in refugee camps during and after the conflict. For example, a fifteen-year-old girl from South Kivu, in the eastern part of the Democratic Republic of the Congo, recently, described her rape and that of her three-year-old sister by the government forces. These rapes were attended by massive violence against everyone in the household:

> There were six soldiers who came into my house. They first raped my three-year-old sister, and then two of them raped me while the others

looted our house. They threw my newborn baby onto the ground, and because of the shock he is in a lot of pain whenever anyone touches his legs. The soldiers were wearing military uniforms and they spoke Kinyarwanda. There were Hutus and Tutsis and other tribes as well. After they raped me, they took my mother away with them. She hasn't come back yet, and I think she must be dead. Five other houses in Kihonga were visited the same night by the soldiers.[9]

The girl had been previously raped the year before, also by government soldiers. The baby boy who was thrown to the floor was born out of that rape. In addition to having to survive two brutal gang rapes in the space of one year, this young girl was also left responsible for her maimed infant son and her three-year-old sister, whose physical and emotional condition can only be imagined after brutal gang rape.

Child survivors and witnesses of sexual assault during genocidal violence often are left to fend for themselves after their parents and other relatives have been killed or kidnapped or after they have been shunned from their families and communities. Human Rights Watch estimates that 400,000 child survivors of the Rwandan genocide were left without one or both parents. While many orphans were taken into the homes of relatives and foster families, others were exploited by unscrupulous people who used them as unpaid domestic servants and field laborers or to obtain the land of their dead family members. Thousands of children live alone on the streets of Rwanda's larger towns and cities, where they are vulnerable to sexual victimization.[10] Children orphaned and displaced by genocide are also vulnerable to being trafficked into the international sex trade. One of the long-term effects of the Cambodian genocide has been a thriving sex tourism industry in the country as well as high numbers of young girls sold to domestic and international traffickers.

Mass Rape

Examinations of rape during conflict and genocide are faced with numerous challenges. First and foremost is the lack of reliable evidence. We know that sexual violence is one of the most underreported crimes during peacetime; during war, there are even more encumbrances faced by victims in reporting these crimes. Young children are perhaps some of the least likely victims to report their experiences of sexualized violence during and after a conflict, due to the fear and self-blame that particularly affect child victims and due to the discomfort of humanitarian aid workers in addressing this particularly traumatic pattern.

Estimates of the number of victims of sexualized violence range widely and are often used for crude political purposes by all opposing sides. For studies of children and sexualized violence during war and genocide, the data set is practically non-existent, since statistics regarding this crime are not generally disaggregated by age.

One of the most common forms of sexualized violence during genocide is mass rape. Mass rape is a feature of all modern instances of genocide, including the Holocaust, and can be considered to be a key indicator and characteristic of genocidal violence. Mass rape characterized the genocides in North America of indigenous peoples, Ottoman Turkey, Nazi-occupied Europe, Japanese-occupied Asia during World War II, East Timor, Biafra (eastern Nigeria), East Pakistan (Bangladesh), Guatemala, Bosnia-Herzegovina, Rwanda, Liberia, Sierra Leone, Uganda, the Democratic Republic of the Congo, Darfur, and Sri Lanka.

While the data suggests that the majority of victims of mass rape are women and girls, in certain conflicts the incidence of rape of men and boys is very high. A survey published in the *Journal of the American Medical Association* found that in the eastern region of the Democratic Republic of the Congo, over 23 percent of men and nearly 40 percent of women reported conflict-related sexual violence, a difference of 17 percent.[11] Furthermore, when we are specifically discussing the subject of child victims of sexual abuse, the gap between prevalence levels among the sexes seems to narrow. An analysis of childhood sexual abuse surveys from twenty-one countries found that 3 to 29 percent of males and 7 to 36 percent of females reported having experienced sexual abuse as children.[12] It is quite possible that during war and genocide male children are violated at rates higher than adult men, putting them closer to the rates of sexual violence experienced by girls during conflict.

In certain conflicts, there is some evidence that children may constitute an overall majority of rape victims. Human Rights Watch reports, for example, that unpublished correspondence with the United Nations Population Fund (UNFPA) suggests that 65 percent of the victims of sexual violence in the Democratic Republic of the Congo in 2008 were children, the majority of them being girls. About 10 percent of the victims were less than ten years old.[13] For a similar time period, the United Nations Office of the Secretary General reported that between 38 and 42 percent of victims of sexual abuse in the Democratic Republic of the Congo were children.[14] Whatever the exact numbers in any conflict, the incidence of child rape and other forms of sexual exploitation during genocide appears to be very high.

As Human Rights Watch points out in its report on sexual violence in the Democratic Republic of the Congo, the consequences of mass rape are particularly disastrous for its child victims.[15] Children suffer in specific ways because of their small size. Many of them die as a consequence of rape, especially in instances of gang rape. Those who survive often face life-long physical disability, including incontinence, infection, and sexually transmitted diseases. In many cases, girl survivors are incapable of conception or of carrying a pregnancy to term. If girls were impregnated by the rapes, they are at a higher risk of developing complications during childbirth. Like adult victims of rape, girls and boys are often rejected by their families. They are even less capable than adult victims of rape of caring for themselves alone, and this puts them at a greater risk of continued sexual violence in the form of repeat rape by armed groups and civilians as well as sexual exploitation by procurers and international traffickers. Girls who are ostracized as a consequence of their rape often find it impossible to marry and hence are deprived of what is often the only route to economic viability. In certain parts of the world, they may be killed by family members seeking to protect family honor. If they bear a child as a result of rape, they are faced with raising it while they are still themselves children and without economic, emotional, and social support from their family and community. While the stigma attached to rape will keep many girls from talking about their experiences and seeking help, we can assume that this is even more true for boys.

During genocide, mass rape can serve many purposes; some of them are linked directly to the genocidal goals of the perpetrators and some are linked to the conditions created by armed conflict, mass upheaval, and refugee flows, all of which break down the traditions, norms, and institutions that protect children from adult violence. A primary motive for—as well as the intent of—mass rape during genocide is the total annihilation of the victim group. Women and girls, as well as men and boys, are instrumentalized before their deaths as objects of humiliation, including sexual humiliation, as a symbol of their total destruction. This was the case in the Holocaust, where it is often assumed that sexual violence was quite limited due to Nazi laws against what was called race defilement. Despite these laws, however, women and girls were raped and otherwise sexually violated throughout Nazi-occupied Europe in their homes, in hiding, at mass execution sites, in ghettos, in "brothels," and in concentration and death camps. The perpetrators were German soldiers, SS men, local police, and non-German soldiers from allied armies, collaborators and, sometimes, fellow prisoners. The vast majority of the victims were killed; many of them were children.[16]

A second motive for mass rape is to terrify populations into fleeing from the territory that the perpetrators seek to control. Mass rape was used for this purpose especially in Bosnia-Herzegovina and Darfur and continues to be in the Democratic Republic of the Congo. The rape of children can be considered to be a very powerful and effective type of terrorization. CNN's Nic Robertson reports that commanders in the army of the Government of Sudan specifically ordered soldiers to rape *children* in Darfur for the purpose of driving out entire communities; soldiers who refused were threatened with death.[17] The famous Ram Plan devised by psychological warfare specialists within the Serbian Army called specifically for the sexual abuse of Muslim women and children as part of an overall strategy of permanently ridding areas, which were perceived to be Serb territories, of their Muslim populations. In fact, it singled out adolescent girls: "Our analysis of the behavior of the Muslim communities demonstrates that the morale, will, and bellicose nature of their groups can be undermined only if we aim our action at the point where the religious and social structure is most fragile. We refer to the women, especially adolescents, and to the children. Decisive intervention on these social figures would spread confusion among the communities, thus causing first of all fear and then panic, leading to a probable [Muslim] retreat from the territories involved in war activity."[18] In Bosnia and Darfur especially, children as young as five years old were sexually targeted as part of an overarching policy of ethnic cleansing that amounted to genocide.

A third motive for mass rape during genocide is to terrorize a population into submission. This is common during counterinsurgencies in which the government using genocidal tactics is not interested in removing a population from its land but rather cowing it into subordination by murdering, raping, and mutilating key symbolic groups within the victim society. There is evidence that the rape of young children is recognized by the perpetrators as a particularly heinous crime and that they utilize it to further terrorize local populations.

A fourth motive for mass rape during genocide is to undermine, both spiritually and physically, a group's ability to reproduce itself into the future. Genocidal conditions within a conflict tend to create the conditions for rape attended by multiple and pronounced forms of physical, emotional, and psychological tortures inflicted intentionally by perpetrators. We see greater evidence of rapes of infants and very old people, for example, as well as a high number of gang rapes, rape used as a weapon of murder, rape documented and consumed by soldiers as pornography through cell phones and other technologies, and rape committed as an "anchor crime" within a litany of atrocities aimed at a particular family or village. In the latter case, girls and boys are often raped in front of parents and community members, are forced to rape each other or older family members, are raped by family members who have been coerced into doing so (often in the hopes of sparing the child's life), and are mutilated and killed alongside family and neighbors. These inversion rituals and ritual desecrations have been pronounced in the Holocaust, the Nanking Massacre, Guatemala, Bangladesh, Bosnia-Herzegovina, Rwanda, Darfur, and the Democratic Republic of the Congo.

Finally, there is the base performative aspect of mass rape that fuels much sexualized violence during genocide. Perpetrators simply treat individual victims, and the smaller familial and local groups to which they belong, as stand-ins for the group at large that is to be destroyed. This is why so many of the victims of these performances are killed afterwards. A common thread in such performances is sexual assault followed by mutilation; this is a fairly common form of genocidal atrocity committed against children and is usually meant for public consumption. During the Rwandan genocide, Hutu genocidaires made it a point to torture children in front of their parents before killing everyone, and frequently this torture involved the mutilation of children's genitals while they were still alive.[19] In a startling passage from General Roméo Dallaire's memoir, *Shake Hands with the Devil*, he describes his realization of the extent of sexual violence during the Rwandan genocide, where it is estimated that between 200,000 and 500,000 women and girls were raped, most of whom were killed or died afterwards. Brutal rape was in fact used as a method of killing:

> I don't know when I began to clearly see the evidence of another crime besides murder among the bodies in the ditches and the mass graves. I know that for a long time I sealed away from my mind all the signs of this crime, instructing myself not to recognize what was there in front of me. The crime was rape, on a scale that deeply

affected me. . . . But if you looked, you could see the evidence, even in the whitened skeletons. The legs bent and apart. A broken bottle, a rough branch, even a knife between them. Where the bodies were fresh, we saw what must have been semen pooled on and near the dead women and girls. There was always a lot of blood. Some male corpses had their genitals cut off, but many women and young girls had their breasts chopped off and their genitals cut apart. They died in a position of total vulnerability, flat on their backs, with their legs bent and knees wide apart. It was the expressions on their dead faces that assaulted me the most, a frieze of shock, pain and humiliation. For many years after I came home, I banished the memories of those faces from my mind, but they have come back, all too clearly.[20]

Frequently during periods of mass rape, children are forced to rape one another. A survivor of the Srebrenica genocide remembers seeing a girl about nine years old and her brother being addressed by Serb forces during the days before the massacres. "At a certain moment some Chetniks recommended to her brother that he rape the girl," she recalled. "He did not do it and I also think that he could not have done it for he was still just a child. Then they murdered that young boy."[21] Often such "inversion rituals"[22] involve a series of atrocities that are linked together by the perpetrator's intent to destroy the spirit and the bodies of a whole community. A woman survivor of a genocidal attack against a community in the Democratic Republic of the Congo reported how unidentified soldiers entered her village and killed the village chief and his children and then proceeded to kill her parents. After this, they ordered her brother to rape her. When he refused, they killed him. Her three children were then murdered—her infant daughter was flung on the ground "like she was garbage"—and the survivor was brutally gang raped and forced into sexual slavery. While there, she witnessed the disembowelment of a pregnant woman, whose baby she was forced to cook and eat along with other captive women. As a consequence of this extended sexual torture, she will undoubtedly suffer lifelong physical disability.

The purposes of forced inversion rituals are manifold. They aim to destroy deep bonds of loyalty, to exploit feelings of responsibility and protectiveness, to target, humiliate, and permanently damage the parents and other adults in the community who are forced to watch, and to provide soldiers with amusement. Children are specific targets of this violence, and their sexualized violation is clearly meant as a direct assault on everything a community cherishes, on its very will to live.

When children are forced to commit crimes against others, including sexual assault, they are often killed afterwards, either when they refuse the command or once they have tried to carry it out.

Sexualized Violence in Confinement

Sexual violence against children during genocide can occur anywhere—in homes, in public places, and in places of confinement, such as detention centers, prisons, internment, concentration, death, and rape camps. In Bosnia-Herzegovina, the genocide committed by Bosnian Serbs with support from the Serbian State under Slobodan Milosevic involved widespread rape in various contexts of confinement, especially "rape camps" of different sizes where women and girls were kept, often with the intent of forcing them to bear "Serb" children (a genocidal phenomenon referred to in the literature as forced impregnation or forced maternity).[23] This incarceration came on the heels of attacks on towns during which women and girls were raped with impunity in front of their families, in basements, in empty apartment buildings, in police stations, schools, movie theaters, and stadiums. A similar pattern existed in East Pakistan (Bangladesh), Rwanda, and Darfur.

During the nine-month war in Bangladesh in 1971, West Pakistan soldiers raped an estimated 200,000 to 400,000 women.[24] Women and girls were frequently raped in front of family members during attacks on villages, after which many of the men were killed. The women and girls were taken to military compounds, where they were kept as sex slaves for the duration of the genocide. Survivors reported that women and girls were often murdered by being bayoneted through their genitals. Mutilation of girls' genitals, especially by bayonets, broken bottles, sharpened sticks, and other such objects, is common in genocide.

Much of the sexualized violence committed during the Holocaust was committed in confinement: in ghettos and concentration and death camps. Furthermore, children in hiding also faced sexual exploitation from their rescuers. German soldiers raped girls in the ghettos in front of their families. They took girls from their families and brought them to military barracks, where the girls were gang raped and killed. In the Lodz ghetto and the concentration camp of Skarżysko-Kamienna, rape of young girls was commonplace. A survivor named Sara M. was raped as a very young girl at the Ravensbrück concentration camp:

> [T]here were two men there and there were some other people in the room, I think. I was put on a table. From what I remember, [it was] a table or could have been a high table. I was very little so it seemed like it was very high up from where I was and I was very violently sexually abused. And I remember being hit, I remember crying and I wanted to get out of there. And I was calling people and screaming and I remember one thing that stands out in my mind, that one of them told me that they would stand me up on my head and cut me right in half. And they wanted me to stop screaming and I've had nightmares about that most of my life.[25]

Concentration and death camps all had brothels made up of women and girls as well as young boys called *Piepels*. A survivor, Yehiel Dinur (known under the nom de plume Ka-Tzetnik 135633), devoted two books of Holocaust fiction to the fates of his sister and brother, both of whom were sex slaves in concentration camps before they were murdered.[26] Girls and boys were also used for painful medical experiments involving sexual organs; many were sterilized, and young women who were pregnant had their babies forcibly aborted. Sexual violation also took other forms. The forced nakedness upon arrival at the camps, as well as the shaving of women's and girls' hair and genitals, also constituted forms of sexual violence, as did the brutal attack experienced by a survivor called Judith in a labor camp when she was eight years old:

> One day I wandered around the camp without telling anyone. . . . I grew tired and sat down on a rock, drawing lazily in the dirt with a stick. I saw ants carrying food and pondered why they were free and I wasn't. Then I saw a tall man wearing a black suit and high boots coming up to me along with his dog. The dog was taller than me, and I was scared of the dog, so he told the dog something in German, and the dog sat still. . . . He asked me my name and then wanted to know whether or not I was a Jew. When I said that I was, he asked me why I wasn't wearing the patch. I said I'd forgotten. Then he took a big stick and swung it into my face, breaking my nose and several teeth. I was bleeding badly, told him I was sorry, and begged him to let me go. He grabbed me and threw me onto the ground, ordering the dog to attack me. The dog bit me and ripped my clothes off. Then the guard came over to me and burned his cigarette into my face. I screamed so loud, hoping that someone would hear me and help me, but nobody did. Then he put his penis inside my mouth and peed. I started choking and vomiting. So he shot me in my leg and left me there alone.[27]

Judith survived and was nursed back to health by nuns who did not know she was Jewish. Once she regained consciousness and told them who she was, they were frightened and had someone bring her back to her mother and other female relatives in the camp. But the guard came looking for her; he accused her mother of stealing her from the Christians on account of her blond hair. Her mother desperately tried to show him Judith's birth certificate, but he tore it apart, grabbed Judith's baby sister, and cut her in two. He then killed her grandmother, who had tried to protect the infant, and shot her mother and aunt. Only Judith and her mother survived the massacre.

Such abject brutality, and the unwillingness of perpetrators to stop at anything, has also been experienced by countless men and boys during genocide. One study of 6,000 survivors of Serb-run concentration camps estimated that 80 percent of male inmates were raped and otherwise sexually violated.[28] Forms of sexual violence included castrating inmates, forcing inmates to castrate other inmates with their teeth, and forcing inmates to rape one another, including fathers and sons. Many men died from this torture or were killed afterwards. Clearly, boys were not spared; instead, they were instrumentalized in inversion rituals involving their own fathers.

Child Soldiering and Sexual Slavery

In genocidal situations where armed groups seek to co-opt the biological power of the civilians they are destroying, the sexual enslavement of young children and their forced recruitment into armed groups go hand-in-hand.[29] Some armed groups appear to use child labor, child sexual slavery, and child soldiers as a means of transferring reproductive units and biological wealth from the communities targeted with destruction to their own group. The children are meant to replenish lost combatants as well as bring new combatants into the world. By and large, boys and girls are recruited for different purposes and given different roles: boys to act as soldiers and girls as domestics and sex slaves. However, the gendered division of labor among child soldiers is not as stark as is sometimes depicted. In Sierra Leone, for example, girls constituted 25 percent of child soldiers in all armed groups fighting in the war that raged from 1991 through 2002. They fought alongside boys and men, witnessed atrocities, and committed them as well, while also being subjected to rape and sexual abuse.[30] Boys, while often used primarily for soldiering and heavy labor, are often also sexually violated while under the control of armed forces.

While the Revolutionary United Front in Sierra Leone, Joseph Kony's Lord's Resistance Army (LRA), which was founded in northern Uganda in 1986 and now operates almost solely in the Democratic Republic of the Congo, and militias operating in the eastern Congo have institutionalized sexual violence within their forces, not all armed groups using child soldiers condone their sexual exploitation. As previously noted, some armed groups, such as those fighting in Colombia, the Philippines, and Sri Lanka, forbid coerced sex with minors and punish it harshly.[31]

A little appreciated consideration in the continuum of sexual violence faced by children in peacetime and in war is the fact that sexual (and other) violence in the home can be a factor in a child's decision to join an armed group voluntarily. In such a case, joining an armed force is an attempt to put an end to sexual violation rather than be subjected to it. Particularly for girls, whose familial and societal status is still much lower than boys in most of the world, armed groups can offer an opportunity for an escape from brutality as well as the chance for employment, education, status, freedom, and adventure, which is not available to them in their peacetime lives. Scholars and human rights practitioners are attempting to appreciate the overlap of experience between boy and girl child soldiers. If girls' actual soldiering is not recognized, they will not be included (as they have not been) in disarmament, demobilization, and reintegration (DDR) programs, which offer them necessary resources and training to return to peacetime life with dignity and independence. Being left out of DDR programs means that girl combatants, many of whom have children who were born as a consequence of sexual exploitation, are given even fewer means than boys to survive, while often facing a harsher reception from family and community upon return. Equally important is the recognition of the extent of sexual abuse of male child soldiers, whose physical and emotional wounds from sexual violence are rarely treated upon demobilization.

Stolen Children and Sexual Trafficking

A slightly different pattern of sexual exploitation involving children was the child kidnapping program of the Argentine military during the country's "Dirty War." As is now becoming well known, during what they called the Process of National Reorganization, military leaders often abducted the young children of dissidents who had been murdered, raising the children as their own. Some of the young children were stolen from families during violent home invasions. Others were born in detention and their mothers killed afterwards. Some mothers may have given birth as a consequence of rape in detention, which was rampant. It is estimated that 500 young children were abducted from murdered parents.[32]

Stealing children is mentioned in the 1948 United Nations Convention on the Prevention and Punishment of the Crime of Genocide (UNGC). Article II(e) of the UNGC defines "forcibly transferring children of the group to another group" as an act of genocide. Stealing children is a policy that is more common in genocidal processes than is often recognized. The wholesale destruction of Jewish children in Nazi Europe can be understood as kidnapping and forcible transfer. The Nazis also kidnapped thousands of "racially valuable" children from homes in South Eastern Europe, Poland, and the Soviet Union to be raised as Germans in Germany. It is estimated that up to 50,000 children were stolen by the SS for this purpose.[33] Forcible transfer was also common in genocidal processes involving indigenous peoples. The best-known cases of this are the North American residential schools and Australia's "Stolen Generation." Sexual violence against children was so rampant in Canadian residential schools that in 1995 a Canadian Supreme Court judge called the schools "nothing but a form of institutionalized pedophilia."[34] The children who were forcibly taken from their Aborigine mothers in Australia were often victimized by sexual predation in the boarding schools and afterwards in their work places.[35]

Processes of genocide can also fuel domestic and international trafficking in children. In Sudan, which has been plagued by genocidal violence perpetrated by the state since the early 1990s, boys and girls from southern Sudan and Darfur have been kidnapped in large numbers and sold into slavery internally in the north and internationally to other Arab countries and Europe. One report exposed the brutal sexual abuse that is routinely committed against boys who are sold to northern households.[36]

Gender-Based Killing

In an attempt to destroy a group, in whole or in part, perpetrators often pursue gender-selective forms of mass killing.[37] There is frequently an age dimension to massacre as well. In the Srebrenica genocide, where an estimated 8,000 Muslim men and boys were selected out from refugees in the safe haven and killed under the pretense of being soldiers, at least 500 victims were under the age of eighteen. Most of these were boys between ten and eighteen years of age, since the Bosnian Serbs defined "battle age" men to include pre-teens and teenagers. During the Darfur genocide, the age and gender groups that lost the greatest number of people to murder and disappearance were young men between the ages of fifteen and twenty-nine on the one hand and girls between the ages of five and fourteen on the other.[38] Janjaweed militias, supported by the armed forces of the Government of Sudan, also singled out male babies to be killed outright during attacks on Darfuri villages (though female babies were also killed in large numbers).

Conclusion

The subject of sexual violence against children during genocide, though difficult to confront, needs to be studied in much greater depth than it has been up to this point. This will require not only that academic researchers write children back into narratives of genocide, but also that human rights researchers develop more sensitive protocols when conducting interviews with survivors of genocidal violence that increase the likelihood that child survivors of sexualized violence are recognized, are encouraged to come forward with their stories, and are given the safe spaces needed to speak about what they have endured.

Sexualized violence against children is part of a much broader gender-based pattern of attack that constitutes the crime of genocide. Some of these patterns can be traced back to peacetime forms of child victimization. Others are particular to the genocidal pattern itself. Sexualized and gender-based violence in genocide has many dimensions, and children can fall prey to one or several of them in the course of a conflict. In many conflicts, children are a primary and intended target of perpetrators' cruelty. They are instrumentalized to damage families and communities to their core, and, as such, children sometimes receive treatment worse than adults, a situation that turns peacetime expectations directly on their heads. The effects of genocidal sexual violence on children, as primary and secondary victims, are so disastrous and so long-lasting that we must begin to understand and speak about genocide prevention as, simply, child protection.

Notes

1. Human Rights Watch, *Lasting Wounds: Consequences of Genocide and War on Rwanda's Children* (New York: Human Rights Watch, 2013), 8.
2. The UN Convention on the Rights of the Child defines a child as "every human being below the age of eighteen years." The full text of the convention is available at http://www2.ohchr.org/english/law/crc.htm (accessed August 20, 2012).
3. War Child UK, *Syria: A War on Childhood* (London: War Child UK, 2012), available at http://www.warchild.org.uk/sites/default/files/Syria%20-%20War%20on%20Children%28final%29.pdf (accessed August 12, 2012); Save the Children, *Untold Atrocities* (London: Save the Children, 2012), available at: http://www.savethechildren.org.uk/sites/default/files/images/untold_atrocities.pdf (accessed 25 September 2012).
4. IASC Task Force on Gender and Humanitarian Assistance, *Guidelines for Gender-based Violence Interventions in Humanitarian Settings: Focusing on Prevention of and Response to Sexual Violence in Emergencies* (Geneva: IASC, 2005), 8.
5. IASC Task Force, *Guidelines*, 7.
6. Paulo Sérgio Pinheiro, *Report of the Independent Expert for the United Nations Study on Violence against Children* (Geneva: United Nations General Assembly, 2006), 10.
7. Elisabeth Jean Wood, "Rape Is Not Inevitable during War" in *Women & War: Power and Protection in the 21st Century*, ed. Kathleen Kuehnast, Chantal de jonge Oudraat, and Helga Hernes (Washington, DC: United States Institute of Peace Press, 2011), 37–63.
8. For a brief overview of the limited literature of the effects of children's exposure to sexual violence against family members, see Zoë Morrison, Antonia Quadara, and Cameron Boyd, "'Ripple effects' of Sexual Assault." *ACSSA Issues No. 7* (Melbourne: Australian Institute for Family Studies, 2007).
9. Human Rights Watch, *Soldiers Who Rape, Commanders Who Condone: Sexual Violence and Military Reform in the Democratic Republic of the Congo* (New York: Human Rights Watch, 2009).
10. Human Rights Watch, *Lasting Wounds: Consequences of Genocide and War on Rwanda's Children* (New York: Human Rights Watch, March 2013).
11. Johnson, K. et al., "Association of Sexual Violence and Human Rights Violations with Physical and Mental Health in Territories of the Eastern Democratic Republic of the Congo," *The Journal of the American Medical Association* 304, no. 5 (2010): 553–62, Available at: http://jama.ama-assn.org.
12. Lara Stempel, "Male Rape and Human Rights," Hastings Law Journal 60 (2009): 605–46.
13. Human Rights Watch, *Soldiers Who Rape, Commanders Who Condone: Sexual Violence and Military Reform in the Democratic Republic of Congo*, July 16, 2009, 7.
14. United Nations Security Council, *Report of the Secretary-General on children and armed conflict in the Democratic Republic of the Congo*, November 10, 2008, Para 42, 43, 44.
15. Human Rights Watch, *Soldiers Who Rape*, 16.

16. Helene Sinnreich, "The Rape of Jewish Women during the Holocaust," in *Sexual Violence against Jewish Women during the Holocaust*, eds. Sonja M. Hedgepeth, and Rochelle Saidel, (Waltham, MA: Brandeis University Press, 2010), 108–23.

17. Nic Robertson, "Sudan soldier: They told me to kill, to rape children," *Cnn.com/world*, March 5, 2009. Available at http://edition.cnn.com/2009/WORLD/africa/03/04/darfur.rape/index.html#cnnSTCText (accessed August 18, 2012).

18. Beverly Allen, *Rape Warfare: The Hidden Genocide in Bosnia-Herzegovina and Croatia* (London/Minneapolis: University of Minnesota Press, 1996), 57.

19. Romeo Dallaire, *Shake Hands with the Devil: The Failure of Humanity in Rwanda* (Berkeley, CA/New York: Carroll & Graf, 2005), 461.

20. Dallaire, *Shake Hands with the Devil*, 429.

21. Munira Šubašić, testimony, Van Diepen/Van der Kroef, Writ of Summons, June 4, 2007. The Hague. Full text, with witness testimonies, Available at: http://www.vandiepen.com/en/international/srebrenica/proceedings-the-hague.html (accessed July 2, 2012).

22. Elisa von Joeden-Forgey, "The Devil in the Details: Life Force Atrocities and the Assault on the Family in Times of Conflict," *Genocide Studies and Prevention* 5, no. 1 (2010).

23. Siobhan K. Fisher, "Occupation of the Womb: Forced Impregnation as Genocide," *Duke Law Journal* 46, no. 1 (1996): 91–133.

24. Lisa Sharlach, "Rape as Genocide: Bangladesh, the Former Yugoslavia, and Rwanda," *New Political Science* 22, no. 1 (2000): 89–102; Angela Debnath, "The Bangladesh Genocide: The Plight of Women," in *Plight and Fate of Women during and following Genocide*, ed. Samuel Totten (New Brunswick, NJ/London: Transaction Publishers, 2009), 47–66.

25. Sinnreich, "The Rape of Jewish Women," 112.

26. Yehiel Dinur, *House of Dolls*, trans. Moshe M. Kohn (London: Frederick Muller, 1956) and *Piepel*, trans. Moshe M. Kohn (London: Anthony Blond, 1961). For a sympathetic discussion of Dinur's controversial work, see Miryam Sivan, "'Stoning the Messenger': Yehiel Dinur's House of Dolls and Piepel," in *Sexual Violence*, eds. Hedgepeth and Saidel, 200–16.

27. Lev-Wiesel and Weinger, *Hell Within Hell*, 50–51.

28. Lisa Sharlach, "Rape as Genocide: Bangladesh, the Former Yugoslavia, and Rwanda," *New Political Science* 22: 1 (2000), 89-102; Angela Debnath, "The Bangladesh Genocide: The Plight of Women," in Samuel Totten (ed), *Plight and Fate of Women during and Following Genocide* (New Brunswick, NJ/London: Transaction Publishers, 2009), 47-66.

29. Janie L. Leatherman, "Seeking Safe Space," *Sexual Violence and Armed Conflict* (Cambridge, UK: Polity, 2011), 89–115.

30. Susan McKay, "Girls as 'Weapons of Terror' in Northern Uganda and Sierra Leonean Fighting Forces," *Studies in Conflict and Terrorism* 28, no. 5 (2005): 388.

31. McKay, "Girls as 'Weapons of Terror,'" 389.

32. Rita Arditti, *Searching for Life: The Grandmothers of the Plaza de Mayo and the Disappeared Children of Argentina* (Berkeley: University of California Press, 1999).

33. Isabel Heinemann, "'Until the Last Drop of Good Blood': The Kidnapping of 'Racially Valuable' Children and Nazi Racial Policy in Occupied Eastern Europe," in *Genocide and Settler Society: Frontier Violence and Stolen Indigenous Children in Australian History*, ed. Dirk Moses (New York/Oxford: Berghahn Books, 2004), 247.

34. Ward Churchill, *Kill the Indian, Save the Man: The Genocidal Impact of American Indian Residential Schools* (San Francisco, CA: City Lights Books, 2004), 62.

35. Moses, *Genocide and Settler Society*; Adam Jones, "Genocides of Indigenous Peoples," *Genocide: A Comprehensive Introduction*, 2nd ed. (London/New York: Routledge, 2006), 105–48.

36. Maria Sliwa, "Sudan Cries Rape: Former Captives Recount the Crime of Boy Rape in Sudan." www.scribd.com/doc/62878277/Sudan-Cries-Rape-Former-Captives-Recount-the-Crime-of-Boy-Rape-in-Sudan (Accessed 11 November 2013)

37. For an overview of this literature, see Adam Jones, "Gendering Genocide," in *Genocide*, 464–98.

38. John Hagen, and Wenona Rymond-Richmond, *Darfur and the Crime of Genocide* (New York: Cambridge University Press, 2009), 212.

Reference

Amnesty International. 2004. *Sudan, Darfur: Rape as a Weapon of War: Sexual Violence and Its Consequences*. London: Author.

Annotated Bibliography

Rita Arditti. *Searching for Life: The Grandmothers of the Plaza de Mayo and the Disappeared Children of Argentina*. Berkeley and Los Angeles: University of California Press, 1999, 251 pp.
    The most comprehensive study to date of the Plaza de Mayo movement and the stolen children in Argentina.
Megan Bastick, Karin Grimm, and Rahel Kunz. *Sexual Violence in Armed Conflict: Global Overview and Implications for the Security Sector*. Geneva: Geneva Centre for the Democratic Control of Armed Forces, 2007, 217 pp.
    A nuanced study of the problem of sexual violence in armed conflict from a global perspective, with special emphasis on its implications for peacekeeping. While there is no particular section dealing with child victims or perpetrators of sexual violence, the study is attentive to the special vulnerabilities of children and mentions them throughout.
Australian Human Rights and Equal Opportunity Commission. "Bringing Them Home: The 'Stolen Children' Report." Sydney, New South Wales: Author, 1997, 680 pp.
    A report of the Australian commission of inquiry established by the federal attorney general in 1995 to investigate the country's policy toward Aboriginal children. The report determined that the child-removal program constituted genocide, a finding that is still controversial in Australia.
Brownmiller, Susan. "The Sexual Abuse of Children," *Against Our Will: Men, Women and Rape*, 271–83. New York: Fawcett Books. 1975.
    The classic feminist text on sexual violence against women, with important analyses of the issues involved in studying the subject as well as useful short

overviews of sexual violence in many wartime contexts and a short section on the sexual abuse of children during peacetime.

Carpenter, Charli R. ed. *Born of War: Protecting Children of Sexual Violence Survivors in Conflict Zones*. Bloomfield, CT: Kumarian Press, 2007, 288 pp.

A seminal collection of essays related to children born of wartime rape, covering theoretical issues related to the subject and case studies of the conflicts in Bosnia-Herzegovina, Rwanda, East Timor, Sierra Leone, and Uganda.

Hagen, John, and Wenona Rymond-Richmond. *Darfur and the Crime of Genocide*. New York: Cambridge University Press, 2008, 296 pp.

A criminological study of the Darfur genocide using data gathered by the US State Department's Atrocities Documentation Team in 2004 that analyzes data according to the gender and age of victims.

Hedgepeth, Sonja M., and Saidel, Rochelle G. eds. *Sexual Violence against Jewish Women during the Holocaust*. Lebanon, NH: Brandeis University Press, 2010, 314 pp.

A ground-breaking work in the study of sexual violence during the Holocaust that brings together the most recent research in the field. Although there are no chapters specifically dedicated to child victims of sexual violence, there are many cases of such discussed throughout the book.

Leatherman, Janie L. "Seeking a Safe Space," *Sexual Violence and Armed Conflict*, 89–115. Cambridge, UK: Polity, 2011.

Chapter on sexual violence against child soldiers, the use of child sex slaves in armed forces, sexual violence against children in IDP camps and in post-genocide societies.

Lev-Wiesel, Rachel, and Susan Weinger. *Hell within Hell: Sexually Abused Child Holocaust Survivors: The Comorbidity of the Traumata*. New York: University Press of America, 2011, 96 pp.

The only published study of child survivors of sexual violence during the Holocaust. The book includes extensive transcriptions from interviews with seven survivors (one man and six women) from the original forty-two interviewed for the study.

Miller, Donald E., Touryan Miller, and Lorna Touryan. "The Experience of Women and Children." In *Survivors: An Oral History of the Armenian Genocide*, edited by Miller and Miller, 94–117. Berkeley/Los Angeles: University of California Press, 1993.

An analysis of first-person accounts of the Armenian genocide with much detail regarding the fates of children.

Moses, Dirk. ed. *Genocide and Settler Society: Frontier Violence and Stolen Indigenous Children in Australian History*. London: Berghahan Books, 2005. 344 pp.

Study of the official policy of Aboriginal child removal in Australia from the nineteenth century through the present day. Although no one chapter focuses on sexual violence per se, this was commonplace particularly in the homes into which girls were placed as domestic servants after graduation from the residential schools.

Shan Women's Action Network. *License to Rape: The Burmese Military Regime's Use of Sexual Violence in the Ongoing War in Shan State*. Chiang Mai: The Shan Human Rights Foundation, 2002, 127 pp.

A study by the Shan Women's Action Network, an NGO based in Thailand, of the systematic sexual violence used by the Burmese Army against civilians in Shan State, Myanmar. The study disaggregates data by the status of the victim as adult or child.

Stiglmayer, Alexandra. ed. *Mass Rape: The War against Women in Bosnia-Herzegovina*. Lincoln: University of Nebraska Press, 1993, 234 pp.

One of the earliest studies of mass rape during the Bosnian genocide, with contributions by some of the most important thinkers in the field. There are no chapters specifically dedicated to child victims of mass rape, but the stories of girl survivors are told throughout.

Totten, Samuel. ed. *Plight and Fate of Women during and following Genocide* (New Brunswick, NJ/London: Transaction Publishers, 2009, 256 pp.

Compendium of short, comprehensive overviews of the fate of women and girls during the genocides in Ottoman Turkey, Nazi-Occupied Europe, East Pakistan/Bangladesh, Cambodia, the former Yugoslavia, Rwanda, and Darfur, as well as topical treatments of rape as genocide, the evolution of gender crimes in international law, the prosecution of gender crimes, and the long-term impact of genocide on women and girls. Each chapter includes an annotated bibliography.

.

10

Child Soldiers: Children's Rights in the Time of War and Genocide

Hannibal Travis and Sara Demir

Introduction

The experiences of children during cases of genocide are varied. Children may be affected as persons succumbing to the deliberate imposition of conditions leading to death from hunger or disease, and as refugees and internally displaced persons, and may even be involved as perpetrators of killings planned by adults. This chapter begins with definitions of children and child soldiers and turns to legal developments surrounding the definitions and their practical impact. The next section of the chapter will deal with genocides involving children or child soldiers in important roles and highlight key aspects of the jurisprudence of the international criminal tribunals relating to child soldiers in the context of genocide or politicide.

In this chapter, the main focus will be on child soldiers in the twentieth and twenty-first centuries. However, child soldiers have existed throughout the history of mankind (Afua 2003). Yet, political and military elites largely neglected and in some ways aggravated the problem until the late 1990s. The large-scale wars and genocides of the twentieth and twenty-first centuries have influenced the development of an international legislation relating to child soldiers.

Scholarship for Children in War and Genocide

Defining a "Child"

An accepted definition of a child according to international law is set forth in Article 1 of the United Nations Convention on the Rights of the Child of 1989 (hereinafter the "CRC"), which provides that: "For the purpose of the present convention a child means every human being below the age of eighteen years, unless under the law applicable to the child, majority is attained earlier."

Defining "Child Soldiers"

While the Fourth Geneva Convention emphasizes child protection in wartime, the Additional Protocols of 1977 "have been the first instruments of international law that addressed the problem of child soldiers" (Topa 2007). Article 77 of Protocol I provides that "the Parties to the conflict shall take all feasible measures in order that children who have not attained the age of fifteen years do not take a direct part in hostilities and, in particular, they shall refrain from recruiting them into their armed forces." Although recruitment of children aged sixteen to eighteen years old was not completely prohibited, Article 77 obligated the states party to it to "endeavour to give priority to those who are the oldest." This development led to the opinion that children under the age of fifteen years enjoy special protection from war, whether or not they are prisoners of war, that is, when they have taken direct part in hostilities and fallen into the power of an adverse party.

Defining "Genocide"

Cultural genocide is a process linked closely to the fate of children, according to the Genocide Convention. The Convention on the Prevention and Punishment of the Crime of Genocide, which was adopted in 1948 and entered into force in 1951, states the following:

Article II: . . . [G]enocide means any of the following acts committed with intent to destroy, in whole or in part, a national, ethnical, racial or religious group, as such:

(a) Killing members of the group;
(b) Causing serious bodily or mental harm to members of the group;
(c) Deliberately inflicting on the group conditions of life calculated to bring about its physical destruction . . . in part;
(d) Imposing measures intended to prevent births within the group.
(e) Forcibly transferring children of the group to another group.

Raphael Lemkin, the individual who coined the term genocide, argued that genocide is often characterized by religious fanaticism, exploitation of weaker victims, separation of families, interference with childbirths and child-rearing, forced conversion to other religions, and subordination of the victim group (quoted in Docker 2008, 68–69).

History of the "Rights of the Child"

An early example of the rights of children and the obligations of states was elaborated by the League of Nations in 1924. There efforts sought to ensure better treatment for, among other children, the tens of thousands of children (Armenians, Assyrians, Assyro-Chaldeans, Russians, and Turks) who became refugees and orphans as a result of World War I, not to mention the Armenian genocide (1915–1921) (Travis 2010, 26). More specifically, the League of Nations adopted the Geneva Declaration in 1924, which stated that "humanity owes to the Child the best that it has to give." The content of the declaration contained five main elements, namely children's rights to development, assistance, relief, protection, and well-being (Geneva Declaration on the Rights if the Child 1924).

During World War II, the devastation experienced by the children of Europe and Asia was incalculable. The material and immaterial losses to children were immense. While millions of children died of starvation and disease, an untold number of others were orphaned, reduced to poverty, and denied medical care. In 1946, the United Nations established the United Nations International Children's Emergency Fund (UNICEF) to provide care for the children in Europe (UNICEF 2012). At the same time, international jurists drafted the Geneva Conventions, which, along with the Hague Regulations and the Additional Protocols to the Geneva Conventions of 1977, make up the fundamentals of international humanitarian law. Particularly noteworthy in this regard is the Protocol Additional to the Geneva Conventions of August 12, 1949, relating to the Protection of Victims of International Armed Conflicts, which calls upon states to refrain from recruiting children under the age of fifteen and to take "all feasible measures" to prevent their fighting (quoted in Dallaire and Beah 2011, 266).

On November 20, 1989, the General Assembly of the United Nations unanimously adopted the Convention on the Rights of Child (CRC). It was the first legally binding international instrument that incorporated the full range of human rights for children (Bang, Tiwari, and Agrawal 2011, 120). Concerning "children in armed conflicts," Article 38 of the CRC builds on the Additional Protocols of 1977 to prohibit recruitment of children under age 15, and requires that those older than eighteen or closer to eighteen years old be recruited prior to those aged fifteen to eighteen (Convention on the Rights of Child 1989, Article 38). The CRC, however, did not necessarily bind non-state entities. It could only impose liability on states parties and retained the age of fifteen as the contours of the ban on children in armed conflict.[1]

As set forth in Appendix A, most UN member states signed the CRC in the early 1990s. Only Somalia and the United States have signed but not yet ratified the convention. In the United States, the rationales of CRC opponents are that the treaty would violate US sovereignty by "supersed[ing] federal, state and local laws, and mandating choices and decisions best left to parents" (Inhofe and Demint 2012). This echoes opposition voiced in the 1980s to ratifying the Genocide Convention.

Defining Child Soldiery as Child Labor

On June 17, 1999, the International Labour Organization adopted the Worst Forms of Children Labour Convention, which entered into force on November 10, 2000. The Convention defines forced or compulsory recruitment of children for use in armed conflict as the worst form of child labor. More specifically, Articles 1–3 state that, "Each Member which ratifies this Convention shall take immediate and effective measures to secure the prohibition and elimination of the worst forms of child labour as a matter of urgency. . . . [Child Labour includes] (a) all forms of slavery or practices similar to slavery, such as the sale and trafficking of children, debt bondage and serfdom and forced or compulsory labour, including forced or compulsory recruitment of children for use in armed conflict; (. . .) (d) work which, by its nature or the circumstances in which it is carried out, is likely to harm the health, safety or morals of children."

Convention 182 of the International Labour Organization (ILO) includes "forced or compulsory recruitment of children for use in armed conflict" as one of the worst forms of child labor (Convention Concerning the Prohibition and Immediate Action for the Elimination of the Worst Forms of Child Labour 1999). The United States, which is a member of the ILO, ratified ILO Convention 182 on December 2, 1999, and it entered into force on November 19, 2000 (International Labour Organization 2012).

The Convention on the Rights of the Child and the Rome Statute of the International Criminal Court appear to permit the volunteering or drafting into military forces of children over the age of fifteen. On

May 25, 2000, the General Assembly of the United Nations adopted the Optional Protocol to the Convention of the Rights of Child on the involvement of children in armed conflict (Office of the United Nations High Commissioner for Human Rights, *Optional Protocol to the Convention on the Rights of the Child*, 2000). This Optional Protocol entered into force on February 12, 2002. This Protocol is the most important and progressive document concerning children in armed conflicts. It prohibits all recruitment—voluntary or compulsory—of children under eighteen years old by armed forces and groups (Dallaire and Beah 2011, 271–72). By 2009, several persons had been held accountable for crimes against children in war (Dallaire and Beah 2011, 289).

The need to increase the protection from involvement in armed conflict is met in part in Article 1 of the Protocol by increasing the age of childhood to eighteen years, providing that: "States Parties shall take all feasible measures to ensure that members of their armed forces who have not attained the age of 18 years do not take a direct part in hostilities" (quoted in US Departments of State, Defense and Justice 2006, 86). And as stated in Article 2, "States Parties shall ensure that persons who have not attained the age of 18 years are not compulsorily recruited into their armed forces" (quoted in Vandewiele 2006, 21, 26).

Another more progressive addition is in Article 4(1), which states that "armed groups that are distinct from the armed forces of a State should not, under any circumstances, recruit or use in hostilities persons under the age of 18 years" (quoted in Vandewiele 2006, 40; see also, Detrick 1999, 734). Besides that, the Protocol elaborated on the need to ensure the physical and psychosocial rehabilitation and social reintegration of children who are victims of armed conflict. It delineates the following goal: "Encouraging the participation of the community and, in particular, children and child victims in the dissemination of informational and educational programmes concerning the implementation of the Protocol" (ibid., 14).

However, a difficulty arises with Article 3, which provides that "States Parties shall raise the minimum age for the voluntary recruitment of persons into their national armed forces from that set out in Article 38, paragraph 3, of the Convention on the Rights of the Child, taking account of the principles contained in that article and recognizing that under the Convention persons under the age of 18 years are entitled to special protection." The question that remains, though, is: When and how can the voluntary recruitment be determined, noting the vulnerability of the children? As Ilona Topa (2007) notes, "The safeguards that have been established to ensure that recruitment is voluntary may be hard to implement" (p. 107).

By 2006, estimates were that hundreds of thousands of children labored as child soldiers around the world (US Senate 2002; UNICEF 2012). In 2008, the United States banned knowingly "recruit[ing], enlist[ing], or conscript[ing] a person to serve while such person is under 15 years of age in an armed force or group" or "us[ing] a person under 15 years of age to participate actively in hostilities," knowing that the person is under fifteen years of age (Child Soldiers Accountability Act 2008). This provision is aimed at child soldiers located outside the United States, and defines "armed group" to include "any army, militia, or other military organization, whether or not it is state-sponsored" (United Nations Committee on the Rights of the Child 2008, para. 64). As a force behind the law, US Senator Dick Durbin argued: "The use of children as combatants is one of the most despicable human rights violations in the world today and affects the lives of hundreds of thousands of boys and girls who are used as combatants, porters, human mine detectors and sex slaves. The power to prosecute and punish those who violate the law will send a clear signal that the U.S. will in no way tolerate this abhorrent practice" (United Nations Committee on the Rights of the Child 2008, para. 83).

The Trafficking Victims Protection Act of 2000, as amended by the Child Soldiers Prevention Act of 2008, makes it a crime to "knowingly provide or obtain the labor or services of a person" by means of (1) force or threats of force or physical restraint to that person or another person; (2) serious harm or threats of serious harm to that person or another person; (3) the abuse or threatened abuse of law or legal process; or (4) any scheme, plan, or pattern intended to cause the person to believe that if that person did not perform such labor or services, that person or another person would suffer serious harm or physical restraint (Child Soldiers Prevention Act 2008). The US law also prohibits peonage, enticement into slavery, involuntary servitude, and attempts or conspiracies to knowingly provide or obtain forced labor, peons, slaves, or involuntary servants (18 U.S.C. §§ 1581, 1583, 1584, 1591, 1592, 1594). The Special Representative of the UN Secretary General for Children and Armed Conflict, Radhika Coomaraswamy, called such changes to the US law a "strong[]" contribution to "the global fight against impunity for the recruitment and use of child soldiers [and that the latter] will be strongly enhanced by the implementation of both acts" (UN Advocate for Children Hails US Legislative Steps 2008).

The President of the United States is permitted by the Child Soldiers Prevention Act of 2008 to provide military aid to countries that he or she knows to be compulsorily recruiting children into their armed forces (Periodic Report of the United States of America, above para. 91). This is consistent with other US laws that allow a waiver of human-rights-related bans on military aid. Absent a presidential waiver, the Act prohibits aid to countries having "governmental armed forces or government-supported armed groups, including paramilitaries, militias, or civil defense forces, that recruit and use child soldiers" (22 U.S.C. § 2370c-1). A child soldier is defined as a person under eighteen years of age voluntarily or compulsorily recruited into governmental armed forces or irregular armed forces, or who "takes a direct part in hostilities as a member of" governmental forces or is "used in hostilities by" irregular forces, "including in a support role such as a cook, porter, messenger, medic, guard, or sex slave" (22 U.S.C. § 2370c). The US Secretary of State is supposed to prepare lists of foreign governments who use child soldiers and such governments are subject to sanctions due to trafficking in persons (22 U.S.C. § 7107(b)).

Interpreting the Genocide Convention

Article II(d) and II(e) of the Genocide Convention relate explicitly to genocidal tactics that affect children disproportionately, insofar as killing, inflicting physical or mental harm, or depriving persons of essential resources may affect all age groups similarly. Article II(d) relates to the act of "imposing measures designed to prevent births within the group," with the intent to destroy the group in whole or in part. The recruitment of children into armed groups and their participation in combat clearly tends to prevent births within ethnic, national, and religious groups. Instead of seeking employment and building stable families, child soldiers develop deviant behavior with respect to societal norms and values. Customarily, children develop their norms and values, partly by their education, partly by their upbringing, and partly by the social context they live in. Child soldiers' upbringing and social context are not conducive to successful reproduction, in that they live on the streets and/or killing fields, with no family, have very little education, and by joining armed groups they sometimes lead lives of killing, torturing, stealing, raping, and committing other atrocities. They even develop pride in being good killers (Harvey 2000).

To increase the attachment of child soldiers to armed groups, leaders of the latter sometimes oblige children to torture and execute the child's own relatives, interrupting cycles of transmission of cultural and social norms to new generations. Understandably, such children may not be accepted in their home village after the cruelties they committed. At the end of their service as child soldiers, because of the cruelties they committed, some of them are destined to have no future outside the army they were compelled to fight for. The participation of child soldiers in conflicts does not only change the life of an individual person, but due to the numbers of children who join the armed forces, it is a practice capable of destroying both "the family and the larger community (Topa 2007; Grover 2012, 149).

In 2012, it was estimated that 300,000 child soldiers took part in more than thirty current conflicts, with little distinction being drawn between boys and girls (UNICEF 2012). Moreover, girls are suffering recruitment in large numbers by armed groups for the purposes of rape and sexual exploitation (Wessels 1997). According to the World Health Organizations, child soldiers range in age from younger than ten years old to adolescence (13–19 years) (Coalition to Stop the Use of Child Soldiers 2004).

Child soldiers are used by governmental forces, guerilla movements, opposition groups, etc. (Topa 2007). All are at constant risk of death, injury and mutilation, torture, arbitrary detention, and mental trauma (Grover 2012, 6, 92, 165, 167, 188, 239, 266, 293).

Child soldiers come into existence in countries where war rages for many years and the civilian population often lives in extreme poverty. Sometimes, street children are forced to join the forces, and sometimes they volunteer out of desperation. Street (or very poor) children may voluntarily join armed groups in order to improve their living circumstances and survive a precarious existence. When children are forcibly recruited, the violators mainly focus on the weak and poor children, who are often street children (Grover 2012, 113–14).

National and international prosecutors should be more attentive to the question of whether the separation of families and abuse of children related to the practice of using child soldiers manifests a genocidal intent or has genocidal effects. Raphael Lemkin regarded separation of families and interference with reproduction as part of a typical pattern of genocidal practices (Travis 2012, 27). Similarly, the International Criminal Tribunal for Rwanda concluded that rape and other sexual violence can amount to the *actus reus* of the crime of genocide because "[i]n patriarchal societies, where membership of a group is determined by the identity of the father, an example of a measure intended to prevent births within a group is the case where, during rape, a woman of the said group is deliberately impregnated by a man of another group, with the intent to have her give birth to a child who will consequently not belong to its mother's group" (Grover 2012, 198). Therefore, "the measures intended to prevent births within the group, should be construed" to include "separation of the sexes. . . ." (UN Secretariat's Draft Genocide Convention, quoted in Abtahi and Webb 2008, 982).

Article II(e) of the Genocide Convention defines genocide as "forcibly transferring children of the group to the other group," with the intent to destroy the group in whole or in part. Advocates of making the Genocide Convention inapplicable to most massacres and ethnic cleansing campaigns, such as William Schabas and Lawrence LeBlanc, find this provision to be "enigmatic" or "out of place" with the rest of the convention. This is because they downplay the treaty's inclusion of the infliction of serious bodily or mental harm as an act of genocide. It may also be because they falsely believe that the Nazis only killed, never kidnapped, children (Mundorff 2009, 79). Despite writing thousands of words between them on the crime of genocide, published by prominent journals and Oxford University Press, among other fora, neither of these scholars saw fit to mention that the "Germanization of Polish children" was a genocidal act in one of the first criminal convictions for genocide arising out of World War II (Mundorff 2009, 81).[2] This omission distorts the concept of genocide not only vis-à-vis World War II but also for all peoples and times.

Contrary to recent attempts to minimize Article II(e), or to render it incomprehensible, the drafting history of the Convention drew on the recent actions of the Nazis when it stated: "The separation of children from their parents results in forcing upon the former at an impressionable and receptive age a culture and a mentality different from their parents. This process tends to bring about the disappearance of the group as a cultural unit in a relatively short time" (UN Economic & Social Council 1947, quoted in Mundorff 2009, 81). Greece led the effort, opposed by the communist bloc, to include Article II(e) in the treaty, at a time when Greek children were suffering widespread conscription by Soviet-backed rebels (Mundorff 2009, 82; see also, Associated Press 1948, 15; Associated Press 1948, 2; Sulzberger 1948, 1).

During the drafting of the Genocide Convention, the Soviet Union tried to restrict the crime of genocide to actions "aimed at the physical destruction" of the group, but this effort failed. Moreover, a push by the UN Secretariat to restrict the "mental harm" clause of the treaty to "mutilations and biological experiments" failed (Travis 2012). These failures resulted in a definition of genocide which includes courses of conduct that do *not* result in physical massacres or mass mutilations. Such a definition echoed Lemkin, who advanced a concept of genocide that included "infringement[s] upon, honor and rights, . . . transgression[s] against life, private property and religion, or science and art, [and] . . . humiliations, debilitation by undernourishment, and danger to health, . . . in violation of the laws of humanity. . . ." (92). In accordance with it, the International Criminal Tribunal for the former Yugoslavia, in its decision on the indictment against Radovan Karadžić and Ratko Mladić, stated "that cruel treatment . . . could constitute serious bodily or mental harm done to members of a group under a count of genocide. . . ." (Prosecutor v. Karadžić and Mladić 1996, 93). The same tribunal concluded "that the forcible transfer of individuals could lead to the material destruction of the group, since the group ceases to exist as a group, or at least as the group it was" (Prosecutor v. Blagojević and Jokić 2005, para. 659).

Theoretical Considerations

Many scholars maintain that genocidal intent should be inferred in circumstances not involving the intent to physically destroy in whole or in part a specific group protected under the convention. For example, Elisa von Joeden-Forgey (2012) has argued that scholars should consider as genocidal "a systematic pattern of atrocity aimed directly at the institutions, symbols, and relations of reproduction as well as the biological capacity to reproduce" (102). In a related vein, David Nersessian (2010) has argued that considering genocide in a broader way, in accordance with Article II(e) of the convention, might help "prevent[] group characteristics (religion, etc.) from being replaced by alien characteristics belonging to a different group" (20). Sonja Grover (2012) points out that removing children from their families and ethnic groups and conscripting them into genocidal armed forces targets the future of the family and potentially the larger group, and indeed threatens them with destruction (148). The International Criminal Tribunal for Rwanda (ICTR) has declared that genocidal intent may be inferred from "culpable," "destructive," or "deliberate" acts, as well as acts that "violate the very foundation of the group," even though they do not kill or prevent births directly (Prosecutor v. Akayesu 1998, para. 523–4; Prosecutor v. Kayishema & Ruzindana 2001, para. 93, 159, 527; Prosecutor v. Musema 2000, para.166).

Some of the same scholars address the plight of children through the lens of the Genocide Convention's Article II(c), which addresses "[d]eliberately inflicting on the group conditions of life calculated to bring about its physical destruction in whole or in part." The actual killing of children or child soldiers during war (or causing of excess mortality among them by exposure to hardships such as deprivation of food, shelter, clothing, health care, sewerage, or other services) could be genocidal under article II(c) of the Genocide Convention and depending on intent. The ICTR has concluded "that the means of deliberately inflicting on the group conditions of life calculated to bring about its physical destruction, in whole or in part, include subjecting a group of people to a subsistence diet, systematic expulsion from their homes and deprivation of essential medical supplies below a minimum vital standard" (Prosecutor v. Musema 2000, para. 157). However, genocidal intent is less likely to be found, and justifiably so, where the government or rebel perpetrators target armed or potentially armed men or boys, as opposed to unarmed men, women, or children. Because males make up the vast majority of armed forces in most conflicts, the gender of the child victims of a killing episode might be highly relevant to the issue of intent.

Child Soldiers as Targets or Victims of Genocide, and as Perpetrators of Genocide

The Indian Wars of the Nineteenth-Century United States

The impetus toward genocide by soldiers seeing themselves as threatened by a population that might commit its youth to combat in the cause of racial survival is visible in American history. In 1864, a book was published in which "the great Indian-fighter Harney" was quoted as saying "'nits make lice'" in support of the view that it would be "justifiable" to "kill all the Indians, men, women and children" (Heard 1864, 187) That same year, Colonel James Chivington reportedly delivered a speech about the Indian wars in which he said, "Kill and scalp all, little and big, nits make lice." (Molholt 2012, 158; Oberholtzer 1917,

342). By 1867, Charles Stickney told the story of one Tom Quick of Ulster County, New York State, who lost his father to the Indian wars and thereafter "was never known to miss an opportunity of killing an Indian, young or old." (quoted in Stickney 1867, 146). He also said by way of explanation, "Nits make lice" (quoted in Stickney 1867, 146). By 1880, Right-hand Thunder, identified as an Indian chief by his publisher, recounted how General Kearney explained white justice when it comes to Indians: "Nits make lice; kill the nits and they will never make lice. . . . [C]hildren may grow into Indians. . . . [S]oon there will be no Indians" (Heard 1864, 187; Molholt 2012, 158; Right-hand Thunder 1880, 233–34; Stickney, 1867, 146).

The Worst Forms of Child Labor during the Ottoman Christian Genocide

Children fell victim to Ottoman military and Kurdish militia massacres between 1914 and 1925. Raphael Lemkin noted, at the outset of his most extended analysis of the Ottoman Christian genocide of this period, that according to an eyewitness statement provided to the American Committee on Armenian and Syrian Relief, Turkish officials began confiscating large amounts of Armenian moneys and goods for use in the war and conscripted hundreds of Armenian boys twelve years old or younger to carry the goods on a death march of some three weeks, reaching from the interior of Anatolia to the Russian frontier, with up to 90 percent dying of beatings, starvation, or the cold as a result (Lemkin 2008, 49). Vahakn Dadrian (2003) pointed out that during the Turkish Military Tribunal of 1919, Turkish officials and eyewitnesses testified to the mass conscription of Armenian girls as sex slaves in Trabzon province on the Black Sea coast of Anatolia (6–7). An Ottoman military officer told his British captors that girls were systematically raped and murdered during the Ottoman Christian genocide (Dadrian 2003, 9). In Urfa, the Edessa or Urhay of Christian learning and heritage, Ottoman military officers and policemen established a brothel of slaves in the Armenian Church (Dadrian 2003, 9). A Swiss eyewitness reported that thousands of Armenian boys were also enslaved for sexual purposes by Ottoman officers (Dadrian 2003, 10). In 1920, a physician with the American Red Cross told the State Department and future President Warren G. Harding that he had personally treated "several hundred Christian children of both sexes," some as young as five years old, victimized by "beastly outrages" (Dadrian 2003, 15).

Minors' Complicity in and Resistance to the Holocaust

As most are well aware, the Hitler Youth had a role in the Holocaust. "At age 13, boys had to join the Hitler Youth Movement, and learn Nazi ideas. Girls joined the League of German Girls" (Senker 2005, 8). The Hitler Youth harassed and abused Jewish students, bringing about a "Nazification" of the schools (Longerich 2010, 76). In 1935, the Hitler Youth attacked the Jews of Berlin in a massive spectacle (Strauss 1980, 313–61). The Hitler Youth elite received military training and were eagerly recruited by the Waffen-SS. Eventually, an entire division of the *Schutzstaffel* (SS) was formed out of the Hitler Youth, including many under the age of eighteen (Williamson 2004, 102). Members of the Waffen-SS were assigned to the Auschwitz death camp and joined the *Einsatzgruppen*, which killed nearly three-quarters of a million Jews in the Soviet Union (Williamson 2004, 229).

The Destruction of Children's Lives in Uganda

Uganda, like many other countries, was forged by the British out of a multinational and multiethnic history into an instrument of forcible assimilation and tribal supremacy (Green 2008, 473–85). The Lord's Resistance Army (LRA) of Joseph Kony utilized up to 25,000 children as soldiers frequently by kidnapping them. In response, the government of Uganda confined up to two million people, including many Acholi, into "concentration camps" where about 1,000 children died weekly by the estimate of World Vision. One author calls it a "secret genocide," "systematically destroying" the Acholi people (Otunnu 2006, 44–45). Between 22,000 and 35,000 minors may have participated in the LRA's activities in some fashion, while others served in the Ugandan army (Drumbl 2010, 34).

The Fate of Children in Rwanda and the Democratic Republic of the Congo (DRC)

In Rwanda, a number of child soldiers are believed to have participated in the 1994 genocide against Tutsi and related war crimes of 1993–1994 (Grover 2012, 161, 212). They sometimes became alienated from their ethnic and national group as a result of their forcible recruitment (Grover 2012, 160–61). Mark Drumbl notes that teenagers "staffed the ranks of the Rwandan Patriotic Army" fighting to topple the Rwandan government in 1993–1994, and that teenagers also participated in the anti-Tutsi checkpoints (Drumbl 2010, 33).

Many Hutu children fled to the DRC (then known as Zaire) after the Rwandan Patriotic Front and factions of the Ugandan army invaded Rwanda (Grover 2012, 160). There, they were subjected to reprisal massacres by Rwandan forces and violence by Hutu warlords (Grover 2012, 160). Paul Kagame of Rwanda worked with Laurent Kabila of the DRC to "dismantle" Hutu refugee camps in the DRC, resulting in large-scale massacres of up to 10,000 people in a matter of weeks, and the displacement of up to 500,000 people in that period (Grover 2012, 161; see also, Arimatsu 2012, 158). The Kabila-Kagame bloc forcibly detained starving children and denied access to humanitarian aid organizations to large numbers of sick and injured civilians including children (Arimatsu 2012, 163). The Rwandan army under Kagame and the Ugandan army under Yoweri Museveni also cut electric power to portions of the DRC, killing a number of hospitalized children (Arimatsu 2012, 181). After the formation of the *Congrès national pour la défense due peuple* by Laurent Nkunda, an agent of Rwandan influence in the DRC, Congolese children suffered one of the worst episodes of mass rape in human history, with about 6,000 treated for it in several clinics in 2008 alone (Arimatsu 2012, 186). Nkunda has enjoyed safe haven and apparent judicial protection in Rwanda since 2009 (David 2011).

Genocide in Southern Sudan and the Darfur Region of Sudan

The genocide in Southern Sudan was prominent for the enslavement of non-Arab African children by the Arab-identifying government in Khartoum. During the 1980s, the Sudanese government clearly targeted children of the indigenous African Dinka group for atrocities, with 40,000 children fleeing the country and 50,000 Dinka girls taken captive (Travis 2010, 442). In 1987, the government issued a decree to kill or capture all male children from Southern Sudan (Travis 2010, 444). This led up to 70,000 to flee on foot to Ethiopia, becoming "Lost Boys" or "Lost Children."

In the late 1980s and early to mid 1990s, a campaign of extermination by the Sudanese government targeted the people of the Nuba Mountains, including Christians, practitioners of animist religions, and less-orthodox Muslims, in what Millard Burr called a pattern of "wholesale murder, abduction, rape, family separation, forced religious conversion, and the forced relocation of tens of thousands of Nuba. . . ." (quoted in Travis 2010, 444). UNICEF claimed that one million Sudanese children died of hunger and disease in 1996–1997 (Travis

2010, 446). The use of Arab militias known as *mujahideen/murahileen* resulted in the kidnapping of hundreds of women and children from the Dinka peoples (Travis 2010, 45). Human Rights Watch reported in 1998 that the government had forcibly recruited thousands of southern Sudanese children into Arab militias (Travis 2010, 446, citing Human Rights Watch 1998). According to Table 10.1, Sudan was second in the world in the number of child soldiers in 1998.

The UN Children's Fund reported that 6,000 child soldiers had been used on both sides of the conflict in Darfur, with far less excuse on the government's side insofar as the government employed hundreds of thousands of adult men in its armed forces and enjoyed an annual income of billions of dollars with which to recruit even more (cited in Drumbl 2010, 33). There were many child victims of genocide in Darfur. As Hannibal Travis (2010) has argued previously:

> The government and *Janjaweed* targeted children of African tribes for murder, in violation of the Convention on the Rights of the Child and with the effect of transferring many children from non-Arab African tribes to Arab tribes, which is a form of genocide under the

Table 10.1.
Child Soldiers, Circa 1998

Country	Number of child soldiers (younger than 16)
Burma	50,000
Sudan	28,000
Rwanda	20,000
Burundi	10,000
Colombia	9,000
Uganda	8,000
Angola	7,000
Congo	6,000
Sierra Leone	5,000
Turkey	3,000
Peru	2,100

Source: Adapted from Perlmutter, W. (2001) "An Application of Refugee Law to Child Soldiers," *Georgetown Public Policy Review*, 6:140, Table 1.

Genocide Convention. Hundreds of children were burned alive or confined in unsanitary internment camps until they passed away from deprivation. In a single massacre in 2004, the Sudanese military and the *Janjaweed* murdered 250 civilians, including a "large number of children" torn from their mothers' protective embrace. (474)

Huge numbers of children fled Darfur as displaced civilians and potential massacre victims, making up a substantial part of 2.5 million persons in flight in 2006 (Travis 2010, 462).

Critical Challenges and Hopes for Progress in the Area

Inadequate Scholarship

There are several challenges confronting this sub-domain of genocide scholarship. Children are often ignored in accounts of genocide in such places as Sudan.[3] Girls remain overlooked in much writing on child soldiers and the fate of children during genocides (McKay 2011, 486–87). They may constitute up to 30 percent of child soldiers in some conflicts, and often suffer mutilation, rape, and death in childbirth related to premature impregnation (McKay 2011, 486–87). Authors writing on the topic of children and genocide have noted that the recruitment of children into armed combat is a red flag of societal collapse and imminent mass killing (Brocklehurst 2006, 173). Scholarship that focuses on the escalation of conflict to levels in which children become involved either as perpetrators or as victims should become the rule rather than the exception in genocide studies and political science.

Future Progress in the Field

International Criminal Court

"On 14 March 2012, the International Criminal Court (ICC) delivered its verdict in the case Prosecutor vs. Thomas Lubanga Dyilo. Mr. Lubanga was convicted for the war crime of conscripting and enlisting children under the age of 15 into the *Forces patriotiques pour la libération du Congo*, and for making them participate actively in hostilities." (UN Secretary-General 2012, para. 235). Although this stands as an important precedent, many countries in which child soldiers have been used have not ratified the ICC treaty, as shown in Table 10.2.

Despite their ratifying the convention, child soldiery in Burundi, Colombia, Peru, or Sierra Leone has not been addressed by the ICC. Article 11 of the Rome Statute of the ICC is presently read to restrict

Table 10.2.
ICC Ratification and Child Soldiers

Country	ICC ratification?
Burma	N
Sudan	N
Rwanda	N
Burundi	Y
Colombia	Y
Uganda	Y
Angola	N
Congo, Dem. Rep.	Y
Sierra Leone	Y
Turkey	N
Peru	Y

the temporal jurisdiction of the court to acts committed since mid-2002 or later in time, depending on the date of ratification by a state. The selectivity and jurisdictional failings of the ICC are, therefore, a major problem.

Global Efforts to End the Use of Child Soldiers

The Optional Protocol to the Convention of the Rights of Child represents the most broad-based effort to end the abuse of children by armed forces and groups. However, a small minority of states ratified it by 2011. UN Secretary-General Ban Ki-moon has urged UN Member States to sign and ratify the Optional Protocol, and then submit reports on their progress toward compliance and implement recommendations by the Committee on the Rights of the Child made to them. He welcomed efforts by states such as Afghanistan, the Central African Republic, Chad, and South Sudan to release children in their armed forces, and punish those who recruited them (UN Secretary-General 2012, Report on Children and Armed Conflict, paras. 237–43). He has solicited donations to help fund and monitor action plans, including the resettlement and retraining of children formerly bound to serve armed forces or armed groups (UN Secretary-General 2012, para. 238). He has also encouraged states "to allow independent access to the United Nations for the purposes of monitoring and reporting on grave violations against children," and to make "specific commitments and measures to address all grave violations against children" (UN Secretary-General 2012, para. 239). Child protection should be mainstreamed into "all relevant mandates of United Nations peacekeeping operations, . . . political and peacebuilding missions, [and] planning . . . processes," he insists (UN Secretary-General 2012, para. 241).

Conclusion

Child soldiery has devastated thousands of lives and played a part in a number of genocides. The international community is making its first efforts toward universal condemnation of the practice; however, these efforts remain fitful and incomplete.

Notes

1. Despite the gaps in the CRC, its Article 30 is a promising avenue for states to end the practice of cultural genocide by ensuring that "in those States in which ethnic, religious or linguistic minorities or persons of indigenous origin exist, a child belonging to such a minority or who is indigenous shall not be denied the right, in community with other members of his or her group, to enjoy his or her own culture, to profess and practice his or her own religion, or to use his or her own language" (Convention on the Rights of the Child 1989). Along with Article 29 of the CRC, respecting parents' "right" to influence the rearing and acculturation of children, Article 30 represents the inverse of genocide by interference with child-rearing (reproductive genocide under Articles II(d)–(e) of the UNCG) (*ibid.*, Art. 29(1)(c)).

2. Schabas mentions "Germanization" in his 600-page treatise on genocide but fails to note that this Germanization was particularly objected to by courts as genocide of Polish children. Schabas 2000, 28, 49–50, 179 Compare Mundorff 2009, 81. The conviction was that of Arthur Greiser, the Nazi governor of western Poland and the first person to be convicted of genocide by a national tribunal in the history of the world. See Schabas 2000, 388.

3. For example, they are virtually ignored by Alex de Waal in *The Oxford Handbook of Genocide Studies*. He mentions rape (on one page of his twenty-page chapter on genocide in northern Africa), but not enslavement of children. The index to the volume does not refer to children, although it does mention rape and notes that rape in Bosnia and Herzegovina receives three pages of analysis. De Waal 2010, 529–49. See also ibid., 663 (index).

References

Abtahi, H., and P. Webb. 2008. *The Genocide Convention: The Travaux Préparatoires*. Dordrecht, The Netherlands: Martinus Nijhoff.

Afua, T.-D. 2003. "Africa's Young Soldiers. The Co-option of Childhood." Institute for *Security Studies Monograph*, No. 8213.

Arimatsu, L. 2012. "The Democratic Republic of the Congo 1993–2010." In *International Law and the Classification of Conflicts*, ed. E. Wilmshurst, 15. New York: Oxford University Press.

Associated Press. 1948. "Many Greek Children Taken from Homeland." *Lewiston Sun* (Maine), June 24, 15.

———. 1948. "Plot to Kidnap Greek Children Laid to Neighboring Nations." *The Milwaukee Journal*, March 1, 2.

———. 2012. "Uganda: Kony 2012." *Africa Research Bulletin* 49: 19208B–19211C.

Bang, A., S. Tiwari, and R. K. Agrawal. 2011 "Legal and Ethical Issues in Infant Growth." In *Handbook of Growth and Growth Monitoring in Health and Disease*, ed. V. Preedy, 115–28. London: Springer.

Brocklehurst, H. 2006. *Who's Afraid of Children?: Children, Conflict and International Relations.* London: Ashgate.

Child Soldiers Accountability Act. 2008. Public Law No. 110–340, Enacted October 3, 2008. http://www.state.gov/documents/organization/135988.pdf.

Child Soldiers Prevention Act. 2008. Enacted as Title IV of the William Wilberforce Trafficking Victims Protection Reauthorization Act of 2008, Public Law No. 110–457, December 23, 2008.

Coalition to Stop the Use of Child Soldiers. 2004. *Child Soldiers. Global Report 2004.* Available at: http://www.child-soldiers.org (accessed September 1, 2012).

Convention Concerning the Prohibition and Immediate Action for the Elimination of the Worst Forms of Child Labour. 1999. Art. 3(a), ILO Convention No. 182 Art. 2, June 17, 1999, 87th Session. Available at: http://www.ilo.org/ipec/Actiononchildlabour/Legalinstruments/ILOConventionsandRecommendationsonChildL/lang--en/index.htm.

Convention on the Rights of the Child. 1989. G.A. Res. 44/25, Art. 30, UN GAOR, 4th Session, Supp. No. 49, UN Doc. A/RES/44/25 (November 20). Available at: http://www.unhchr.ch/html/menu3/b/k2crc.htm.

Dadrian, V. 2003. "Children as Victims of Genocide: The Armenian Case." *Journal of Genocide Research* 5 no. 3: 421–37.

Dallaire, R., and I. Beah. 2011. *They Fight Like Soldiers, They Die Like Children: The Global Quest to Eradicate the Use of Child Soldiers.* New York: Bloomsbury Publishing.

David, K. M. 2011. "Congo-Kinshasa: Nkunda's Case Not Easy, Says Rwanda." *Daily Nation*, January 20. Available at: http://allafrica.com/stories/201101200874.html.

De Waal, A. 2010. "Genocidal Warfare in North-east Africa." In *The Oxford Handbook of Genocide Studies*, ed. A. D. Moses, and D. Bloxham, 529–49. Oxford: Oxford University Press.

Detrick, S. A. 1998. *Commentary on the United Nations Convention on the Rights of the Child.* Dordrecht, Netherland: Martinus Nijhoff.

Docker, J. 2008. "Are Settler-Colonies Inherently Genocidal?" In *Empire, Colony, Genocide Empire, Colony, Genocide: Conquest, Occupation, and Subaltern Resistance in World History*, ed. A. D. Moses, 81–98. New York: Berghahn Books.

Drumbl, M. 2010. *Reimagining Child Soldiers in International Law and Policy.* Oxford: Oxford University Press.

Geneva Declaration on the Rights of the Child. 1924. Available at: http://childrensrightsportal.org/childrens-rights-history/references-on-child-rights/geneva-declaration/.

Green, E. 2008. "Understanding the Limits to Ethnic Change: Lessons from Uganda's 'Lost Counties.'" *Perspectives on Politics* 6 (3): 473–85.

Grover, S. 2012. *Child Soldier Victims of Genocidal Forcible Transfer: Exonerating Child Soldiers Charged with Grave Conflict-related International Crimes*. London: Springer.

Harvey, R. 2000. "Recruitment and Deployment of Child Soldiers." *Children and Armed Conflict Occasional Paper Series*, University of Essex. Available at: http://www.essex.ac.uk/armedcon/News%20Folder/Future/2000News/Comments/DraftOPCS.htm

Heard, I. 1864. *History of the Sioux War*. New York: Harper & Brothers.

Hovannisian, R. 1967. *Armenia on the Road to Independence*. Berkeley and Los Angeles: University of California Press.

———, ed. 1986. *The Armenian Genocide in Perspective*. New Brunswick, NJ: Transaction Publishers.

Hulme, K. 2008. "Child Soldiers in International Law (Review)." *Modern Law Review* 71 (3): 496–99.

Human Rights Watch. 1998. *Famine in Sudan*. Available at: http://www.hrw.org/reports/1999/sudan/index.html and http://www.hrw.org/reports/1999/sudan/SUDAWEB2-01.htm.

Inhofe, J., and J. Demint. 2012. "U.N. Treaties Mean Lost U.S. Sovereignty." *The Washington Times*, July 25, n.p.

International Labour Organization. 2012. *Child Labour and Armed Conflict* (Dec. 2012). Available at: http://www.ilo.org/ipec/areas/Armedconflict/lang--en/index.htm.

Joeden-Forgey, E. von. 2012. "Gender and the Future of Genocide Studies." *Genocide Studies and Prevention*, April 7, 89–107.

Lemkin, R. 1943. *Axis Rule in Occupied Europe*, New York: Carnegie Endowment for International Peace.

———. 2008. *Raphael Lemkin's Dossier on the Armenian Genocide*. Glendale, CA: Center for Armenian Remembrance.

McKay, S. 2011. "Girls in Armed Groups." *The Encyclopedia of Peace Psychology*. New York: Wiley. Available at: http://onlinelibrary.wiley.com.ezproxy.fiu.edu/doi/10.1002/9780470672532.wbepp121/abstract (accessed October 5, 2012).

Longerich, P. 2010. *Holocaust: The Nazi Persecution and Murder of the Jews*. New York: Oxford University Press.

Molholt, S. 2012. "American Indians in Print Advertising Since 1890." In *American Indians and Popular Culture*, ed. E. Hoffman, 151–64. Santa Barbara, CA: ABC-CLIO.

Mundorff, K. 2009. "Other Peoples' Children: A Textual and Contextual Interpretation of the Genocide Convention, Article 2(e)." *Harvard Journal of International Law* 50 (1): 61–128.

Nersessian, D. 2010. *Genocide and Political Groups*. New York: Oxford University Press.

Office of the United Nations High Commissioner for Human Rights (2000). *Optional Protocol to the Convention on the Rights of the Child*. May. Available at: http://www2.ohchr.org/english/law/crc-conflict.htm.

Oberholtzer, E.P. 1917. *A History of the United States since the Civil War: 1865–68*, vol. 1. New York: The Macmillan Co.

Otunnu, O. 2006. "The Secret Genocide." *Foreign Policy*, July–August, No. 155, 44–46. Available at: http://www.jstor.org/stable/25462062

Prosecutor v. Akayesu, Case No. ICTR-96-4-T, Trial Chamber, Judgement (September 2, 1998). Available at: http://www.refworld.org/docid/40278fbb4. html, and http://www.unhcr.org/refworld/publisher,ICTR,,,40278fbb4,0. html.

Prosecutor v. Blagojević and Jokić, Case No. IT-02-60-T, Trial Chamber, Judgement (January 17, 2005). Accessed at: http:// www.refworld.org/docid/47fdfaf51a. html and http://www.icty.org/x/cases/blagojevic_jokic/tjug/en/bla-050117e. pdf.

Prosecutor v. Kayishema & Ruzindana, Case No. ICTR-95-1-T, Appeals Chamber, Judgement (Reasons) (June 1, 2001). Available at: http://www.refworld. org/docid/48abd5760.html 1.http://69.94.11.53/ENGLISH/cases/KayRuz/ appeal/3d.htm#_ftnref221.

Prosecutor v. Musema, Case No. ICTR-96-13-A, Trial Chamber, Judgement and Sentence (January 27, 2000). Available at: http://www.refworld.org/ docid/48abd5791a.html, http://www1.umn.edu/humanrts/instree/ICTR/ MUSEMA_ICTR-96-13/MUSEMA_ICTR-96-13-A.html.

Prosecutor v. Radovan Karadzić and Ratko Mladić, Review of the Indictments pursuant to Rule 61, Case Nos. IT-95-5 and IT-95-18 (July 11, 1996). Available at http://www.haguejusticeportal.net/Docs/CourtDocuments/ICTY/ Karadzic_Review_indictment_EN.pdf.

Right-hand Thunder. 1880. *The Indian and White Man: Or, the Indian in Self-defense*. Indianapolis, IN: Carlon & Hollenbeck.

Schabas, W. 2000. *Genocide in International Law: The Crime of Crimes.* New York: Cambridge University Press.

Senker, C. 2006. *Surviving the Holocaust.* Chicago, IL: Raintree, 8.

Stickney, C. 1867. *A History of the Minisink Region*. Middletown, NY: Finch and Guiwits.

Strauss, H. 1980. "Jewish Emigration from Germany: Nazi Policies and Jewish Responses." *Leo Baeck Institute Yearbook*, no. 25, 313–361.

Sulzberger, C.L. 1948. "Abductions by Greek Rebels Spur Vast Child Aid Project." *New York Times*, June 21, 1.

Tirman J. 2011. *The Deaths of Others: The Fate of Civilians in America's Wars.* New York: Oxford University Press.

Topa, I. 2007. "Prohibition of Child Soldiering—International Legislation and Prosecution of Perpetrators." *Hanse Law Review: The E-Journal on European, International, and Comparative Law 3*. Available at: http://www.hanselawreview.org/pdf5/Vol3No1Art06.pdf.

Travis, H. 2012. *Genocide, Ethnonationalism, and the United Nations: Exploring the Causes of Mass Killing Since 1945*. London: Routledge.

———. 2010. *Genocide in the Middle East: The Ottoman Empire, Iraq, and Sudan.* Durham, NC: Carolina Academic Press.

UN Committee on the Rights of the Child. 2008. *Optional Protocol to the Convention on the Rights of the Child on Involvement of Children in Armed Conflict: Periodic Report of the United States of America and U.S. Response to Recommendations in Committee Concluding Observations of June 25, 2008*

(January 22, 2010), para. 64. Available at: http://www.state.gov/documents/organization/135988.pdf.

UN Economic & Social Council. 1947. *Draft Convention on the Crime of Genocide*, UN Doc. E/447 (June 26, 1947).

United Nations. 2008. UN Secretariat's Draft Genocide Convention, UN Doc. No. E/AC.25/W.1.

UN Secretary-General. 2012. *Report on Children and Armed Conflict*, UN Doc. No. A/66/782 & S/2012/261 (April 26).

UN Children's Fund. 2012. "Factsheet on Child Soldiers." Available at: http://www.unicef.org/emerg/files/childsoldiers.pdf (accessed September 1, 2012).

UN Children's Fund. 2012. "About UNICEF: Who We Are." May 25. Available at: http://www.unicef.org/about/who/index_history.html.

US Departments of State, Defense and Justice. 2006. *Response to Additional Questions of Sen. Jesse Helms*. US Senate Executive Reports: United States Congressional Serial Set, Serial No. 14751. Washington, DC, United States Government Printing Office.

US Senate. 2002. *Senate Executive Report No. 107-4* (June 12). US Senate Executive Reports: United States Congressional Serial Set, Serial No. 14751. Washington, DC, United States Government Printing Office.

Vandewiele, T. 2006. *A Commentary on the United Nations Convention on the Rights of the Child Optional Protocol: The Involvement of Children in Armed Conflicts*, vol. 51. Dordrecht, the Netherlands: Martinus Nijhoff.

Wessells, M. 1997. "Child Soldiers." *Bulletin of the Atomic Scientists*, November–December. Available at http://pangaea.org/street_children/africa/armies.htm (accessed September 1, 2012).

Williamson, G. 2004. *The SS: Hitler's Instrument of Terror*. Minneapolis, MN: Zenith Press.

Zabir, S. 1988. *The Iranian Military in Revolution and War*. New York: Routledge.

Annotated Bibliography

Allen, Tim. *Trial Justice: The International Criminal Court and the Lord's Resistance Army*. London: Zed Books. 2006, 176 pp.

"The first major case before the International Criminal Court is the appalling situation in northern Uganda where Joseph Kony's Lord's Resistance Army abducted thousands, many of them children, and systematically tortured, raped, maimed and killed them. This book argues that much of the antipathy to the ICC is based upon ignorance and misconception. Drawing on field research in Uganda, it shows that victims are much more interested in punitive international justice than has been suggested, and that the ICC has made resolution of the war more likely."

Convention on the Rights of the Child. G.A. Res. 44/25, Art. 30, UN GAOR, 4th Session, Supp. No. 49, UN Doc. A/RES/44/25, November 20, 1989. Available at http://www.unhchr.ch/html/menu3/b/k2crc.htm.

The Convention on the Rights of Child (CRC) is a binding treaty intended to promote the full enjoyment of human rights by children. Concerning "children in armed conflicts," Article 38 builds on the Additional Protocols to the Geneva Conventions of 1977 to provide that

(1) States Parties undertake to respect and to ensure respect for rules of international humanitarian law applicable to them in armed conflicts which are relevant to the child;

(2) States Parties shall take all feasible measures to ensure that persons who have not attained the age of fifteen years do not take a direct part in hostilities;

(3) States Parties shall refrain from recruiting any person who has not attained the age of fifteen years into their armed forces. In recruiting among those persons who have attained the age of fifteen years but who have not attained the age of eighteen years, States Parties shall endeavour to give priority to those who are oldest; and

(4) In accordance with their obligations under international humanitarian law to protect the civilian population in armed conflicts, States Parties shall take all feasible measures to ensure protection and care of children who are affected by an armed conflict.

Drumbl, M. *Reimagining Child Soldiers in International Law and Policy*. New York: Oxford University Press, 2010, 276 pp.

The author analyzes the problem of child soldiers from a variety of perspectives. In doing so, he points out that child soldiers may not be legally responsible for committing genocide or other extraordinary international crimes due to the greater responsibility of the adults who recruit or employ them. He mentions only one genocide, that in Rwanda, but comments on other conflicts across the globe.

Dunson, Donald H. *Child, Victim, Soldier: The Loss of Innocence*. Maryknoll, NY: Orbis Books, 2008, 145 pp.

"The rebel group in Uganda known as the Lord's Resistance Army has abducted children, boys and girls, to serve as soldiers and to provide sexual services. Torn from their families in the dead of night and forced to carry out terrible acts, including murdering family members and other children, they bear terrifying scars on their bodies, minds, and souls. Fr. Dunson lets their stories be heard, often in their own voices, telling of their hurts and needs, but also of their hopes for the future. His text, accompanied by powerful photographs taken by Gerald Straub, also reflects on the presence of evil in the world and the need for healing."

Everett, J. "The Battle Continues: Fighting for a More Child-Sensitive Approach to Asylum for Child Soldiers." *Florida Journal of International Law* 21, no. 2 (2009): 285–356.

During the 1990s, there were 300,000 child soldiers, concentrated in Africa, where up to 100,000 children were implicated in the practice in 2004, although children have also been used as soldiers in Asia, the Middle East, Latin America, and Europe. The law applicable to refugees from persecution could provide a mechanism for providing these children with protection and a safe haven. The term "refugee" applies to a child if, owing to well-founded fear of persecution on account of ethnicity, membership in a particular social group, or other protected factors, he or she is unable or unwilling to avail him or herself of his or her country's protection and is unable or unwilling to return. The author argues that the asylum law of the United States should be revised to broaden the availability of asylum to former child soldiers, consistent with the Convention on the Rights of Children.

Grover, S. *Child Soldier Victims of Genocidal Forcible Transfer: Exonerating Child Soldiers Charged with Grave Conflict-Related International Crimes*. London: Springer, 2012, 302 pp.

"This book provides an original legal analysis of child soldiers recruited into armed groups or forces committing mass atrocities and/or genocide as the victims of the genocidal forcible transfer of children."

Happold, M. "Child Soldiers: Victims or Perpetrators?" *University of La Verne Law Review* 29, no. 1 (2008): 56–87.

The author argues, among other things, that child soldiers cannot contribute to genocidal intent, owing to their age and immaturity, and other factors such as duress.

Kahn, Leora, and Luis Moreno-Ocampo. *Child Soldiers*. New York: Powerhouse Books, 2008, 120 pp.

"Child Soldiers focuses on countries with a history of child warfare, as captured by photographers and writers from across the globe. The book explores the children's time as combatants, as well as their demobilization and rehabilitation." *Child Soldiers* features the work of nine prominent photographers, who have covered the use of children in combat around the world. Contributing writers include Jo Becker, Children's Rights Advocacy Director for Human Rights Watch, Jimmie Briggs, journalist and author of *Innocents Lost: When Child Soldiers Go to War* (Basic Books, 2005), Senator Dick Durbin of Illinois, Luis Moreno-Ocampo, International Criminal Court Prosecutor, Emmanuel Jal, a Sudanese musician and former child soldier, and Michael Wessels, a professor of psychology at Columbia University.

Lonegan, B. "Sinners or Saints: Child Soldiers and the Persecutor Bar to Asylum." *Boston College Third World Law Journal* 31, no. 1 (2011): 71–99.

The author points out that US law has many examples of rules and precedents that recognize the lesser criminal culpability of children. He notes, further, that the fate of child soldiers often fits the criminal-law defense of duress, most notably the elements of suffering an imminent threat of death or serious bodily injury, a lack of viable alternatives to criminal activity, and a direct causal relationship between the criminal activity and the bodily harm feared.

Machel, Graça. *Impact of Armed Conflict on Children, transmitted by Note of the Secretary-General*. UN Doc. A/ 51/306, August 26, 1996, http://www.unicef. org/graca/.

Estimates indicated that in some 25 wars and conflicts, armed groups used about 200,000 child soldiers under sixteen years old in 1988. The author contends that "children are often press-ganged from their own neighbourhoods where local militia or village leaders may be obliged to meet recruitment quotas," notably in Ethiopia, Guatemala, and Sudan. He adds that, "For girls, recruitment may lead to sex slavery. . . . Many [children] have been physically or sexually abused by the very forces for which they have been fighting, and have seen their parents killed, sometimes in the most brutal manner, in front of their eyes."

Mundorff, K. "Other Peoples' Children: A Textual and Contextual Interpretation of the Genocide Convention, Article 2(e)." *Harvard Journal of International*

Law 50, 2009. Available at: http://www.harvardilj.org/site/wp-content/
uploads/2010/07/HILJ_50-1_Mundorff.pdf.

The author engages in a thorough review of the drafting history and context of Article 2(e) of the Genocide Convention. He makes the important point that Greece, which was suffering mass child abductions blamed on communist armed groups, was the driving force behind the provision. Article 2(e) was deliberately included in the treaty, and probably at some political cost to the small countries pressing for it, after the Soviet Union denied that the transfer of children could be genocidal, and after the Soviet satellite of Poland also opposed the transfer clause. Greece ensured the inclusion of the clause after it threatened to be dropped, at a time when the world knew that Greece was suffering the mass abduction of its children by communist rebels supported by Bulgaria and derivatively by the Soviet Union. This drafting history will be important to future cases involving child soldiers.

Singer, Peter Warren. *Children at War.* New York: Pantheon Books, 2005, 269 pp.

"Analyzes the growing use of children as soldiers in global conflicts, explaining how youngsters are recruited and abducted, indoctrinated, trained, and utilized as warriors; how changes in weapons technology and a breakdown of global order have led to the phenomenon."

De Temmerman, Els. *Aboke Girls: Children Abducted in Northern Uganda.* Kampala: Fountain Publishers, 2001, 160 pp.

"In October 1996, one hundred and thirty nine girls were abducted from St Mary's College, in northern Uganda. In an act of extraordinary courage, Sister Rachele, the Italian deputy headmistress, followed the abductors. Her journey took her to the Lord's Resistance Army, led by Joseph Kony, where she managed to secure the release of the majority of the girls. What happened to the remaining thirty girls and thousands of other children who have disappeared from their homes and schools in northern Uganda since the arrival of the Lord's Resistance Army? In this book journalist Els De Temmerman reconstructs the journey of two Aboke girls who managed to excape and one of the abductors, a fourteen year old boy who was part of Kony's elite troops."

UN Office for the Coordination of Humanitarian Affairs. *Sudan: Conscription of Children, Sexual Abuse Unabated in Darfur—UN Envoy, 2012,* 2012. Available at: http://www.irinnews.org/printreport.aspx?reportid=69882

In 2012, Radhika Coomaraswamy, the UN Special Representative to the Secretary-General on Children and Armed Conflict, held a press conference in Khartoum, Sudan, in which the issues of child soldiers and rape were addressed. She reported that the government of Sudan recognized that "child recruitment and sexual violence" were occurring and promised reforms, but had not been implemented. She also noted that medical data suggested that sexual violence occurred at high levels in Darfur. One planned reform called for the UN to visit military "camps" to ascertain whether children were present. The report noted that an African Union force of 7,000 troops found it difficult to promote peace in Darfur, from which two million people had been driven by force, and where, via a rough estimate, 200,000 people had been killed.

UN Secretary-General. *Children and Armed Conflict in Iraq: Report of the Secretary-General*, UN Doc. S/2011/366, June 15, 2011.

The report confirms that "children were used as suicide bombers by insurgent groups, including Al-Qaida in Iraq, throughout the reporting period." It notes that children are being exploited for their perceived lack of threat, which makes them easier to send through security checkpoints. Remote detonators have been used on children carrying explosives on behalf of Al-Qaida. "In 2008, an official of the Ministry of the Interior publicly claimed that Al-Qaida in Iraq had used 24 children as suicide bombers in the previous two years." The problem persisted in 2009 and 2010. Sunni tribes allied with the government after defecting from Al-Qaida forces in 2005 also employed children in a 100,000-strong militia known as "Awakening Councils." The report states that the full scope of children's involvement in fighting in Iraq is difficult to ascertain because the poor security situation precludes a complete study of the subject.

UN Secretary General. *Children and Armed Conflict*, UN Doc. No. S/2012/261, April. 26, 2012.

In this report, the Secretary General notes that his Special Representative for Children and Armed Conflict filed an *amicus curiae* brief before the International Criminal Court (ICC), contending that a broad interpretation of the term "participate actively in hostilities" in Article 8(2)(b) (xxvi) of the Rome Statute of the ICC, defining the crime of using children in armed forces or armed groups, should be interpreted broadly to include "a wide range of activities, from those children on the front line (who participate directly) through the boys and girls who are involved in a myriad of roles that support the combatants," the central question being whether the child's role "exposed him or her to real danger as a potential target" (para. 236). The ICC's decision confirmed that the Special Representative for Children and Armed Conflict was correct: that "conscription" and "enlistment" are both forms of "recruitment" of children into armed groups under Article 8. The report concluded

> Reports of child casualties in the course of military operations, including the use of explosive weapons, aerial bombardments and drones, continue to be of concern, and I remind all parties of their obligation under international human rights law and international humanitarian law, in particular the principles of distinction and proportionality and the duty to protect children and prevent violations, to take all necessary precautions to avoid civilian casualties. I strongly urge them to ensure that they continuously review tactical directives for the better protection of children during the conduct of military operations, and that military and police personnel are sensitized to the protection of children's rights under national and international laws.

List of Contributors

Jeffrey C. Blutinger is an associate professor in the History Department at California State University, Long Beach, and holds the Barbara and Ray Alpert Endowed Chair in Jewish Studies. Among his publications are: "An Inconvenient Past: Post-Communist Holocaust Memorialization," *Shofar: An Interdisciplinary Journal of Jewish Studies* 29, no. 1 (Winter 2011) and "Bearing Witness: Teaching the Holocaust from a Victim-Centered Perspective," *The History Teacher* 42, no. 3 (2009): 269–79. He also organizes the annual Eugene and Eva Schlesinger Teacher Workshop on the Holocaust, which trains teachers in the Los Angeles and Orange County areas on how to teach the Holocaust in schools.

Asya Darbinyan is the deputy director of the Armenian Genocide Museum-Institute (AGMI), and a graduate student in Armenian History and Genocide studies at AGMI of National Academy of Sciences of the Republic of Armenia. She has a Masters of Arts in International Relations at Yerevan State University. The working title of her doctoral thesis is "Humanitarian Assistance Provided by the Near East Relief to Armenian Orphans during and after the Armenian Genocide."

Sara Demir completed her studies in International and European law at the University of Leiden. Her thesis at Leiden was previously published as "The Atrocities against the Assyrians in 1915," *Journal of Assyrian Academic Studies* 25 (2011): 40–77.

Amanda Grzyb is an assistant professor of Information and Media Studies at Western Ontario University. Her teaching and research interests include Holocaust and genocide studies; media and the public interest; social movements and media; among others. She is currently engaged in several research projects, including, for example, field research at genocide memorial sites in Rwanda, and a book, with Samuel Totten, on the two most recent crises in the Nuba Mountains,

Sudan. In 2009, she edited *The World and Darfur: International Response to Crimes against Humanity in Western Sudan* (McGill-Queen's University Press).

Rubina Peroomian (born in Tabriz, Iran) holds a PhD in Near Eastern Languages and Cultures from University of California, Los Angeles (UCLA). Her dissertation (1989), published as a book, *Literary Responses to Catastrophe: A Comparison of the Armenian and the Jewish Experience* (Atlanta, GA: Scholars Press, 1993) marked her debut in the field of genocide studies. She has taught Armenian language and literature at UCLA, and is currently a research associate in the Department of Near Eastern Languages and Cultures.

She has contributed research articles to scholarly journals such as the *Journal of the Society for Armenian Studies*, *Pakin* (an Armenian literary journal), the *Journal of Genocide Research*, and *Genocide Studies and Prevention: An International Journal*.

Her major publications in the field of Armenian Genocide studies include *Literary Responses to Catastrophe: A Comparison of the Armenian and the Jewish Experience* (1993); *And Those Who Continued Living in Turkey after 1915* (2008, 2012); and *The Armenian Genocide in Literature, Perceptions of Those Who Lived through the Years of Calamity* (2012).

Colin Tatz is a visiting fellow in Politics and International Relations at the Australian National University, Canberra, Australian Capital Territory (ACT) and director of the Australian Institute for Holocaust and Genocide Studies, Sydney, New South Wales, Australia. His areas of research are race politics, Holocaust, and genocide studies. Among his works on genocide are *With Intent to Destroy: Reflecting on Genocide* (Verso, 2003) and (as editor) *Genocide Perspectives* I (1997), II (2003), III (2006), and IV (2012).

Henry C. Theriault is professor in and chair of the Department of Philosophy, Worcester State University in the United States, where he has taught since 1998. He earned his PhD in Philosophy from the University of Massachusetts in 1999. He is also chair of the Armenian Genocide Reparations Study Group and lead author of its forthcoming report. He teaches courses on genocide, mass violence against women, long-term justice for mass violence, and other related topics.

Some of his forthcoming and recent publications are "The Challenge of the Armenian Genocide for 21st Century Turkey: Responsibility and

Reparation toward Resolution," in Proceedings of the "1915 Within Its Pre- and Post-Historical Periods: Denial and Confrontation" Symposium (in Turkish, forthcoming); "Reparative Justice and Alleviating the Consequences of Genocide," in *The Armenian Genocide and International Law*, edited by Antranik Dakessian (forthcoming); "From Unfair to Shared Burden: The Armenian Genocide's Outstanding Damage and the Complexities of Repair," *Armenian Review*, special issue: The Global Reparations Movement (forthcoming); "Against the Grain: Critical Reflections on the State and Future of Genocide Scholarship," *Genocide Studies and Prevention* 7:1 (Spring 2012); and "The Mass Atrocity Response Operation Handbook: New Possibilities or the Same Old Militarism," *Genocide Studies and Prevention* 6:1 (Spring 2011).

Samuel Totten is a genocide scholar based at the University of Arkansas, Fayetteville.

In July and August of 2004, Totten served as one of twenty-four investigators on the US State Department's Darfur Atrocities Documentation Project whose express purpose was to conduct interviews with refugees from Darfur in order to ascertain whether genocide had been perpetrated or not in Darfur. Based upon the data collected by the team of investigators, US Secretary of State Colin Powell declared, on September 9, 2004, that genocide had been perpetrated in Darfur, Sudan, by the Government of Sudan troops and the *Janjaweed.*

For the past nine years he has conducted research into the Darfur Genocide (2003 to present) and the Nuba Mountains Genocide (late 1980s into the 1990s) in refugee camps along the Chad/Darfur border and in the Nuba Mountains. He was most recently in the Nuba Mountains between December 25, 2012 and January 5, 2013.

From 2003 to 2013, Totten served as the editor of *Genocide: A Critical Bibliographic Review* (New Brunswick, NJ: Transaction Publishers). The three most recent volumes (not counting the current one) in the series are entitled: *Fate and Plight of Women during and following Genocide* (2009), *The Genocide of Indigenous Peoples (with Robert Hitchcock)* (2011), and *Impediments to the Prevention and Intervention of Genocide* (2013).

From 2006 to 2013, he served as founding coeditor of *Genocide Studies and Prevention: An International Journal*, the official journal of the International Association of Genocide Scholars (University of Toronto Press). In 2008, he served as a Fulbright Scholar at the Centre for Conflict Management at the National University of Rwanda.

The books he has written, co-authored and co-edited on genocide include: *Dictionary of Genocide* (Westport, CT: Greenwood Publishers, 2008); *Genocide in Darfur: Investigating Atrocities in the Sudan* (New York: Routledge, 2006); *An Oral and Documentary History of the Darfur Genocide* (Santa Barbara, CA: Praeger Security International, 2010); and *We Cannot Forget: Interviews with Survivors of the 1994 Genocide in Rwanda* (New Brunswick, NJ: Rutgers University Press, 2011); *Genocide by Attrition: Nuba Mountains, Sudan* (New Brunswick, NJ: Transaction, 2012); and *Centuries of Genocide: Critical Essays and Eyewitness Accounts—4th Edition* (New York: Routledge, 2013). Totten is currently completing a book of essays tentatively entitled *The Prevention of Genocide: A Sisyphean Task? A Collection of Essays*, and the second edition of *Genocide of Attrition: Nuba Mountains, Sudan* (Transaction Publishers).

Hannibal Travis is professor of law, FIU College of Law. He earned his JD at Harvard University Law School in 1999.

His publications include *Genocide, Ethnonationalism, and the United Nations: Exploring the Causes of Mass Killing since 1945* (London: Routledge, 2012) and *Genocide in the Middle East: The Ottoman Empire, Iraq, and Sudan* (Durham, NC: Carolina Academic Press, 2010).

Among his articles and book chapters on genocide are "Genocide by Deportation into Poverty: Western Diplomats on Ottoman Christian Killings and Expulsions, 1914-1924," in Shirinian (Ed.) *The Ottoman Turkish Genocides of Anatolian Christians: A Common Case Study* (forthcoming, 2014); "The Construction of the 'Armenian Genocide': How Genocide Scholars Unremembered the Ottoman Assyrians and Greeks," in Hinton, Irvin-Erickson, and La Pointe (Eds.) *Hidden Genocides: Power, Knowledge, and Memory* (Rutgers University Press, 2013); "The Assyrian Genocide: A Tale of Oblivion and Denial," in Lemarchand (Ed.) *Forgotten Genocides* (University of Pennsylvania Press, 2011); "The International Arms Trade and the Prevention of Genocide: The Law and Practice of Arming Genocidal Governments," in Totten and Hitchcock (Eds.) *Impediments to the Prevention and Intervention of Genocide* (Transaction, 2012); "Genocide in Sudan: The Role of Oil Exploration and the Entitlement of the Victims to Reparations," in Guiora (Ed.) *The Top Ten Global Justice Law Review Articles 2008* (Oxford University Press/Oceana, 2009); "On the Original Understanding of the Crime of Genocide," *Genocide Studies and Prevention* 7 (2012); and "The Assyrian Genocide and Middle East Studies," in *Journal of Assyrian Academic Studies* 25 (2012).

Elisa von Joeden-Forgey served as a visiting scholar in the Department of History at the University of Pennsylvania for several years, where she taught courses on genocide, human rights, war, and imperialism. She is currently a visiting professor in the Holocaust and Genocide Studies Program at Richard Stockton College of New Jersey. Her work on German imperial history has been published in several journals and collected volumes. Her current research on gender and genocide has appeared in the *Journal of Genocide Studies and Prevention*, the *Oxford Handbook on Genocide*, the collected volume *New Directions in Genocide Research*, and the forthcoming *Hidden Genocide: Power, Knowledge and Memory* and volumes 11 and 12 of *Genocide: A Critical Bibliographic Review*. She is currently completing a book on gender and the prevention of genocide which will be published by the University of Pennsylvania Press.

Index

Darfur genocide and black African children (*continued*)
   violence against black African children, 167–168,
death camps (Nazi), 89–91, 105, 112, 205, 208–209
   Auschwitz-Birkenau, 89–91, 98, 101, 112, 231
death marches
   during Armenian genocide, 33, 44, 47–48
death squads, Guatemala, 137
deportations, 61–63, 90
   during Armenian genocide, 61, 63
   during the Holocaust, 90
denialism
   that the treatment of Aboriginal children constitutes a case of genocide, 8, 10, 12–16, 26–27, 30, 35
      Windshuttle, Keith, 14–15
   in regard to the fact of the Armenian genocide, 37, 39, 41, 72
diaries
   about the Armenian genocide, 72–73, 75
   by children during the Holocaust, 94–95
"disappearances" (enforced) of children during genocide, 197
   Argentina, 216
   Darfur, 213
   Guatemala, 124, 131, 135, 137, 145
Doctors' Trial, 105, 112–113, 115, 118

Egoyan, Atom, 36
eugenics
   in Australia, 5, 8–9, 24–25
   eugenicist fantasy of Australian settlers, 5
   Nazi eugenics, 105–121, 115–119
      approaches of, 106–108
         sterilization, 108–110
         murder, 110–112
      The Doctors' Trial, 105, 112–113, 115, 118
      "medical" experimentation on disabled children, 112
      Kinderaktion, 105
      T-4 eugenics campaign, 86–87, 100, 105–121

eugenics fantasy, 5
   of Australian settlers, 5

fetuses, destruction of during genocide, 2
   during the Darfur genocide, 171,
   during the 1994 genocide in Rwanda, 149
The Forty Days of Musa Dagh, 36

gang rape, 198, 201
   long-term psychological development of young rape victims, impact on, 197
   of Darfurian girls during genocide, 168–169, 184, 189, 198, 201–202
   during the Holocaust, 208
   Mayan girls during Guatemalan genocide, 127, 131
gender-based killing during genocide, 212–213
   in Srebrenica, 212–213
genocide of children
   Armenian children, 29–83
   Australian Aboriginal children, 5–21
      Bringing Them Home, 11–13
   black African children of Darfur, 167–193
   Tutsi and moderate Hutu in Rwanda (1994), 147–165
Genocide Convention (United Nations Convention on the Prevention and Punishment of the Crime of Genocide) (UNCG), 6, 10–11, 31, 236
   Intent (issue of), 6
      case of "Stolen Children" (Aboriginals of Australia), and, 6, 19, 23–24
      child removal with intent (Aboriginals of Australia), 6–8
      the "science" of removal, 8–10
Gorky, Arshile, 36–37
Guatemala, genocide in, 123–145
   babies (murders of during), 123–124, 126, 141
   the civil patrol system, 128, 131, 143
   Commission for Historical Clarification, 124, 126, 135, 137, 139, 141, 144–145
   counterinsurgency operations, 123–124, 140, 142
   death squads, 137